# UNCOMMON DEFENSE

# UNCOMMON DEFENSE

## INDIAN ALLIES IN THE BLACK HAWK WAR

John W. Hall

HARVARD UNIVERSITY PRESS

Cambridge, Massachusetts, and London, England

2009

*Library of Congress Cataloging-in-Publication Data*

Hall, John W., 1972–
Uncommon defense : Indian allies in the Black Hawk War / John W. Hall.—1st ed.
p. cm.
Includes bibliographical references and index.
ISBN 978-0-674-03518-8 (cloth : alk. paper)
1. Black Hawk War, 1832. 2. Black Hawk, Sauk chief, 1767–1838.
3. Indians of North America—Government relations—1789–1869. I. Title.
E83.83.H335 2009
973.5'6—dc22      2009016110

*For Heidi*

# Contents

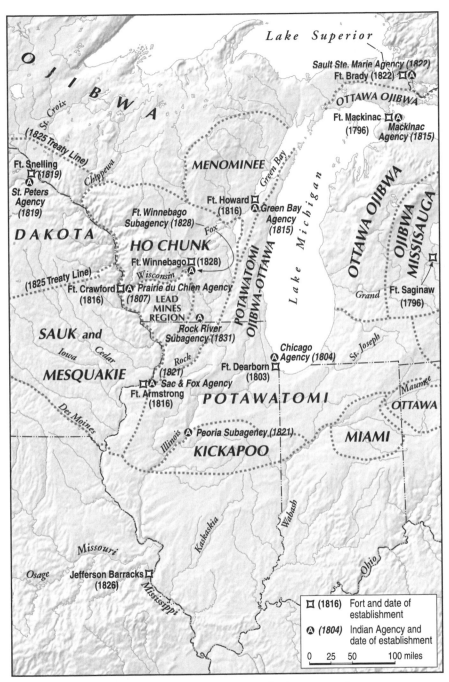

American occupation of the *pays d'en haut*, 1796–1831

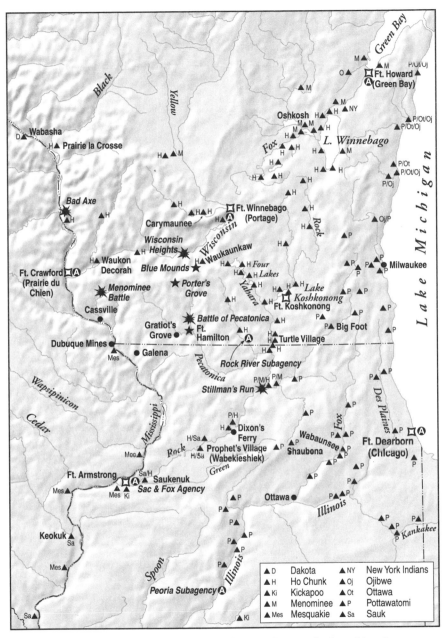

Distribution of Indian villages on the eve of war and selected battles

# Uncommon Defense

# INTRODUCTION

Some men looked away while others fixed their eyes with morbid curiosity on the spectacle of Dr. Addison Philleo amputating the arm of a child.[1] Having just concluded the Black Hawk War by raining fire on the forlorn survivors of Black Hawk's band as they attempted to swim across the Mississippi River, Illinois volunteers now took account of the damage they had wrought. A single ball had nearly separated the limb from the gaunt little boy's body before killing his mother. Indeed, most of the Sauk casualties at the Battle of Bad Axe were women and children—all of them were near starvation. "It is to be hoped, that the women and children fell by random shots," U.S. Army officer Philip St. George Cooke mused, but he knew full well "that a frontiersman is not particular, when his blood is up, and a redskin in his power."[2] Illinois volunteer John Wakefield acknowledged that "it was a horrid sight to witness little children, wounded and suffering through the most excruciating pain," but consoled himself that "they were of the savage enemy, and the common enemy of the country."[3] Another frontiersman displayed no remorse whatsoever, observing after he killed an infant, "Kill the nits and you'll have no lice."[4] Meanwhile, a short distance away, another Indian—a Menominee warrior—lay dead. While Sauk corpses, scalped and stripped of their teeth, were left to float down the Mississippi, this warrior received a military burial with full honors, and U.S. Army soldiers interred him beside their own dead.[5]

In April 1832, a Sauk war captain named Black Hawk and approximately one thousand followers crossed the Mississippi River into Illinois to reoccupy ceded lands in defiance of the United States. Although Black Hawk's band was made up of women and children as well as warriors, this act sparked a panic among Anglo-American frontier settlers as local newspapers conjured an Indian invasion and Illinois governor John Reynolds requested federal troops and called up the militia. Over the ensuing four months, federal and state forces under Brigadier General Henry Atkinson pursued Black Hawk's band through the Old Northwest, finally obliterating its emaciated remnants as they attempted to recross the Mississippi on 2 August 1832. Standard historical accounts see the war as a disgraceful landgrab by Indian-hating frontiersmen, but this view fails to explain the behavior of more than seven hundred Menominees, Dakotas, Ho Chunks, and Potawatomis who made common cause with the United States during the Black Hawk War.

This unlikely alliance is difficult to comprehend. On a historical stage populated by racist frontiersmen, capricious army commanders, venal federal Indian agents, and a Native hero in the mold of Tecumseh, the United States' Indian allies appear to be fools who fought on the wrong side of the contest. Indeed, some of their descendents are at a loss to explain the alliance, not wishing to believe that their forefathers helped defeat a nascent pan-Indian movement or facilitated Indian removal. Scholars of the war have, to one degree or another, endorsed this interpretation by variously describing the American allies as "mercenaries," "guerilla fighters for their white overlords," and "treacherous Indians" who betrayed Black Hawk when they "should have been his friends."[6] Others have developed a more empathetic understanding of these Indians but nevertheless depict them as hapless victims of white exploitation.[7] None fully comprehends the nature of the alliance that developed between these tribes and the United States. Nor do they acknowledge the significance of Indian participation in the Black Hawk War, which, although militarily negligible, represented a turning point in the history of the Old Northwest and, indeed, of the United States.

For over two hundred years, the tribes of the western Great Lakes (also referred to as the Old Northwest, the Upper Mississippi, and the *pays d'en haut*, or upper country) had been in direct contact with Europeans. First appearing in the region in 1634, the French sought furs and, to a lesser extent, converts to the Catholic faith. They found a region in disarray. European demand for North American peltry (especially beaver) had already radically altered the economies of eastern tribes, which waged wars of conquest to acquire additional hunting lands. Refugees of these conflicts fled westward in the "Great Dispersal" of the mid-seventeenth century, overpopulating Wisconsin and threatening the existence of its indigenous tribes. Capitalizing on these Indians' fragile state, the French offered an economic and military alliance with the tribes of the *pays d'en haut* that eventually stemmed the tide of Iroquoian expansion and restored stability to the region. Affecting the title Onontio (Great Mountain), French governors exercised paternalistic leadership of this alliance, but the Indians never regarded themselves as subjects of the French king. Instead, the French-Indian alliance rested on a foundation of reciprocity and mutual obligation. If the Indians permitted Onontio to mediate their disputes, they also demanded of him the largesse and leniency of a kindly father figure. Contesting Britain's colonial ambitions and laying nominal claim to over half the continent with fewer than one thousand French soldiers at his disposal, Onontio could ill afford to disappoint the expectations of his "red children."[8] Although rocky at times, this relationship proved mutually beneficial and provided an important precedent for interracial cooperation that the Indians hoped to emulate in the future.

Britain's victory in the Seven Years' War (also known as the French and Indian War in North America) did not augur well for the Indians of the *pays d'en haut.* By the 1763 Treaty of Paris, France's North American possessions passed to British control, requiring the Indians to seek trade and rapprochement with their recent enemies. Whereas military necessity had compelled the French to spend lavishly on their Indian allies, British administrators regarded the Indians as conquered subjects and drastically curtailed the budget for Indian diplomacy. Uninterested in the protocols of reciprocity established by their French predecessors, British traders compounded the problem by cheating the Indians.[9] In a series of attacks remembered as Pontiac's Rebellion, the Indians protested these transgressions and compelled the British to reappraise their policy. Yet while the Crown's subsequent handling of Indian affairs conformed more closely to Native expectations, American colonists resented policies designed to preserve the Indians and their land at the expense of American expansion—an imposition that contributed to the decision for revolution in 1775. Unsurprisingly, the Indians of the *pays d'en haut* generally supported or sympathized with the British in the ensuing contest, which persisted in various forms until the conclusion of the War of 1812. Victorious, the Americans belatedly extended their suzerainty over the *pays d'en haut* in 1816. Despite their recent animosity toward the Americans, the Native residents greeted the occupiers with the anticipation that the victors would now don the mantle worn previously by the French and British. When passed to the officers of the U.S. Army and the agents of the Office of Indian Affairs, however, the mantle fit poorly.

Initially, U.S. officials seemed unlikely patrons. Occupying a country populated by recently hostile Indians and the remnants of previous colonial regimes, the Americans conducted themselves as conquerors. Due largely to the Natives' eagerness to resume trade, however, relationships between the Indians and their American administrators warmed, and it appeared as though the Americans would indeed assume the paternalistic obligations of Onontio. In his place, the Americans offered the "Great Father," the president of the United States. Learning from their previous mistakes in the management of Indian affairs, the Americans resolved to turn over a new leaf in the Old Northwest, extending treaties of trade and friendship to their former antagonists and—ostensibly—conforming to the Indians' expectations of alliance politics. In their federal Indian agents and the army officers who accompanied them, the Natives saw shadows of Onontio and heard echoes from the Great Mountain.

The Americans differed markedly from their French and British predecessors, however, and over the course of the 1820s and 1830s the Indians became aware that familiar forms did not fit their new circumstances. Like their predecessors, the Americans represented themselves to the Indians in martial ceremonies that, implicitly and explicitly, venerated the accomplished warriors of both cul-

tures. But while the French and subsequently the British had regarded the Indians as indispensable military allies, the Americans
considered the martial "savage" an existential threat to the security
of the frontier and, by proscribing intertribal warfare, denied him
opportunities for future glory. Similarly, the Great Father revealed
that, though he was interested in sustaining the fur trade while it
lasted, he ultimately intended that the Indians surrender the chase
in favor of intensive agriculture. While the Indians resented this
imposition upon their traditional economy and gender roles (for
they uniformly considered farming to be women's work), the Americans' program of "civilization" bespoke a more profound distinction between the Great Father and his predecessors. Invested in the
fur trade and eager to keep the *pays d'en haut* beyond the control of
their colonial competitors, the French and British regimes had encouraged the hunt and, by extension, Indian occupancy of their
lands. By the time of the American arrival, however, the Indians
had already exhausted most of the region's peltry, and natural resources such as lead and timber promised more substantial returns—without need of an Indian labor force. By introducing the
Indians to small-plot farming, the Great Father hoped he could in-
duce the Indians to sell their "surplus" lands and open the way for
American development and settlement. While the French and British had needed the Indians, the Americans needed the Indians
gone.

If this now-familiar narrative seems to have been inevitable, it
is only in retrospect. At the time of the Black Hawk War, the Indians of the *pays d'en haut* had been acculturated to nearly two centuries of military and economic alliance with a European, colonial
power. Little in their collective experience suggested that race figured prominently in white conceptions of alliance. The French, af-

ter all, had made war against the British, who subsequently fought against their American cousins—in all instances with significant Indian assistance. Nursing their own share of intertribal animosities, the Indians saw nothing unseemly in the Europeans' behavior. Frequent intermarriage between French fur traders and Indian women had reinforced an earlier alliance with enduring kinship bonds that remained manifest in Franco-Indian trading towns throughout the region. And while the residents of these villages forged a unique, métis identity, they provided a very visible reminder that race did not determine loyalty in the *pays d'en haut*. Friends were friends and enemies were enemies, regardless of the color of one's skin.

In their early dealings with the region's Native population, the Americans did not compel the Indians to reappraise this conviction. In justifying his proscription of intertribal warfare, the Great Father explained that he loved all of his "children" equally, thereby evoking Onontio, who employed similar language to resolve intra-alliance disputes. But the Great Father was not the Great Mountain, and the Americans proved inept at arbitrating disputes between the Indians fairly. The extent of the Americans' inadequacy did not become evident until the Great Father was called upon to mediate disputes between his red and white children. Only then did the Indians of the *pays d'en haut* begin to discern the primacy of race to American conceptions of alliance. Coming first in a trickle, eventually a deluge of miners occupied Indian lands in the 1820s. A rough-and-tumble lot, these men shared the same complexion and language of the federal officers who had preceded them, but they possessed dissimilar values and loyalties. Typical of the pioneer wave that had steadily eroded Indian land holdings in the years since the American Revolution, these newcomers were men known for their love of hard drink and hatred of the Indian. Heretofore only modestly successful at maintaining peace between the Indian tribes, federal officers now had to maintain the peace between Indians and frontiersmen—and failed spectacularly at both in 1832.

To its indigenous participants, the Black Hawk War was a convergence of two conflicts. The better known of these was the Indian struggle to retain lands east of the Mississippi in the face of white expansion. This tragic endeavor involved more than Black Hawk and his followers. Elsewhere in Illinois over the course of the 1820s, the Potawatomis and Ho Chunks endured abuse at the hands of settlers and witnessed the erosion of their sovereignty. Enjoying Potawatomi sympathy (if not overt support), some Ho Chunks offered a violent protest in what became known as the Winnebago War of 1827. Rather than showing Americans the error of their ways, this brief conflict revealed to the Ho Chunks and Potawatomis the relative weakness of their position—and the probable consequences of again opposing the Americans by force of arms. The Black Hawk War thus put the Potawatomis and certain Ho Chunk bands in a very awkward position. On the basis of shared experience and, in some cases, intermarriage, many Ho Chunk and Potawatomi bands sympathized with Black Hawk; indeed, in several instances, they joined his war against the Americans. Yet leaders of these tribes realized that the citizens of Illinois would use the actions of a disaffected few to condemn each tribe in its entirety. Facing the prospect of uncompensated removal, the Potawatomis and some Ho Chunk bands effected a measured alliance with the Americans by offering scouts. Designed to demonstrate fealty to the Great Father while avoiding direct confrontation with the Sauks and Mesquakies, this policy offered these communities a conscionable (albeit tricky) solution to a seemingly impossible situation.

Yet not all Indians who opposed Black Hawk did so under du-
ress, for the Black Hawk War also involved an intertribal conflict
that had smoldered for decades. Together with Ho Chunk bands residing on the Wisconsin River, the Dakotas and Menominees harbored an enmity for the Sauks and Mesquakies that had its roots in
the seventeenth and eighteenth centuries. American efforts to quell
this antagonism proved ineffective, and flimsy peace settlements
fell apart in 1830 and 1831. Unwilling to submit to arbitration in the
first place, each party to the conflict held the meddling Americans
at least partly responsible for their latest losses. As victims of the
most recent reprisal, the Menominees consented to let the Great
Father dispense justice on their behalf, but they urged alacrity.
When the Americans disappointed this expectation, the Menominees spent the winter of 1831–1832 planning a renewed offensive
with their Dakota and Ho Chunk allies. Intent on striking their
foes with or without American leave, Black Hawk's reoccupation of
Illinois in April 1832 and defeat of a militia battalion the following
month presented the Menominees, Dakotas, and Wisconsin River
Ho Chunks an unanticipated opportunity. Contravening official
policy and popular sentiment, Brigadier General Henry Atkinson
summoned these tribes to make war on their common enemy. Having chafed under American restraint for years, elements of these
tribes welcomed the call. Waging their own war parallel to that of
the Americans, these groups actively sought combat with Black
Hawk's band and, when they found it, exacted bloody retribution.

Despite the diversity of motives among (and, in the case of the
Ho Chunks, within) these tribes, they each allied with the United
States against Black Hawk to serve the best interests of their people
in a time of considerable change, and they did so in accordance
with protocols they had negotiated with earlier European powers.

In accepting military aid from the Indians, the Americans drew upon the uncomfortable precedents of their colonial predecessors but proved amateurish and often reluctant in comparison. Far from being manipulated, the government's Indian allies were the true architects of an alliance that served their own ends first and always. Seeking to strike traditional tribal enemies, extract political advantage and material gain from the Americans, and fulfill important male gender expectations, these Indians generally achieved their objectives—but they also helped create conditions that wrought permanent change on the world in which they lived. When the Menominees, Dakotas, Ho Chunks, and Potawatomis sent their warriors against Black Hawk, they deployed their forces within the last remnants of a cosmopolitan domain that was neither wholly Indian nor wholly European. But in so doing, they helped stabilize a region in turmoil and inadvertently opened the gates to a new wave of settlement that ultimately consumed this vestige of colonial North America. Indeed, with the final operations of Menominee and Dakota warriors in August 1832, the last chapter in the colonial history of the western Great Lakes gave way to the subsequent narrative of Manifest Destiny.[10]

To understand this critical shift fully, it is essential to explore the Black Hawk War (to the extent possible) from the perspective of its Native participants. To that end, the various Indian groups that played a part in this story are referred to in the same manner by which they referred to themselves. Hence, the Sioux, Chippewas, Winnebagos, and Foxes are here given as the Dakotas, Ojibwas, Ho Chunks, and Mesquakies, respectively.[11] These tribal distinctions do not represent discrete political units but identities based on a shared language and culture. Hence, the decision to ally with the

United States was always local rather than tribal, and the alliance of particular bands of these four tribes should not be misconstrued as a "tribal" alliance. As the cases of the Potawatomis and (more vividly) the Ho Chunks illustrate, different bands of the same tribe could and did pursue wildly divergent policies.

This episode of intercultural military contact in the western Great Lakes following the War of 1812 provides a case study of the employment of indigenous forces by a "conventional" military power. A ubiquitous feature of colonial military ventures, the practice of waging proxy war through indigenous allies or auxiliaries has retained considerable relevance in the early twenty-first century, when the U.S. military has embraced the practice of working "by, with, and through" local forces in pursuit of national security objectives. Despite the economic and romantic allure of "irregular" and "unconventional" operations, their historical record is uneven at best. Rarely—even in the most celebrated instances—have both partners to these uneven alliances realized their ambitions. More typical is the Black Hawk War, in which all parties found their allies wanting in some regard. The weaker party in such relationships has often arrived at George Washington's realization that "there can be no greater error than to expect, or calculate upon real favours from Nation to Nation. 'Tis an illusion which experience must cure, which a just pride ought to disregard."[12] Prudently, then, indigenous allies such as the Ho Chunks have exhibited only half-hearted commitment to their supposed benefactors. Yet if the sponsors of proxy war have been disappointed by the lackluster contributions of their indigenous allies, the cost borne by these partners has been the greater. As the Potawatomis, Ho Chunks, Dakotas, and Menominees discovered during the Black Hawk War, the promises proffered by the minions of one Great Father proved nothing more than idle words under the administration of another. Far from unique, their experience is worth remembering for those who would make such promises again—and those who would listen to them.

# I

## ROOTS OF CONFLICT

In a ritual common to northern Wisconsin in the seventeenth century, a Menominee hunting party of eight to ten men set out to hunt along the Peshtigo River. This particular morning was notable because the party carried firearms afield for the first time. The excitement occasioned by this inaugural gunpowder hunt was heightened by the knowledge that a *manitou* (spirit) had directed it. One of the hunters invoked a dream in which spirits directed him to obtain a rifle and ammunition from the white men who traded in nearby Green Bay. He and his fellows obeyed the solemn edict of the spirit world, and their families prepared for a celebratory feast in anticipation of a successful hunt. Unable to foresee the day's events, the Menominees did not realize that they were, in fact, preparing for a mourning feast.

When the hunting band brought their canoes to rest on the shores of the Peshtigo, an alien Indian, armed and painted for war, emerged from the woodline and startled the Menominees. The narrator of the dream raised the weapon ordained by his vision, took aim, and fired. The Sauk warrior, who had come forward to offer a friendly greeting, fell dead. Seeing their comrade fall, the remainder of the Sauk war party, which had prepared an ambush for their Ojibwa enemies, issued the war whoop and sprang upon the Menominees. Surprised, the hunters retreated to their canoes. Those who made it that far soon drowned in the Peshtigo River, as the Sauks riddled their fragile vessels with arrows and watched as the water swallowed both canoes and pilots.[1] The accidental encounter gave rise to an enmity that would last for nearly two hundred years, up to the Black Hawk War.

Most narratives of the Black Hawk War begin on 3 November 1804. On that day, hoping to make amends for the killing of a white settler and to secure a treaty of friendship with the United States, a Sauk and Mesquakie delegation inadvertently ceded all of their territory east of the Mississippi River to an opportunistic territorial governor (and future president) named William Henry Harrison.[2] The U.S. Senate ratified this treaty, but the affected tribes did not, and when they refused to vacate their former lands in the early 1830s, war resulted. This story line, while vital to understanding Black Hawk's motives in the spring of 1832, meant nothing to the Menominees, Dakotas, Ho Chunks, and Potawatomis who opposed him later that summer. Nor does it help explain their decision to align with the United States. For several of these tribes, the Black Hawk War was another in a series of battles that stretched back over generations. Contemporary white observers ascribed these "ancient" conflicts to "savage" bloodlust without seriously considering their origins or significance to the involved communities—a mistake repeated by many historians. But understanding these Indians' actions during the Black Hawk War requires familiarity with the events that shaped intertribal political relations over the preceding two centuries. It is there that the roots of intertribal animosities can be found, as well as the ways in which Native conceptions of warfare and alliance with European powers evolved and informed Indian practices in 1832. The American narrative of the Black Hawk War may begin in 1804, but the Indian story begins much earlier.

The Sauks on the Peshtigo River were among the more recent of a wave of interlopers who appeared on Menominee lands in the mid-seventeenth century. Approximately fifty years earlier, in the early 1600s, the Menominees and their western neighbors, the Ho Chunks, enjoyed exclusive occupation of what is presently Wisconsin. Calling themselves Kayaes Matchitiwuk ("original men" or "original people"), the Menominees had inhabited northern Wisconsin for at least three thousand years.[3] Oral tradition maintains that they have always lived in Wisconsin and that the two principal clans of the Menominees, Bear and Thunder, originated around the mouth of the Menominee River and at Lake Winnebago, respectively.[4] Speaking an Algonquian language, the pre-Columbian Menominees shared many cultural similarities with neighboring Algonquian tribes such as the Ojibwas, Ottawas, and Potawatomis, but the Menominees were unique in their affinity for their Siouan neighbors to the west, the Ho Chunks.

Tracing their own origins to the Red Banks on the east shore of Green Bay and calling themselves the people of the "Big Voice," the Ho Chunks enjoyed a reputation among their neighbors as a particularly powerful and bellicose people.[5] By their own oral tradition, the Ho Chunks wished for war so that they would have the opportunity to slay as many of their enemies as possible.[6] When denied the martial glory of combat, Ho Chunk men diverted themselves by playing "the kicking game," a contest in which two men kicked one another until one could bear it no longer.[7] Not surprisingly, the Ho Chunks guarded their domain with uncommon ferocity and allegedly ate Ottawa envoys seeking to establish trade.

Such treatment sat poorly with the Algonquians of the eastern Great Lakes, who by the early seventeenth century were armed and supplied by the French. In a series of campaigns, the Algonquians reduced the once populous Ho Chunks to four or five thousand souls, who consolidated into a single village. Here, fortune continued to turn against them, and disease ravaged the Ho Chunks, killing over half of the remaining population.[8] Although at that point numbering only about 1,500, the Ho Chunks mounted a retaliatory raid against the nearest of their aggressors, the Mesquakies, who had encroached on Ho Chunk lands and occupied the eastern shore of Lake Winnebago. Five hundred warriors launched their canoes into this large lake, but a tempest struck the unfortunate party, and not one of its number saw land again.[9]

Taking sympathy on the hapless Ho Chunks, the Algonquians ceased hostilities, and the Illinois Confederacy even offered aid to ease Ho Chunk suffering. Although they needed the assistance, the Ho Chunks worried more about the spiritual consequences of leaving their dead unavenged. Accordingly, the Ho Chunks murdered a large party of diplomats from the heretofore beneficent Illinois tribe. Their otherworldly concerns thus addressed, the Ho Chunks attended to more pragmatic problems. Realizing that the Illinois—and perhaps other offended tribes—would respond to their treachery, the Ho Chunks fortified themselves on a single island on Lake Winnebago. The Illinois, having devoted an entire year to mourning their dead, waited for winter, when nature furnished an ice bridge to the Ho Chunk fort. Upon entering the village, however, the Illinois warriors discovered that their quarry had vacated it to engage in their winter hunt. For six days, the Illinois tracked the Ho Chunks, who traveled in one body for security.[10] Their concentration only made it easier for the Illinois to obliterate their foes.

While the Illinois generally granted mercy to Ho Chunk women and children, only a handful of warriors escaped. In 1640, Jesuit priest Claude Allouez reported that the Ho Chunks had been "almost wholly destroyed by the Illinois."[11]

On the verge of extinction, the Ho Chunks reconciled with the Mesquakies, who had themselves been driven from their native Michigan by the Ojibwas.[12] Seeking refuge rather than war, the Mesquakies migrated westward through Wisconsin and, by the early seventeenth century, occupied the western fringes of Menominee and Ho Chunk land in the Fox River Valley.[13] The Menominees extended hospitality to their Algonquian relatives. Through the practice of *apēīkon ahkīhih* (to sit down upon), the Menominees granted the Mesquakies permission to occupy Menominee land while withholding some usufructuary rights.[14] Remaining at the sufferance of the Menominees, the Mesquakies were welcome so long as they did not abuse the Menominee resources at their disposal. The Mesquakies and the Menominees remained allies until the very early eighteenth century.[15] In future years, the Ho Chunks also cemented an alliance with their former enemies and partly restored their population through intermarriage with the Mesquakies.[16]

The unlikely harmony achieved by the Menominees, Ho Chunks, and Mesquakies did not last. Beginning in the mid-seventeenth century, the Native peoples of Wisconsin became party to a conflict with origins across the Atlantic. European fashion of the day placed a high demand on North American furs—especially beaver pelts. The demand transformed the economies of the Iroquois of New York and the Algonquians of Lower Canada, who rapidly depleted their own supplies of fur-bearing animals. Allied with the British, the Five Nations of the Iroquois Confederacy represented the preeminent military power on the continent, and it expanded westward and northward in search of new hunting grounds. This expansion led to conflict with the various Algonquian tribes that traded their furs with the French. Better organized and armed, the Iroquois displaced one Algonquian population after another, creating a refugee crisis that culminated at the far end of the Great Lakes.[17]

Strangers began to appear in 1634, when the French visited Wisconsin for their first time. Preceded by French trade goods and diseases, the arrival of the newcomers wrought little immediate change. In the ensuing decades, however, Sauks, Potawatomis, Kickapoos, Miamis, and even Huron refugees moved into Wisconsin to escape from the Iroquois and to hunt for furs. Menominee oral tradition suggests that the first encounters were not uniformly violent and that the Menominees may have extended the hospitality of *apēīkon ahkīhih* to the Sauks. The Sauks lived in the very midst of the Menominees and maintained a village at the mouth of the Oconto River on Green Bay. Relations between the two tribes were cordial until the incident on the Peshtigo River. Afterward, both sides tried to make amends, but intractable Sauk warriors continued to claim Menominee lives. Ultimately, the Sauks exhausted Menominee goodwill, and the tribes became inveterate foes.[18] Now overwhelmed by aliens, the Menominees resurrected their traditional military alliance with the Ho Chunks to defend their sovereignty. Still no match for their many and populous enemies, the Menominees teetered on the brink of extermination by 1669.[19] To make matters worse, the invaders carried not only firearms but also European diseases, which threatened to terminate the tenuous existence of Wisconsin's original inhabitants.[20]

Ironically, the Menominee and Ho Chunk survivors managed

to escape extinction due to their inherent weakness and the persistent threat posed by the Iroquois. Militarily impotent, both tribes sought rapprochement with the new Algonquian powers of Wisconsin, with whom they intermarried. In doing so, the Ho Chunks and Menominees began the slow process of recovering their populations and forming the kinship ties that, in Native communities, provided the foundation for political alliances. Yet, while amorous affection was vital to Menominee and Ho Chunk survival, fear and war completed their deliverance. Facing renewed aggression by the Iroquois Confederacy, which sought prisoners to replace its own war dead and furs for their British trading partners, the refugee tribes of the western Great Lakes cast aside their antipathies for each other to form a military alliance under the aegis of New France.

Plagued by a variety of congenital defects that ultimately led to its fall, New France needed Indian allies as much or more than they needed New France. While the English had transported married families into its colonial settlements, New France was almost entirely male, made up of Jesuit missionaries and hardy fur traders. As moral compasses, the priests proved less effective than English wives, who offered their men more than pious admonitions. Undeterred by Jesuit objections, French fur traders routinely consorted with Indian women.[21] Many Native leaders condoned the unions, which promised to reinforce the fictive bonds of trade with more binding kinship ties and "transformed French traders into Indian husbands, fathers, and brothers."[22] In this way, the simple rules of supply and demand gave way to Native expectations of reciprocity and mutual obligation. Indeed, by the end of the seventeenth century the French fur trade was less a commercial enterprise than a demonstration of Onontio's faithfulness to his allied Indian kin.[23]

By virtue of geography, some tribes were better situated than others to capitalize on the French alliance. The establishment of French trade hubs at Michilimackinac and Green Bay conveyed special privileges to the tribes that inhabited those places: the Ojibwas, the Ottawas, and—at Green Bay—the Potawatomis. Like the Sauks and Mesquakies, the Potawatomis originally inhabited the Michigan peninsula but fled to Wisconsin to escape the Iroquois. Settling on the shores of Green Bay, which by 1677 was home to an estimated twenty thousand Indians and had become the western epicenter of the French fur trade, the Potawatomis controlled access to the French fur traders and thereby enjoyed a prominent status among their fellow tribes.[24]

Evolving conceptions of tribal leadership allowed the Potawatomis to capitalize on their fortune. Respected advisors rather than executives, traditional civil chiefs of Algonquian cultures led by persuasion and lacked coercive authority. Moreover, the formulation of policy was typically the business of bands or villages, not tribes. This diffusion of power frustrated the French, who preferred to deal with Indian leaders who spoke for the tribe as a whole. Although no such leaders existed in Native society, the Potawatomis contributed to the invention of the "alliance chief," who accepted increased authority in return for loyalty to both the French and his own tribe. These liaisons could maintain their position only so long as they met the not always complementary expectations of their dual constituencies. Such a task demanded rare talent, and liaisons between the French and Algonquians often achieved status beyond their ordinary station in life in recognition of their abilities. The accumulation of too much privilege or the display of hubris, however, could erode support for an alliance chief. The more successful liaisons in the *pays d'en haut*, of which Onanghisse of the Potawatomis was prototypical, were careful to place the good of their primary constituency and the alliance as a whole before personal interests.[25] The practice and office of the alliance chiefs established an important precedent among France's Indian allies, who learned the value (and, later, necessity) of relying on trusted liaisons to conduct diplomacy with their European counterparts.

United, the Algonquians, Ho Chunks, and French turned back the Iroquois tide and even induced the mighty Five Nations of the Iroquois Confederacy to sue for peace. At the Grand Settlement of 1701, the Iroquois vowed to remain neutral in the continuing contest between France and Britain and agreed to abandon their annexed hunting territories west of Detroit.[26] Their homelands liberated, most of the Michigan tribes returned to their native soil, restoring to the Menominees and Ho Chunks control of their domains. Significantly, however, the Sauks and Mesquakies remained in Wisconsin.

While the Potawatomis typified the best case of accommodation with the French regime, the Mesquakies represented the opposite. Occupying the western edge of the Menominee and Ho Chunk country at the time of the "Great Dispersal" of refugee tribes into Wisconsin, the Mesquakies responded to the influx by migrating southwestward toward the portage of the Fox and Wisconsin Rivers. Here, the Mesquakies encountered the Dakotas, the easternmost of the Sioux tribes who, like their linguistic cousins the Ho Chunks, were reputable warriors. Although yet unaware of the strategic significance of "the Portage," which linked the Great Lakes to the Mississippi River, the Dakotas jealously guarded their hunting grounds, and they forcibly evicted the intruders.[27] These initial clashes between the Dakotas and Mesquakies gave rise to a mutual animosity between the two peoples that waxed and waned over the ensuing years, persisting through the Black Hawk War.

Chastened, the Mesquakies fell back to the area around Green Bay, which by this time was home to several new immigrant groups. Already expelled from Michigan by the Ojibwas and from south-central Wisconsin by the Dakotas, the Mesquakies erected oaken palisades and constructed earthworks to prevent their further displacement.[28] Jesuits who began to proselytize among these fortifications described the Mesquakies as "given to hunting and warfare"—vocations that did not endear them to their new neighbors.[29] Consequently, Father Claude Allouez reported that the other Wisconsin tribes held the Mesquakies "in very low estimation."[30] Regardless, the Mesquakies were able to rally the support of various tribes in intermittent forays against their new western antagonists, the Dakotas, for whom the Mesquakies nursed a special hatred. Although the Dakotas outnumbered the Mesquakies, the latter were better armed due to their proximity to the developing French trade entrepôt at Green Bay. Their advantage proved short-lived, however, as an Ojibwa-Dakota armistice opened French trade to the latter tribe in 1679. Supplied with French arms and ammunition by Ojibwa middlemen, the Dakotas gained an advantage over the Mesquakies in the next decade.[31]

Blaming the French for their reversal of fortune, the Mesquakies courted the Iroquois and began to raid French traders on Wisconsin waterways. A violation of intertribal law and *apēīkon ahkīhih,* Mesquakie piracy incurred the wrath of the French and their trading partners. Even the Menominees, who had remained friendly to the Mesquakies throughout their tenure in Wisconsin, now turned against them.[32] Hoping to defuse the situation, the French invited the Mesquakies to relocate to the new French fur trading hub at Detroit, where they would enjoy a direct exchange free of middlemen. Two Mesquakie villages accepted the offer, but then made a nuisance of themselves by abusing other tribes and boasting that they would seek a trade relationship with the British. Their behavior exhausted the patience of the French as well as most of the Michigan Indians, who urged the French to eliminate the Mesquakies once and for all. In 1712, the French-Indian alliance nearly accomplished this objective following a sensational siege, but the Mesquakie communities that had remained in Wisconsin adopted a conciliatory tone and deflected French wrath, albeit temporarily. In 1727, the French denied the Mesquakies a role as middlemen in the fur trade by establishing a new trading post on the upper Mississippi that provided direct access to the Dakotas and their relatively bountiful supply of furs. Despite the counsel of seasoned leaders, young Mesquakie warriors retaliated against the French and their few remaining allies. As a result, by 1729, the Mesquakies stood alone.[33]

Among the last to abandon the Mesquakies were the Ho Chunks, who, like the Menominees, had accommodated the Mesquakie migration to Wisconsin and intermarried with them. Recognizing the foolhardiness of standing with the Mesquakies against the combined force of the French-Algonquian alliance, the Ho Chunks elected to reconcile with Onontio. To prove their loyalty, they performed his bidding by joining Ottawa and Ojibwa warriors in attacking Mesquakie settlements. Incensed, in early 1730 the Mesquakies laid siege to the Ho Chunks, who again took refuge in their island stronghold. French and Menominee forces from Green Bay eventually lifted the siege, but the Mesquakie estrangement from their Wisconsin allies was nearly complete.[34]

Thereafter, Onontio exhorted his Indian children to wipe the Mesquakies from the earth, a task at which they nearly succeeded later that year. Afterward, the Mesquakie survivors—perhaps fewer than two hundred—sought refuge with the Sauks, with whom they were intermarried and who had begun to question New France's genocidal policy toward the Mesquakies. The Sauks bravely defended the last remnants of the Mesquakie people, but they could not withstand the combined power of the Menominees, Ho Chunks, and other Indians, who drove the newly formed Sauk-Mesquakie confederation down the Fox River Valley.[35]

By the conclusion of what became known as the Fox Wars, the character of warfare had changed in the *pays d'en haut*. Even before the "Beaver Wars" against the Iroquois, Indian men fulfilled the complementary roles of hunters and warriors. While the former provided nourishment, the latter provided prestige and respectability. Indoctrination began early: they slept in cradles decorated with bows and arrows as infants, practiced archery and wrestling at a young age, and learned to venerate war veterans through ceremonies and oral tradition.[36] The Menominees believed that the path of a warrior began in the womb, where the red war god Minisíno-häwätûk preordained his success in battle and the length of his life.[37] Successful warriors in all tribes received eagle feathers for killing a foe, notched their war clubs to record their exploits, and expected to be memorialized in song and legend. In addition, because offices of civil and spiritual leadership often were awarded on the basis of heredity, war provided the primary means for social advancement. Put simply, young Indian men from every tribe in the region aspired to become accomplished warriors when they grew to maturity.[38]

Still, their ambitions were held in check by the civil leaders and women of their villages. While neither group had the authority to forbid warfare outright, they imposed checks and balances on the bellicose passions of youth. Civil leaders could decree that a venture under consideration was inimical to the interests of the tribe and deny participants the pomp and circumstance that usually accompanied sanctioned ventures.[39] Worse yet, civil leaders and women could reproach returned warriors for their actions and thereby deprive them acknowledgement and honor. Women could further dissuade military action by refusing to perform their traditional duties as logisticians, compelling the warriors to abandon their cause or carry on with empty haversacks and worn-out moccasins.

But the protracted warfare that wracked the Great Lakes region during the late seventeenth century increased the prestige of war leaders, and martial prowess became the most exalted virtue in men.[40] Ominously, war leaders began to usurp the authority of civil chiefs, and warriors paid less heed to the objections of their women, undermining the traditional balance of power within Indian communities. In many tribes, particular clans directed warfare and diplomacy, and these clans now assumed unprecedented importance. Among the Mesquakies, conversely, the business of war became so important that its traditional stewards, the Fox Clan and the Kiyagamohag warriors' society, relinquished their prerogative to the rest of the tribe.[41] By the time of the Grand Settlement of 1701, the western Indians had endured a generation of continuous warfare. After the settlement, their children participated in the wars against the Mesquakies, and their grandchildren participated in the climactic struggle between Onontio and the British king during the French and Indian War.[42] Whereas military experience had been a virtue in the past, by the mid-eighteenth century it was a mandatory rite of passage. According to Black Hawk, young Sauk men were not even permitted to marry until they had proven their mettle in combat.[43] In 1827, Indian agent Thomas Forsyth described the significance of warfare to Sauk and Mesquakie society:

> Young Indians are always fond of war, they hear the old Warriors boasting of their war exploits, and it may be said, that the principle of war is instilled into them from their cradles, they therefore embrace the first opportunity to go to war even in company with a strange Nations so that they may be able to proclaim at the dance, I have killed such a person, &c. &c. One or more Indians of the same Nation and village may at the same time fast, pray, and consult their Munitos or Supernatural Agents about going to war. The dreams they have during their fasting praying &c. determines every thing, as they always relate in public the purport of their lucky dreams to encourage the young Indians to join them . . . and if the warriors believe in his dreams &c. he is never at a loss for followers.[44]

The Sauks and Mesquakies were typical rather than unique, and by the time of the American Revolution, the western Great Lakes had developed into a land of martial peoples who were habituated to warfare and alliance with a European power.

This conditioning served the Sauks and Mesquakies well as they migrated westward to escape Onontio's vengeance and, later, to distance themselves from the persistent Ojibwa-Dakota contest for control of the upper reaches of the Mississippi. By the beginning of the nineteenth century, the Sauks and Mesquakies resided in about a dozen villages on either bank of the Mississippi between the mouths of the Wisconsin and Des Moines Rivers. Here, the Mesquakies gradually rekindled their old animosity for the Dakotas, who were widely regarded as the most warlike of all tribes on the upper Mississippi.

Even upon first contact with Europeans, the Dakotas exhibited the sort of militaristic tendencies that the Algonquians acquired only with the passage of time. When Pierre Radisson visited the Dakotas in the 1650s, he made careful note of the men he encountered but neglected the women altogether. According to Gary Clayton Anderson, the oversight was understandable: "The lapse illustrates the chauvinistic nature of Sioux society; most functions revolved around the excitement of the chase and the glories of war."[45] Indeed, prepubescent Dakota boys accompanied their fathers to war at the tender age of nine or ten so that they might learn their future vocation. In recognition and fear of their martial abilities, some Frenchmen referred to the Dakotas as the "Iroquois of the West."[46] One French commandant regarded the Dakotas as superior, claiming that "they surpass the Iroquois in bravery and courage" and used their bows and arrows as pillows, suggesting that they were ready for a fight even as they slept.[47] The Dakotas' Algonquian neighbors in Wisconsin shared this impression and, according to French observers, were terrified of the eastern Sioux.[48]

The warlike disposition of the Dakotas appears to have been a product of their economy, in which hunting provided their primary means of subsistence.[49] Unlike the Algonquians of Wisconsin, whose diverse economies relied far more on agriculture, fishing, and gathering, the Dakotas required vast expanses of untrammeled hunting land to provide an adequate supply of calories and protein. Hence, sustaining their population required the Dakotas to guard their domain with singular determination—and population growth compelled wars of conquest. The advent of the fur trade did not improve the situation. If anything, it increased competition over a limited commodity with almost limitless demand—a circumstance that all but guaranteed conflict with fellow Indians, especially the Ojibwas and Mesquakies.

While the contested hunting grounds around the upper reaches of the Mississippi fueled a seemingly endless war between the Dakotas and Ojibwas, the Dakotas reserved special opprobrium for the Mesquakies on account of their taxation of trade on the Fox River. This practice victimized the Dakotas more than any other tribe. With no feasible alternative but to ship their furs up the Wisconsin and Fox Rivers to Green Bay, the Dakotas were unwilling benefactors of the Mesquakies until the French established a western trading post in 1727. When the Mesquakies protested by raiding French commerce, the Dakotas willingly participated in the final French campaign against the Mesquakies. The Mesquakies' eventual defeat represented a tremendous boon to the Dakotas, who achieved ascendancy in the western fur trade by the mid-1730s.[50]

Having achieved economic security, the Dakotas acquiesced to Sauk and Mesquakie settlement in Iowa and along the banks of the Mississippi over the next twenty years. Despite their historical animosity with the Mesquakies, the Dakotas—like many tribes in the region—had begun to question Onontio's willingness to extirpate an entire people and took pity on their vanquished foes.[51] Even in concert with the Sauks, the harrowed Mesquakies posed no threat to the mighty Dakotas, who could field as many warriors as any other tribe in the region.[52] In fact, young Mesquakie warriors looking to establish themselves sometimes joined Dakota war parties as they crossed the Mississippi to strike members of the Illinois Confederacy.[53] Inexorably, though, the Sauk and Mesquakie position improved while the supply of fur-bearing animals diminished. By the end of the eighteenth century, the mutual loathing of the Dakotas and Mesquakies had not only been resurrected, but it had pulled in the Sauks and attained unprecedented intensity.

For the most part, however, the French carefully guarded against the escalation of intertribal squabbles even as they imposed the wrenching economic changes that gave rise to many of the disputes. For the officials of New France, the prevention of conflict between their Native allies was a matter of good politics and better business. The "Fox Wars"—New France's nearly successful bid to eliminate the Mesquakies as a people—were both an exception to and a manifestation of this principle. The campaign against the Mesquakies was an unusual instance in which the French regarded a single tribe as being so disruptive to both the Algonquian alliance and the fur trade that it had to be eliminated. At his best, Onontio learned to mediate disputes between his various Indian children, lavishing them with presents to maintain order and goodwill. Despite the cost, he was willing to make this investment. Hopelessly outnumbered by English colonists, France's North American colonial empire rested on the stability of its Algonquian alliance and hard-earned Iroquois neutrality.[54]

Imperial ambition may have compelled France to construct a remarkable, intercultural alliance, but this same ambition proved its undoing. Hoping to contain Britain's North American colonies east of the Appalachian Mountains, in the mid-eighteenth century French officials contested British expansion into the Ohio River Valley. Here, Onontio's kinship alliance had the shallowest of roots, and he relied on the military power of his western Indian allies. In the main, these Indians were more than willing to go to war at Onontio's behest. As war-making had become the premier occupation among Indian men and French officials attempted to resolve intertribal disputes peacefully, assailable enemies became a precious commodity in the *pays d'en haut*. Consequently, young warriors were willing to travel great distances in search of martial accomplishment. Moreover, Onontio compensated them with trade goods, provisions, and the prospect of war booty, thereby compounding the already strong incentive to make war.[55]

But the French and Indian War (1754-1763) taxed the Franco-Algonquian alliance beyond its limits. Maladroit French administrators demanded too much and gave too little, while military commanders from the Continent misused allies they considered more distasteful than necessary.[56] Perhaps nowhere was this more evident than at Fort William Henry in 1757, where the Marquis de Montcalm's mismanagement of two thousand Indian allies resulted in the famous "Massacre" of Fort William Henry, in which warriors violated the European terms of surrender to reap the Indian fruits of victory. The event proved calamitous for New France, as Britain prosecuted the remainder of the war with indignant vigor, and the disaffected western Algonquians returned to their wigwams.[57] France suffered a decisive defeat, and Onontio, the Great Mountain, turned to dust.

Vengeful over real and imagined atrocities committed by various Native groups during the war, the victorious British initially treated the Indians like conquered subjects. With varying degrees of concert, Indian groups from Michigan to Georgia responded violently to British pretensions during Pontiac's Rebellion, which compelled a reappraisal of Britain's postwar Indian policy.[58] By their actions, the Indians made it clear that they were not defeated and that the British would have to accord themselves with Indian expectations if they desired stable relations. Desirous of maintaining the peace they had just won at extraordinary cost, the British redressed Indian grievances and moved to contain their principal cause: American colonists.

To this end, the British continued to vest responsibility for Indian diplomacy in the offices of royal "superintendents for Indian affairs" rather than returning it to the jealous colonial assemblies, whose members were more concerned with tapping the economic potential of their newly won continent than with establishing friendly relationships with the Natives. Indeed, in the wake of a particularly brutal race war along the Pennsylvania and Virginia frontiers, such a goal appeared unobtainable, and British administrators realized that the fragile peace on the frontier depended on the segregation of whites and Indians. Hence, the British issued a royal proclamation in October 1763 that forbade American colonists from violating the sanctity of the trans-Appalachian Indian country. Often cited as among the earliest in a catalog of offenses that culminated in the American Revolution, the Proclamation of 1763 also announced Britain's assumption of the duties of Onontio.

Over the ensuing decade, the British replicated many of the functions earlier fulfilled by the French.[59] Initially, the relationship was almost entirely commercial. Although the Indians were growing increasingly dependent on European trade goods (and the British could offer these goods in greater quantities, in higher quality, and at lower prices than had the French), British traders soon realized that the economy of the *pays d'en haut* operated on more than the laws of supply and demand. The privilege of conducting commerce with the Indians was contingent on demonstrations of reciprocity, and the British learned the necessity of reconstituting a kinship-based trading network. Rather than squeezing out the French and métis traders who remained, the British co-opted not only the individual traders but also their invaluable networks.[60] Typically, American merchants were shut out from this trade, which simultaneously forestalled the development of commercial relationships between Americans and the western Indians and contributed to a mounting disaffection among American colonists for the Crown's Indian policy—indirectly encouraging cooperation between the British and the Indians in a venue other than trade.

For many Indian groups, the American Revolution was very similar to the French and Indian War. While many eastern Indian groups labored (often unsuccessfully) to maintain neutrality and a few allied with the Americans, most considered their interests best served by alliance with the British, with whom they were already bound by trade and who seemed to be the lesser of two evils. Having not relied extensively on Indian allies since the seventeenth century, however, the British proved amateurish in sponsoring an Indian war, and many of the king's eastern allies paid dearly for their decision to oppose the Americans.[61] But the Indians of the Old Northwest had enjoyed considerable success against the Americans and remained largely beyond the vindictive reach of the colonists. Undefeated, they conceded nothing to the Americans, who in any event lacked the strength to evict the British from their western posts. British suzerainty over the western Great Lakes remained intact until 1795, when the British garrisons began to withdraw to Canada in accordance with the provisions of Jay's Treaty. This agreement, however, upheld British trading privileges in American territory, and the British continued to administer Indian affairs from nearby Malden in Canada.

Militarily impotent, the Americans took meager steps to exert their influence in the region. In 1797, the Americans unsuccessfully challenged the British fur trade monopoly by occupying Michili-mackinac.[62] Five years later, Indian-white disturbances in southern Illinois prompted the government to station a company of troops at Kaskaskia. The following year, another company established Fort

Dearborn at the mouth of the Chicago River on the south end of Lake Michigan.[63] The Americans did not make a concerted effort to extend their hegemony over the region, however, until the 1803 Louisiana Purchase at once expanded American claim to the western Great Lakes region, established the need for a military administration of the new possession, and excited further economic competition with Great Britain.

This economic competition came to a head in the War of 1812. While the Americans had made only temporary inroads among the Indians of the Upper Mississippi, the British exerted considerable influence through their network of fur traders, many of whom were French or métis and retained kinship ties to their trading partners. Consequently, when the Battle of Tippecanoe and the War of 1812 brought war to the *pays d'en haut,* many Native groups again aligned with the British. As in the American Revolution, neutrality proved elusive, and Indian groups chose their allies by carefully considering their prospects for success and the best interests of their people.[64] Unfortunately for the Indians, their best interests and their best prospects proved mutually exclusive, and by 1814 even the most ardent of Britain's Indian allies sensed the impending American victory. Although he had worn the rank of a British general officer and led his people against the Americans in two wars, the Dakota chief Wabasha laid down his tomahawk and prepared to make peace with the Americans.[65] In defeat, the British offered a demonstration of loyalty to their Indian allies, demanding that the Americans not punish the Indians on account of their participation in the war. Yet while the Treaty of Ghent nominally restored the status quo ante bellum, it provided no effectual barrier to American expansion into Indian lands.[66]

Following the War of 1812, the inhabitants of the *pays d'en haut* lived in a new world. For the past two hundred years, European powers had engaged with them in economic and military partnerships, the first compelled by commercial interest, the second by necessity. Antagonism between the French and British and, later, British and Americans had rendered Indian warriors invaluable to successive European regimes. By 1815, the Indians of the *pays d'en haut* were a martial people accustomed to alliance with powerful, European powers. The contest for control of the Great Lakes region had been decided, however, and Indian warriors were no longer in high demand. They previously had been able to leverage their indispensability to their advantage, compelling both the British and the French to conform to Indian expectations of reciprocity. These days were now at an end; the Americans were coming.

# 2

## A New Onontio

In the years following the War of 1812, the United States finally extended its suzerainty over the Old Northwest. Beginning in 1816, the U.S. government established military posts and Indian agencies along the Fox-Wisconsin waterway to secure the fruits of America's recent victory and sever the Indians' ties to their British "father." Denied succor by their former British allies and eager to resume trade, most Indian groups reconciled with the Americans, who, for their part, administered a relatively benign Indian policy. Over the course of a quarter-century of trial and error, U.S. officials learned what the British had divined decades earlier: peace on the frontier required fair dealings with the Indians and the protection of their lands from illegal white encroachment. Hence, the Americans who appeared in the *pays d'en haut* in 1816 attempted to replicate many of the diplomatic forms of their European predecessors, offering the "Great Father," the U.S. president, as a new Onontio. In other regards—especially the Americans' insistence that the Indians cease all intertribal conflict—the Indians discerned alarming departures from the French and British precedent. Still, the Indians lacked alternatives and generally embraced the Americans as their new allies in trade and—eventually—arms.

The Americans were not complete strangers to the Indians of the Upper Mississippi, who called their white neighbors *gchimookmaanan* (Big, or Long, Knives) on account of the swords worn by an earlier generation of English colonists. The Indians had, of course, fought two wars with the Americans over the past forty years, and the Indians on the banks of the Mississippi River had maintained sporadic diplomatic contact with the Americans since the time of the Louisiana Purchase. With good reason, the Indians regarded the Americans as a warrior people; uniformed officers conducted warfare and diplomacy among the Indians, suggesting a similarity to the Indians' own office of "war chief." Following the American Revolution, British-allied Indians treated with George Rogers Clark, who seemed in some ways familiar to them because of his stature as a warrior. The Indians paid deference to the swaggering American general, although he overestimated the significance of his purely military victories.[1] Yet Clark's methods provided the Americans with what they considered a working model for the management of Indian affairs in the Old Northwest. In the future, all diplomacy between the Indians and the United States would take place in a distinctly military milieu, which was designed to both impress and intimidate the Indians.

Zebulon Pike adhered to this model in 1807, when he traveled up the Mississippi to scout locations for military posts from which the army could erode the influence of British traders among the Indians. During his trip, Pike discovered the internecine conflict between the Dakotas and the Ojibwas. Because the former agreed to sit with Pike in council, the army officer concluded that they were the less offensive of the two parties, and he pledged to assist the Dakotas militarily should the Ojibwas refuse to accept a negotiated peace. Accustomed to the French model of Indian diplomacy, the

Dakotas welcomed Pike's proposal to construct forts in the region, which the Indians construed as trading houses. They balked, however, at Pike's designs on arbitrating the Dakota-Ojibwa conflict. For their part, the Ojibwas had no more interest in a settlement than did their foes. Yet, Pike reported that he "*commanded* them, in the name of their great father, to make peace," and he pompously assumed that they would obey.[2] Further offending his hosts, Pike demanded that they relinquish the medals bestowed upon them by the British, which conveyed to their wearers the honor of alliance chiefs.[3] Despite Pike's transgressions, the Indians of the Upper Mississippi were encouraged by the prospect of a lively trade with the Americans.

Yet even in this regard the Americans disappointed them. In 1808, the army constructed a fort at the mouth of the Des Moines River to extend American military and economic influence over the Sauks, Mesquakies, and Dakotas. With the exception of the Sauks, most tribes welcomed the Americans and their trade goods. American traders were more interested in expanding westward into the Missouri River Valley and in leaving the Upper Mississippi trade to the British, who were more than willing to enter American territory illegally and offer their superior trade goods. The British also established an entrepôt at St. Joseph's Island, which offered the Indians a convenient trading site outside of American territory.[4] Disappointed in the Americans' failure to assume fully the mantle of Onontio, many Indians turned again to the British, who were more than happy to oblige.

Only after the War of 1812 did the Americans exhibit any serious interest in establishing a permanent presence in the region. American motives were at once economic, military, and humanitarian. Foremost, Americans wished once and for all to disassociate the Indians from the British, who continued to tap the valuable fur trade from afar and, according to many suspicious Americans, to agitate the Indians against the Americans.[5] Accordingly, the Americans embarked upon an ambitious program of fortification construction aimed at subduing the Indians and severing their British ties. In the words of one officer, "The intervention of a fortress between an Indian and his home, is an insuperable obstacle to distant warfare."[6] Even Thomas Forsyth, later renowned as one of the most capable and conscientious Indian agents, subscribed to the necessity of the fortifications because they "would keep the Indians in awe, and might be the occasion of preventing many accidents."[7] In 1816, the army constructed Fort Howard at Green Bay and Fort Crawford at Prairie du Chien. Where they did not build fortifications, soldiers marched through the Indian country simply to show the flag and demonstrate military presence. Two such ventures in 1817 and 1818 seem to have impressed the Dakotas considerably.[8]

In their quest to insulate the Indians from British influence, the Americans received significant assistance from an unexpected quarter: British Canada. The intrigues of private Canadian traders notwithstanding, officers of the British Indian Department steadfastly adhered to the provisions of the Treaty of Ghent—to the great disappointment of the affected Indians. From Canada, the British continued to humor their former allies in council, offering presents to assuage Indian frustration and British guilt. But British agents delivered a consistent message to their former allies: their own Great Father, the King, was at peace with the Americans, and the Indians could no longer look to him for support.[9] As bafflement gave way to bitterness over their betrayal, most Indians reconciled themselves to a new, American order. By 1819, Indian agent Thomas Forsyth was able to note that "the Indians on the Mississippi, I am happy to say, from the best information I can collect, are perfectly peaceable." Even the Sauks—who, along with the Mesquakies, Kickapoos, and Ho Chunks of the Rock River in Illinois had been among the last tribes to sign peace treaties with the United States— appeared to be warming to the Americans.[10] These Indians, Forsyth reported, "do not appear to express such a high opinion of their British Father as formerly; but, on the contrary, they begin to think that their American Father has the strongest arms, and his medicines are the best."[11]

The American program of fort building contributed to this new assessment, but its principal effects were economic rather than military. When, in 1819, Colonel Henry Leavenworth traveled up the Mississippi to establish Fort Snelling at the confluence of the Minnesota and Mississippi Rivers, Thomas Forsyth attempted to allay any anxiety occasioned by the arrival of a substantial military force. Among the Dakotas, Forsyth emphasized the economic benefits of the planned fort. In addition to providing the Indians convenient access to essential services such as blacksmiths, the post, according to Forsyth, would double as a government-administered trade "factory."[12] A critical component of American Indian policy from 1795 until 1822, the factory system existed to increase U.S. influence over the Indians "by administering to their wants, increasing their comforts, and promoting their happiness."[13] Completed in 1820, Fort Snelling at once curtailed the influence of Canadian traders in the region and offered an American enterprise to take their place.[14] Just as the French construction of a trading post on the Upper Mississippi in 1727 had proved a significant economic boon for the tribe, the arrival of the Americans promised to reinvigorate the Dakota economy. Forsyth recorded that a chief named Little Crow voiced pleasure about the impending fortress construction, for "the Sioux would now have their Father with them."[15] In Green Bay, the reception was much the same, especially among the métis population, which quickly grasped the economic potential of the new garrison.[16] In contrast, métis and French traders of Prairie du Chien—a bastion of pro-British sentiment—were put off by the army commanders, who occupied the village with the haughtiness of conquerors. Relations did not improve in 1817, when Lieutenant Colonel Talbot Chambers assumed command. A notorious drunkard whom the army cashiered in 1826, Chambers sentenced Jacques Menard to twenty-five lashes for reproaching the colonel for his drunken, lustful pursuit of an unwilling young woman.[17] Economic imperatives and the arrival of more temperate officers helped alleviate the situation, but Prairie du Chien was unique for the distance that remained between its Francophone citizens and U.S. administrators.

The Indians may have wished to restore the fur trade to its former prominence, but they were less certain about the cannon-toting bluecoats garrisoning the most martial of trading posts. Although the various contingents were miniscule by European standards (typically two infantry companies for each remote post), their purpose was not entirely clear to the Indians. While the French and British had maintained soldiers in the remote reaches of the *pays d'en haut,* they had typically done so within the context of broader colonial contests. But the Americans were not at war, and they preached steadfast neutrality in Indian affairs. What purpose were the soldiers to serve? In the corridors of American government, the forts were meant to subdue the Indians, but this was never communicated to them. Forsyth assured the Dakotas that the army was there for their benefit and protection, and that "their enemies would not be allowed to injure any of the Sioux Indians at or near the fort." He added, however, an important caveat: "but at the same time the Sioux must not injure the Chippewas that might visit the fort."[18] Echoing Pike's earlier admonishments, it seemed that the soldiers were intent on preventing warfare between the Indians.

In Green Bay, which many officers regarded as the most important location in the region, the Americans paid the Menominees the diplomatic courtesy of requesting permission to erect a fort on their lands.[19] The American commander and his officers sat in council with the famous Menominee chief Tomah, who addressed the group with flattery. "My Brother! How can we oppose your locating a council-fire among us? You are too strong for us. Even if we wanted to oppose you, we have scarcely got powder and shot to make the attempt." In this last statement, Tomah meant to communicate not only that his Menominees posed no threat to the Americans but that they were a people in need, subtly implying that the Americans could demonstrate their beneficence by easing his people's privation. Tomah explicitly requested only one favor from the Americans: "that our French brothers shall not be disturbed or in any way molested." Contingent upon this request, he said, "You can choose any place you please for your fort, and we shall not object."[20]

The Ho Chunks were not so acquiescent. Following their victory over the Sauks and Mesquakies in the preceding century, the Ho Chunks had expanded south and westward to occupy the hunting lands of their vanquished foes. Although their population had by this time rebounded to approximately 4,500 persons living in nearly forty villages stretching from the lower Rock River to Lake Winnebago, the Ho Chunks retained the fiery belligerence of a people who had narrowly survived extermination.[21] Among other Algonquian customs, the Ho Chunks adopted the earlier Mesquakie practice of levying tribute on those traversing the Fox River. Despite signing a treaty of goodwill with the Americans in St. Louis on 3 June 1816, the Ho Chunks continued this practice and were rumored to remain on the British payroll.[22] Upon learning of the American force at Green Bay, the Ho Chunks sent a deputation to protest the intrusion. A chief informed the American commander "that if his object was peace, he had brought more with him than was necessary to treat; but if his object was war, he had brought too few to fight."[23] The officer responded by showing the chief ten or twelve large cannon, which seemed to alter the Ho Chunk's initial calculation.[24] The Ho Chunk deputation departed without incident, but relations between the tribe and the army remained tense.

Over the next decade, Americans' opinion of the Ho Chunks ranged from loathing to admiration. One idea, however, remained constant: that the Ho Chunks were "a bold and warlike tribe."[25] Among early American civilians in Green Bay, these characteristics could cause considerable alarm. In 1822, a missionary schoolteacher observed a Ho Chunk war dance in which "their stalwart men, [and] Amazonian women" displayed their "independent mien, athletic figures, and defiant bearing." Although clearly impressed, the teacher noted that "none could endure the scene unmoved—unappalled."[26] Others disagreed. Perhaps raised to admire demonstrations of martial prowess, the son of Fort Snelling's commander opined, "These people have more courage, and more national character, than any tribe of the North West. Drunkenness is not so common among them as among other tribes, and they are not so fond of mixing blood with the whites."[27] Because of their reluctance to intermarry with whites, the Ho Chunks had not developed the kinship networks that tied other tribes to the French and (to a lesser extent) the British. Although they had fought beside the

French, Pontiac, and the British, the basis of the Ho Chunks' various alliances remained almost entirely military and was designed to preserve their existence as an independent people.[28] Even by the time of the Black Hawk War, some Ho Chunks exhibited no interest in normalizing relations with the Americans. A visitor to Green Bay in the summer of 1832 described the Ho Chunks as "tall in figure, haughty in his mien, proud of his nationality, and ever ready for war," adding that "he . . . repulses the advance of the white man."[29] Relatively unimpressed by American military power, the Ho Chunks fired on soldiers who refused to pay their Fox River toll and continued to demand tribute from military detachments traversing the Fox River as late as 1830.[30]

In stark contrast to the Ho Chunks, tribes that had enjoyed privileged stations under the French regime were quick to adapt to the American presence—and to make the Americans adapt to theirs. Formerly the hosts of significant French trade entrepôts at Green Bay and Lake Pepin on the Upper Mississippi, the Menominees, Potawatomis, and Dakotas exerted considerable influence over the Americans through their relatives in Green Bay, Chicago, and Prairie du Chien. Unimpressive to American eyes, these cosmopolitan, "Creole" villages were in fact important sites of economic and cultural exchange.[31] At the time of the Americans' arrival, the leading citizens of these communities were French or métis traders. Fluent in several languages, and despite varying degrees of fluency in English, these traders won early appointments as justices of the peace and other civil offices from the territorial governors. Although most of the métis regarded army officers as capricious and overbearing, métis people rendered vital services to federal Indian agents, who employed them as interpreters, guides, and couriers to the Indian country.

First authorized by Congress in 1793, Indian agents conducted the day-to-day business of managing federal-Indian relations from agency houses among the Indians, usually at a common site with a military post and (until 1822) a trade factory. While the soldiers awed the Indians and the government factor supplied them, the Indian agent dispensed annuities (perennial payments for ceded territory) and endeavored to administer federal Indian policy. For much of the nineteenth century, this policy aimed at "civilizing" and assimilating Indians into the dominant white society by exposing them to European agricultural practices and notions of individual property ownership. Despite rabid anti-Indian sentiment along the frontier of white settlement, Secretary of War William Crawford was sincere in 1816 when he wrote, "It is the true policy and earnest desire of the Government to draw its savage neighbors within the pale of civilization" rather than "to extinguish the Indian title, and settle their lands as rapidly as possible." The latter course, Crawford contended, would result in "continual warfare, attended by the extermination or expulsion of the aboriginal inhabitants." Aware that such an outcome suited some Americans just fine, Crawford admonished, "The correctness of this policy cannot for a moment be admitted. The utter extinction of the Indian race must be abhorrent to the feelings of an enlightened and benevolent nation."[32] Hence, while the army came among the Indians to awe them into submissiveness, the Indian agents came as advocates of beneficent paternalism—agents of a distant but omnipotent leader who would provide for the Indian's needs, afford them "occasional asylum" when chastised by enemies, and furnish "redress for any grievances."[33] In place of the "Great Mountain," Onontio, the Americans offered a "Great Father," the President.

Despite the similarity of the name and the paternalistic pretensions, the Great Father was notably inferior to his French—and even British—predecessor in many ways. Immediately noticeable to the Indians was the poor quality of American trade goods, which—with the single exception of tobacco—were so inferior to British manufactures that the Indians assumed that any article of shoddy workmanship was American-made.[34] Often the government-paid factors were of no better quality than the goods they dispensed. One of the first American residents of Green Bay deadpanned that the factor at that place was "as well fitted for the trust as any citizen totally unacquainted with the Indian country, its trade and inhabitants, could be—that is, not fitted at all." Devoid of any knowledge of the Indians and peddling the "sleazy, woolen blankets, cheap calico, and . . . poor unserviceable guns" furnished by the government, the factor stood no chance when competing with private métis traders (usually employed by British trading companies in Canada) who had dealt with the Indians for generations. Consequently, "during his four years' trade," the Green Bay factor "did not secure fifty dollars worth of peltries."[35] Other factors fared no better, and in 1822 Congress ended the factory system, which had incurred financial losses in every year of its existence and failed to demonstrate any progress toward its designed objectives of "civilizing" the Indians and distancing them from the British.[36]

In 1819, Sauk and Mesquakie agent Thomas Forsyth ascribed lingering affection for the British among the Indians to not only the superiority of their trade goods but also the superiority of their Indian agents, who uniformly spoke Native languages and were familiar with their customs. In contrast, "A man is appointed an agent in the interior of the Union, who perhaps never saw an Indian until he came to the agency. How, then, can it be supposed that a man who knows nothing about Indians, can do anything with them?"

Forsyth pilloried his colleagues for their ignorance of "Indian character" and their propensity to "promise fifty things to the Indians with a prior intention to put them off." He warned, "As long as we continue to pursue our present ignorant system of Indian affairs, we will always be in the dark, and the hatred of the Indian race will be handed down to successive generations."[37]

Warranted in some cases, Forsyth's criticism did not do justice to many of his contemporaries, such as Henry Schoolcraft, who became one of the best-known ethnologists of his day. As Forsyth indicated, Indian agents achieved their office by political appointment rather than familiarity with the Indians, and few possessed any special qualifications for dealing with Indians. Still, the men who won these appointments (which were ratified by the Senate) were mainly ambitious, talented, and educated men who threw themselves wholeheartedly into the business of learning their trade and the Indians they served. While certainly not as adept at their craft as had been the French commandants of a century past, they were not wholly incompetent, and they certainly are not to be confused with the infamously corrupt Indian agents of a later generation. The success of the various Indian agents inevitably depended upon the character of the individual agent and, according to historian Francis Paul Prucha, the United States was fortunate to have enjoyed the services of "a number of capable and distinguished men of character and integrity that gave stature to the office of Indian agent."[38] If inferior to their predecessors, the U.S. Indian agents were usually the most accessible and sympathetic Americans known to the Indians, and—however poor their diction—they spoke a familiar language of alliance.

But Forsyth was not alone in his fear that the agents were making promises they could not keep. Adhering to customary forms of

Indian diplomacy, agents spoke on behalf of their Great Father and pledged his undying affection and loyalty for his red children. Believing that they were dealing with true spokesmen for the president, the Indians were initially unaware that they were in fact communicating with lower-level functionaries of an inconstant government. Undermanned and underfunded, the agents were responsible for the administration of an ambitious and important federal program in some of the most desolate corners of the nation. And they did so from an ambiguous legal foundation that excited the jealousies of some authoritarian army commanders, who resented the agents' prerogative. Recognizing that their organization was insufficient for the task at hand, Secretary of War John C. Calhoun established the Bureau of Indian Affairs within his department in 1824. To chair this important body, he appointed Thomas McKenney as Superintendent of Indian Affairs. Unfortunately, Calhoun established this office without legal authorization, and McKenney found himself powerless to effect meaningful change; he lamented that his extralegal bureau was "too powerless to be effective, and too responsible for its feebleness."[39] He championed legislation that would put the Indian Office on firmer footing, but it was never put to a vote during his tenure, and he rightly feared that "we shall go on slip-shod, as we have gone on."[40] Compelled by events, Congress finally passed the legislation advocated by McKenney in 1832—two years after McKenney left office.[41] (Believing that McKenney's loyalty to the Indians was stronger than his attachment to the president, Andrew Jackson dismissed McKenney in 1830.)

Much of McKenney's frustration sprang from the fact that officials charged with executing American Indian policy could not agree on its proper course. Although later remembered as a champion of Indian removal, McKenney was foremost an advocate of a program of "civilization," believing that it was the government's duty to wean the Indians from their "savage" habits through literary and moral instruction so that they could eventually assimilate into Anglo-American society. In the southern United States, McKenney relied on the evangelical zeal of missionaries to effect this object, but such ex officio agents were sparse in the Old Northwest, and the business of civilizing fell principally to the Indian agents and army officers, who did not uniformly subscribe to McKenney's vision. Brigadier Edmund Pendleton Gaines, commander of the Western Department of the U.S. Army for most of McKenney's tenure, openly criticized McKenney's emphasis on *"literary* and *moral instruction"* and instead advocated vocational and military training for the Indians.[42] Believing the Indians possessed virtues absent in white men, Gaines favored only partial acculturation that would enable the Indians to live peaceably beside the Americans without surrendering their Native culture entirely.

Part of this culture, Gaines recognized, was exaltation of the warrior. Rather than eradicate Indian martial values, as McKenney and many missionaries intended, Gaines hoped to put them in the service of the United States. Reflecting on America's doleful performance in the War of 1812, Gaines asserted, "The only possible means of avoiding a recurrence of some of the worst of those evils is to instruct, civilize, and thus secure to ourselves the friendliness and future services of these numerous tribes."[43] Most Americans, he knew, dreaded the prospect of arming the Indians, but he insisted that "no nations can field better light troops than most of these Indians."[44] Moreover, Gaines insisted that Indians had always evinced themselves to be steadfast and loyal when they had been treated fairly. Although this precondition had left the United States with a shallow pool of historical experience on which to draw, Gaines argued that, if the past performance of America's Indian allies had left something to be desired, it was "because we forbid their fighting in the manner best known to them, viz.: *as savages* are in the habit of fighting." As proof, he pointed to the effectiveness of Britain's Native allies against the Americans, who fought in their traditional modes of war.[45]

Like McKenney, Gaines demanded fair dealing with the Indians and exhibited sincere concern for their welfare. His admiration of Native warrior values, however, put him at odds with McKenney, and the superintendent resented what he regarded as unenlightened meddling. Gaines, meanwhile, recommended that Congress charge the administration of Indian affairs to army officers, who, he argued, wielded more authority and garnered more respect among the Indians. Gaines recommended that majors of cavalry simultaneously serve as Indian agents and the commanders of large companies of mounted infantry.[46] Learning of the proposal, McKenney scoffed, "No man who knows his Alphabet in Indian concerns can listen a moment to it. Officers of the Army to manage Indians!"[47] Despite his flippant dismissal of Gaines's proposal, McKenney realized that it was not without substance. The Indians did, in fact, afford greater respect to military officers, and Indian agents routinely affected military titles on the basis of often brief and ancient militia service. Even McKenney himself saw fit to don a uniform when conducting his first treaty negotiations with the Ojibwas in 1826.[48]

Whatever their disagreements over policy, Gaines and McKenney both recognized the Indians' admiration of military strength. In all important affairs, the Indian agent and the army commander represented the United States alongside each other, usually in the shadow of an American fortification. If an army post was not near-by, an infantry company accompanied the treaty commissioners, partly for security but mainly to conduct parades and in-ranks in-spections for the benefit of the Indians, who were impressed with such martial theater regardless of its tactical value. For reasons of economy and convenience, the Americans preferred to treat with Indians at army posts, which obviated the need to detail a military escort for the commissioners and tended to avoid the "introduc-tion among the Indians of spirituous liquors," which almost always disrupted the proceedings.[49] Initially, the Americans conducted di-plomacy in this martial milieu to awe the Indians, but they soon learned that the Indians themselves preferred a military setting. In their experience, army officers were among the most trustworthy Americans they had encountered, and the presence of uniformed soldiers offered the Indians some confidence that they were not be-ing cheated. Moreover, the Indians were indeed impressed with demonstrations of military strength. Gaines recognized that "that the presence of a military force" did not operate "upon the fears of the Indians" but rather appealed to their "chivalric spirit."[50] As the most manifest evidence of the Great Father's power, the army was intended to convince the Indians of the folly of opposing the Amer-icans by force of arms. Instead, it convinced many Indians that the Americans were allies worth embracing.

The primal urges of the military officers and some Indian agents may have furthered among the Indians the conviction that the Americans were interested in resurrecting a multidimensional alli-ance that, adhering to the French precedent, involved a union based on blood as well as arms and trade. White women had always been rare in the *pays d'en haut,* and American women were rarer yet; the only unmarried American woman at Fort Snelling in 1823 was claimed by a lieutenant when she was only fifteen.[51] Inevitably, and like the French voyageurs before them, federal officers sought and found carnal comfort in the lodges of nearby Indian villages. Never given to regard chastity as a virtue in the first place, the Indians assented to these liaisons in the reasonable belief that they would yield the nearly indestructible kinship bonds upon which meaningful alliances must rest. At first, however, the officers apparently regarded their affairs as mere dalliances. Dr. Muir, the surgeon at Fort Snelling, married his Mesquakie consort only to endure the merciless taunting of his fellow officers, which compelled him to abandon both his wife and their child. When she traveled nine hundred miles by canoe with only the company of their infant to be reunited with her husband, however, Muir relented, surrendering his army commission and settling down with his multiethnic family in Galena, Illinois.[52] Over time, Muir's colleagues abandoned their own inhibitions, and at one point all but two of Fort Snelling's officers had taken common-law wives among the Indians. Although less common among the Indian agents, two notable cases beg mention. At the Saint Peters Agency adjacent to Fort Snelling, Agent Lawrence Taliaferro wed the daughter of the Dakota war chief Cloud Man.[53] Fort Snelling's schoolmaster, John Marsh, also took a Dakota bride, mastered the language of her people, and became the subagent at Prairie du Chien.

Despite the probably apocryphal rumor that Zachary Taylor initially disapproved of Jefferson Davis's courting Taylor's daughter on account of Davis's cavorting with Indian women, commanders do not seem to have discouraged their officers from the practice (although, in an army plagued by desertion, no evidence suggests that enlisted men were permitted to do so).[54] Some regarded their attachment as sacred, and at least one officer fought a duel over an insult directed at his bride.[55] Agents Taliaferro and Marsh were devoted husbands and, by extension, friends to the Dakotas, the latter even losing his post as subagent because his superior believed him to be *too* partial to the tribe.[56] Most military officers, meanwhile, appear to have regarded their Indian lovers fondly, but few took their wives and children with them when they transferred to different duty stations. Among those rumored to leave behind their métis children were Jefferson Davis and William S. Harney. According to one soldier, "the alliance between officers and children of the forest was close, if not enduring."[57] Although most marriages did not last, the Indians did not necessarily regard the departure of husbands as unconscionable abandonment. In accordance with their own practice, marriages were often of short duration, and both men and women commonly took several spouses in their lifetimes. Fragile though the bonds of matrimony may have been, the kinship ties manifest in the métis children endured.

Sent to the region to humble the Indians, army officers also appealed to the Indians' conception of a cross-cultural alliance. Alarmed at first, the Indians grew accustomed to the forts' cannon and the presence of armed troops at councils. As mentioned earlier, these spectacles likely pleased the Indians as symbols of military strength and experience.[58] The Indians themselves sent both "war chiefs" and "civil chiefs" to represent their people in council, and the Americans' practice seemed to suggest a degree of cultural congruence and a shared affinity for military strength. Although army officers enjoined their Indian counterparts to lay down the hatchet and live at peace with their neighbors, Indian leaders could not help but notice that the Americans showed deference to established Indian warriors. According to a missionary who later worked among the Dakotas, they "might be told that it was wrong to kill women and children, but he who had the most eagle feathers on his head was sure to attract the most attention and also to be treated with the greatest consideration."[59] When, after the War of 1812, the United States offered to the Indians treaties of peace and friendship, the latter could just as easily perceive the U.S. Army as an opportunity as a threat; the Americans' willingness to take wives among their people seemed to remove any ambiguity. To the Indians, who generally categorized all other groups of people as friends or enemies, the Americans appeared to be very powerful friends indeed, and the prospect of allying with them seemed to offer an opportunity to place American military power at their disposal. After all, Pike, Forsyth, and other spokesmen of the Great Father promised to chastise the enemies of those Indians loyal to the United States. None of them could envision how the terms of the alliance would change once the principal enemies of the loyal Indians were whites rather than other Indians.

In the early years of American occupation, however, such concerns were distant, if they entered Indian consciousness at all. Although the Americans spoke the language of Onontio somewhat awkwardly and their trade goods left much to be desired, they resurrected many of the earlier vestiges of alliance relied upon by the French and British. Operating from a handful of posts separated by hundreds of miles of wilderness, the Indian agents found it infeasible to deal with dozens of disparate bands as distinct political entities. Just as the French regime had relied on "alliance chiefs," the Indian agents necessarily vested power in "principal chiefs" willing to represent all bands within the administrative lines of agency jurisdiction. Although some Indians resented the erection of such synthetic chiefdoms, which elevated those best able to deal with the white man on his own terms, the practice was not unknown to

France's former allies.[60] This fact did not escape Thomas McKenney, who later cited French and British precedent to justify the naming of a principal chief for the Menominees and the manufacture of three hundred silver medals bearing the likeness of President Jackson to award to principal chiefs (although the government neglected to replace the British medals Zebulon Pike had taken from the Dakotas until 1833).[61]

Perhaps the most important—and problematic—way in which the Americans echoed earlier practices of the French and British was in their mediation of disputes among the region's various tribes and bands. While the Americans did not share their predecessors' interest in assembling a large, multitribal military alliance, they did share the Europeans' keen interest in profit, especially after 1822, when John Jacob Astor's American Fur Company quickly filled the void left by the demise of the factory system. The pursuit of profit encouraged the Americans to seek peace. War diverted Indian men from the hunt—some permanently—and threatened the lives and capital of whites engaged in the fur trade. Although renowned for his compassion for the Indians, even Thomas McKenney could not discount the financial imperative for maintaining peace: "The great sufferers in general contests of this sort, next to the Indians, are the traders. The hunting parties are broken up by these wars, and there is a corresponding reduction in their returns, and a loss to the companies."[62]

Yet the motive for maintaining the peace was not entirely economic. Intent on converting the Indians to full-time agriculturalists, proponents of the civilization program recognized the importance of curtailing traditional male pursuits (which frequently put them in conflict with the fur traders, who were not at all eager to see the Indians abandon hunting). War, which provided the only venue for male social advancement, had to go. Denied the ability to gain honor and station by arms, the theory went, Indian men would necessarily take up the plow and adopt a more domesticated mode of life. This required Indian men not only to abandon that which defined them as male but also to take up farming, a quintessentially female vocation in Indian society. Not surprisingly, the Indians exhibited little enthusiasm for the venture. Although it became evident to some that the goal of transforming the Indians into Christian farmers was infeasible, the supposed imperative of pacifying the Indians intensified throughout the 1820s—for they could not be removed to the trans-Mississippi West while at war with one another.[63] Wisely, American officials never communicated this motive for pacification to the Indians.

Indian agents appealed to the Indians to quit their wars on humanitarian grounds. According to Thomas McKenney, "Humanity directs that these people, who sport so with each other's lives, should be counseled frequently, and led, if possible, to cherish the more agreeable state of peace and friendship." Unless the Americans weaned the Indians from their warrior ways, it appeared inevitable that they would "fight on until some one or other of the tribes shall become too reduced and feeble to carry on the war, when it will be lost as a separate power."[64] The Indians were unmoved by such logic, which appeared flawed to them. Warfare was neither unnatural nor inhumane, but instead a vital component of their culture and the basis for many societal structures. Despite the excesses of the Beaver Wars and the Fox Wars—arguably products of European instigation—Indian warfare remained limited in scope and duration. Their fragile, subsistence economies dependent on regular production from every hunter, Indians were averse to inflicting, as well as sustaining, large numbers of casualties.

Because most Indian groups shared a relatively benign interpretation of warfare, they were bemused and later frustrated by American admonitions to refer all grievances to the Great Father for arbitration. In 1819, Thomas Forsyth asked the Dakota chief Little Crow about the possibility of ending the incessant Dakota-Ojibwa feud. Little Crow replied that it would be easy enough to secure a peace, but that the consequences would be doleful for the Dakotas. Each year, Little Crow asserted, the Ojibwas and his people would lose a man or two to the conflict, but the boundary between the two remained relatively static. In the event of peace, "we, the Sioux, would lose all our hunting grounds on the north-east side of the river; why then . . . should we give up such an extensive country to another nation to save the lives of a man or two annually[?]" In his journal, Forsyth admitted, "I found the Indian's reason so good, that I said no more on the subject to him."[65]

As Little Crow indicated, intertribal conflict and bloodshed were in fact valued devices for the resolution of outstanding grievances. Most Indian societies adhered to remarkably similar legal systems characterized, like most facets of Indian life, by reciprocity. Lives lost normally had to be "covered," or compensated for, by a like number of lives from the offending group. If the killing occurred within the population of the same clan or group, resolution was usually swift, and frequently the murderer would submit himself to the mercy of the aggrieved family. Transgressions that crossed tribal boundaries, however, were more difficult to arbitrate, and long-standing animosities between tribal enemies were often the product of unresolved feuds. When Indians killed members of allied tribes—a happenstance often occasioned by alcohol—tribal leaders moved quickly to defuse the situation. In 1819, a drunken Menominee stabbed a Dakota man near Fort Crawford. Although the young Dakota survived the assault, his tribesmen seized and bound the offender. Rather than impose punishment in kind, Dakota leaders had the Menominee brought before them, presented him with gifts, and compelled him to eat from the same dish with his recovering victim, thereby forgiving his sin and averting a confrontation between allies.[66] Other tribes were less magnanimous. Perhaps because of their earlier travails, the Ho Chunks were hardly inclined to grant amnesty to any party and, indeed, regarded the lives of their own worth more than the lives of any other Indians. According to the son of an army officer with a liberal view of Indian justice, "No tribe consider revenge a more sacred duty than the Winnebagoes. It is their ancient custom to take five lives for one, and it is notorious on the frontiers, that no blood of theirs has been shed, even in modern days, that has not been fully avenged."[67] This bellicose policy appears to have served the Ho Chunks well; once on the verge of extinction, they had no natural enemies when—or until—the Americans arrived.

Although desirous of peace with the Ho Chunks, the Americans set out to eradicate their notions of justice. In July 1820, Michigan Territory governor Lewis Cass, whose domain encompassed all of modern Michigan and Wisconsin, attempted to negotiate a settlement between the Ojibwas and the Dakotas at Fort Snelling. It established a pattern that became all too familiar over the ensuing years: faced with a carrot-or-stick proposition by the United States, each party (both of which only represented portions of their respective tribes) reluctantly conceded to the American-brokered settlement, which would remain in effect only a matter of months before some new incident rekindled the conflict and occasioned another settlement. Ostensibly, the forward-positioned garrisons of American soldiers served as a deterrent against intertribal violence, but these forces were essentially toothless in practice. Engagements in internecine tribal squabbles routinely amounted to no more than a half dozen casualties total; the government learned about them well after the fact; and each of the belligerents exercised effective, preemptive diplomacy with the United States—pleading their innocence to their respective agents and begging their Great Father to redress the wrongs committed by their nefarious foes. Agents routinely endorsed the version of events related by their own charges, with different agencies thus proposing divergent responses. The government then resorted to arbitrating anew. The army could do little more than seize hostages from the offending tribes to be held until the surrender of the perpetrators, who where then subjected to American justice. Given the nature of the scant evidence available, these suspects were often acquitted after lengthy detention.

Perhaps aware that submitting the Indians to European justice produced discontent among the Indians, a few American administrators—particularly army officers—adopted a pragmatic accommodation with Indian modes. In 1827, a party of Dakotas treacherously killed some Ojibwas with whom they were smoking a pipe of peace near Fort Snelling. Colonel Josiah Snelling, commander of the post that bore his name, seized some of the perpetrators. Rather than submit them to the laborious American justice system, however, Snelling handed them over to the Ojibwas to do with as they pleased: "I deliver them into your hands," he told them. "They have deserved death, and you may inflict it, or not, as you think proper. . . . I wash my hands of the matter."[68] Snelling was careful to ensure, however, that the executions occurred beyond the shadow of his fort and the sight of his garrison. He also demanded that the Ojibwas dispose of the bodies so as not to excite the passions of the neighboring Dakotas.[69]

Although the Indians preferred Snelling's solution, it ran the risk of sullying the Great Father's impartiality (as in fact happened in this case). Moreover, it ran counter to the established goal of eradicating the Indians' revenge-based justice system. Consequently, the Indian Office insisted that the standard mode of redressing Indian grievances involve the apprehension of the principal offenders, followed by trial and punishment. In the event that the offending tribe refused to surrender the perpetrators, the agent was to cooperate with the local military commander to undertake coercive measures. Under no circumstances were agents to permit Indians to take matters into their own hands.[70] The absolute prohibition on resolving their own disputes frustrated the Indians considerably, but most Indian groups submitted to their Great Father's will and permitted him to dispense justice on their behalf. They did so, however, not out of fear of military retribution but due to the influence of Indian agents like Lawrence Taliaferro, whose kinship ties permitted him to work within the Dakota political system.[71] He exercised a dutiful impartiality and earned the sobriquet "Four Hearts" because of his unusual fairness to Americans, Britons, Frenchmen, and Indians.[72]

By 1822, most of the Indians of the Upper Mississippi Valley and the officers of the American government had reached an accommodation. Although some army commanders could be capricious and overbearing (on rare occasion even submitting Indians to harsh, military punishments), most officers developed considerable empathy for the Indians. As Edward Coffman has revealed by his meticulous examination of their correspondence and professional journals, officers of the era usually regarded the Indians as tragic victims of both circumstance and—as soon became evident in this region—white frontiersmen.[73] Drawn predominantly from educated families in the East, many officers subscribed in some degree to the archetype of the "noble savage," and very few expressed the patently racist view of Judge Advocate of the Army Samuel Storrow, who, while conducting an inspection of the western posts, "found none of the high qualities which they have been so lavishly imputed to them; nothing to justify the contradictory expression of *savage virtue*, or to warrant the belief of a radical difference between the Arab, the Algerine, or the Indian."[74] Those who lived on the frontier and among the Indians knew better. According to Juliette Kinzie, wife to an Indian agent at the Portage, the wretches observed by Storrow had been subjected to "the debasing influences of a proximity to the whites, . . . which no one will admit with so much sorrow as those who lived among them, before this signal change had taken place."[75] Although most frontier officers considered the Indians benighted, Captain Henry Smith expressed the predominant sentiment of the army officers when he wrote that the Indians were "almost always 'more sinned against than sinning.'"[76]

Among those who sinned against the Indians were the enlisted soldiers of the army garrisons. Often immigrants, the soldiers exhibited the same opprobrium for the Indians that marked the frontiersmen. Although discharged soldiers were known to take Indian wives and engage in trade, commanders recognized the prudence of limiting contact between soldiers and Indians. Infamously, unscrupulous fur traders victimized Indians during the annual payment of treaty annuities by plying them with liquor and cheating them of all of their money for mere trifles. Not to be outdone, soldiers swindled the Indians with what little they had. According to one soldier, "The Indians would pay any sum for an ornament that pleased them, and the soldiers would sell pewter buttons and scales, costing 6 or 8 cents, for as many dollars."[77] Conscientious commanders held their subordinates responsible for offenses against the Indians. In Green Bay in 1832, a drunken soldier stabbed the Menominee war chief Poegonah (Big Soldier) in the thigh with his bayonet. A witness later recalled that "the old chief seized the soldier, disarmed him with one hand, and grabbing him by the throat with the other, threw him to the ground, calling him a dog, and alleging that if he were an enemy, he would take his life for his insolence." The commander of Fort Howard at that time took no issue with Poegonah but had the offending soldier whipped before an assemblage of Indians.[78] On other occasions, the Indians did not need American commanders' assistance to redress grievances against enlisted men. In 1822, an Indian woman killed one soldier and wounded another when they attempted to steal her whiskey.[79]

Fortunately for all involved, conflicts between soldiers and Indians were rare, and the army came to depend on the Indians to render essential services for its remote garrisons. Fort Winnebago, constructed at the Portage in 1828, was so isolated that it received mail only once every two or three months. "There was, however, no lack of meat," veteran John Dean recalled, because the Indians kept "the garrison well supplied with venison, wild ducks, and other game."[80] Dean also stated that it was common practice for the army to employ Indians or métis to track down deserters, trailing them to Chicago, where the bounty hunters identified the fleeing soldiers to authorities.[81]

By employing Indians to track fugitive whites and dispensing harsh justice against soldiers who abused the Indians, American officers may have contributed to a belief among the Indians that the Americans did not discriminate on the basis of race. While successive frontiers of Indians to the east had learned otherwise, the Indians of the Upper Mississippi Valley had remained relatively isolated from the brutal race wars of the eighteenth century—and from the "nativist" movements they inspired.[82] While the teachings of the Delaware prophet Neolin and the Shawnee prophet Tenskwatawa had helped forge a pan-Indian consciousness among tribes to the east, those of the *pays d'en haut* retained their traditional conceptions of identity and alliance. Their experiences offered little precedent for solidarity on the basis of race. Rather, these Indians were well accustomed to allying with whites against "fellow" Indians and other whites. When private American fur traders moved into the region following the demise of the factory system in 1822, the Indians saw further evidence that the Great Father reserved no special status for his white children.

Most Indians welcomed the American Fur Company traders. Unlike the government factors, the traders traveled throughout Indian country rather than requiring the Indians to transport their furs to the factories. More importantly, John Jacob Astor understood the Indian market and furnished articles in which the Indians were interested: British-manufactured trade goods and liquor.[83] As the doleful effects of alcohol on their communities became apparent, some Indian leaders began to preach temperance, but liquor remained a high-demand staple of the fur trade. One of the supposed benefits of the factory system had been its ability to limit the supply of alcohol among the Indians. With the demise of that system, private traders realized that they needed to offer whiskey to remain competitive, and unethical traders came to appreciate how easily an inebriated Indian and his furs were parted. The Indian Office and the army did not look kindly on the trade in whiskey, which was conducive neither to the stability of the frontier nor to the "civilization" of the Indians.[84] For their own part, the traders resisted the federal government's initiative to convert the Indians to small-plot agriculture. Because their own livelihood depended on the Indians' skill as hunters, the fur traders and their employers actively dissuaded the Indians from adopting the economic reforms advocated by the American government and even tried to undermine treaties between the Indians and the government if such treaties promised to deprive Indian hunters of fur-rich hunting lands. Hence, an antagonism developed between federal officials and the fur traders. By 1831, an anonymous observer in St. Louis (likely Thomas Forsyth, who by that time had been relieved of his post as agent) wrote, "The American Fur Company seems to have made war upon the agents in all of the Missouri country, except one or two who belong to them."[85] Meanwhile, the agents made war on many of the traders, who became persona non grata in Prairie du Chien and other hubs of regional commerce. Fully engaged with each party of this dispute, the Indians saw little evidence of a singular American identity.

Until the mid-1820s, the Indians had not encountered American settlers in large numbers. Painfully aware of the likely consequences of such contact, this suited the U.S. government just fine. As early as 1788, Secretary of War Henry Knox lamented the role of frontier whites in fomenting Indian wars.[86] He discerned a pattern that would repeat itself for over a hundred years with disastrous consequences for the Native peoples of the continent. In wanton violation of existing treaties defining the boundary between U.S. and Indian territory, squatters and land speculators constructed houses and planted crops on unceded land while abusing the local Indian population. Thus confronted, the Indians responded in one of two ways: by appealing to the government for redress or by forcibly evicting the interlopers. In the former case, leading citizens among the squatters eloquently pleaded ignorance of the treaty line and appealed to the government to secure an additional cession of land from the Indians lest they forfeit the considerable capital they had already invested in "improvements" upon the land. Almost invariably, the government responded favorably to these entreaties, and it was by this process that the United States eliminated the claim to most Indian lands over the next century. When the Indians responded to the intrusions with force, however, white frontiersmen generally responded with a vengeance, inciting a bitter brand of warfare that offered no protection to noncombatants. Because of a disparity in numbers and the vulnerability of the Indian villages, the whites uniformly prevailed in these contests, and the "belligerent" Indians were made to relinquish territory without compensation as reparations. Thus, however the Indians responded to the squatters, their land eventually passed from their control, prompting Knox to reflect that "a future historian may mark the causes of this destruction of the human race in sable colors."[87]

Knox recognized a problem that had been evident to the British colonial administration decades earlier: security on the western frontier required the separation of the white and Indian populations. Unable to maintain this separation in the past, the Americans resolved to get it right following the War of 1812. The Treaty of Ghent had confirmed American territorial possessions that far exceeded the needs of the population, and the government demurred at the prospect of purchasing more lands from the Indians due to the "propensity of our frontier settlers to spread over the surface of every cession, however distant," to instigate conflict with the Natives.[88] Only in the Southeast, where the boundaries established by the 1783 Treaty of Paris and the Louisiana Purchase had put the Indians in close contact with "civilization" and left them "exposed to the contagion of its vices," did the U.S. government endeavor to gain title to additional Indian lands—and only with the "voluntary consent" of the owners.[89] In the Old Northwest, however, President James Madison ordered "the necessary measures for removing all white persons who have intruded and settled upon the lands of the Indians," including the use of U.S. troops.[90] This was more than a hollow proclamation, and an early American resident of Green Bay averred that the Indians, the French, and the army all discouraged settlement in Wisconsin until the 1830s, by which time John Quincy Adams and Andrew Jackson had reversed the course set by Madison.[91] "If any attempted to 'squat' upon the lands," Henry S. Baird testified, "they were forcibly removed at the point of a bayonet, or prosecuted by the United States officials as trespassers upon Indian lands."[92]

Undeterred, some ambitious Americans opened business in the region as tenants of the métis, French, or Indians. Not surprisingly, their relations with government officials—especially army officers— were acrimonious. According to one resident, "the officers of the army treated the inhabitants as a conquered people, and the commandants assumed all the authority of governors of a conquered country."[93] Henry Baird, who noted the steadfastness with which the army defended Indian lands, complained that the army subjected early Americans to martial law:

> It occasionally happened that some military genius, possessed of more tinsel than discretion, became the commanding officer, and to mark the era of his reign, would exercise his "little brief authority" in an arbitrary manner, and thus contrive to render the condition of the citizens as uncomfortable as possible. Instances of high handed oppression and injustice were, in the early days of our

history, frequently committed by some military martinet,
upon the persons, liberty or property of those whom
they were sent to protect.[94]

Baird's conviction that the army was there to protect *him* no doubt
gave rise to his indignation; few army commanders perceived their
duty in such terms. More concerned with upholding the letter of
the law, commanders exhibited little concern for the interests of
frontier Americans. If they built houses on Indian lands, soldiers
tore them down; if they cut trees on Indian lands without permission, the army confiscated the timber.[95] Some army commanders
earned the enmity of American entrepreneurs by sheltering their
soldiers from the collection of outstanding debts, but the principal grievances always revolved around the guardianship of Indian
rights.[96]

In this regard, perhaps no officer was as despised by his fellow
Americans as Major David Twiggs. Twiggs, who later gained infamy
for turning his entire command over to the Confederacy at the outbreak of the Civil War, oversaw the construction of Fort Winnebago
in 1828 and commanded its garrison until 1831.[97] One early Wisconsin resident described him as "a large, portly, pompous man" with
"a reputation of being an arbitrary, overbearing officer." Another
called him "A little god, who could do as he pleased, in his own estimation."[98] John Dean, who served under Twiggs, acknowledged
that Twiggs "left no very favorable record, or impression among the
people" and that he was "severe and unreasonable with his men,
and domineering over all who came within his reach."[99] Tales of
Twiggs horse-whipping his own surgeon, confining a soldier to "the
hole" for six months, and binding another to a tree, where he was
whipped for a period of days, gained currency among the Ameri-

cans, who regarded Twiggs as a special sort of evil.[100] But a member of one of the most prominent Ho Chunk families remembered Twiggs as "a good man" who "very often furnished us with shot and powder to shoot geese with."[101]

Martinets were not uncommon in the army of the nineteenth century—Lieutenant Colonel Talbot Chambers was relieved for ordering the ears of one of his soldiers lopped off as a punishment—but Twiggs was particularly objectionable to whites due to his unwavering enforcement of the trade and intercourse laws, which had governed white-Indian relations since 1790.[102] Although he may have been cruel, Twiggs enforced the law to its letter, even requesting the Ho Chunks' permission to cut the timber with which his men constructed Fort Winnebago.[103] Pioneers Daniel Whitney and Ebenezer Childs claimed to possess similar permission, but Twiggs responded decisively to complaints from the Ho Chunks, burning $1,000 worth of shingles cut by the two men.[104] For his actions, Twiggs found himself called into civil court, where the judge determined that he had exceeded his mandate.

The case was far from exceptional. In 1824, Mackinac Indian agent George Boyd sent a party of Ottawas to arrest an outlaw trader named William Farnsworth, who had gone among the Menominees without a license. Delivered to him by a band of Ottawas sent for that purpose, Boyd confiscated Farnsworth's trade goods and flogged and detained the Grand River Indians who had illegally conveyed him. The same evening, however, a Mackinac village court presided over by Justice John Dousman brought charges against Boyd, his Ottawas, and Major William Whistler (then commanding at Mackinac). The Ottawas were released on the grounds that they had only followed orders, but both Boyd and Whistler were found guilty of aiding and abetting the "robbery" of Farnsworth and for flogging the Grand River Indians. Both federal officers were forced to post their own bail and were eventually acquitted by a higher court, which was not beholden to local interests.[105] Over the next several years, sentiments even in Washington began to favor private citizens when they ran afoul of the trade and intercourse acts. In 1829, Major Stephen Watts Kearny of Fort Crawford seized lumber cut on Indian lands by Jean Brunet of Prairie du Chien. Brunet sued both Kearny and Indian agent Joseph Street, and a circuit court awarded damages.[106] The government eventually reimbursed its officers (although Twiggs, who had neglected to keep receipts, paid his own attorney's fees), but it was clear that a gap was growing between federal Indian policy and popular sentiment during the 1820s. As westerners accrued congressional representation throughout the decade and even elected one of their own to the presidency in 1828, the views of the federal government shifted to fall in line with those of its frontier constituents. When Congress reluctantly awarded Twiggs partial compensation in 1832, it warned that officers and agents acting on behalf of the Indians were being "watched with jealousy by Congress for the security of the people" and that the overzealous public officer would, in the future, pay his own court costs "without any hope or prospect that he will obtain relief by applying to Congress."[107]

In the half dozen years following the War of 1812, the Indians of the Old Northwest and the agents of the U.S. government achieved an accommodation. Dependent on European trade goods and inured to the necessity of a white patron, most Indians acquiesced to the Americans' arrival and sought to recreate the symbiotic relationships they had known under the French and Brit-

ish regimes. Bound by the Treaty of Ghent to respect tribal sovereignty, the Americans resolved to turn over a new leaf in their
spotty record of managing Indian affairs and conformed to Indian expectations in many regards. Contentious issues, however, remained: traders offered better goods but defiled Indian society with
liquor; the government denied Indians the freedom to settle their
own disputes and, in the process, frustrated the ambitions of
young warriors; and Indians resisted American overtures toward
"civilization." Meanwhile, the Indians of the Rock River—refugees
from the French regime rather than its beneficiaries—eyed suspi-
ciously the American occupiers. The Sauks and some of their Mesquakie allies continued to nurse a grievance against the United
States dating back to 1804, when the Sauks supposedly surrendered
all of their lands in Illinois to the Americans in return for annuities. The Sauks protested the legitimacy of the treaty, but the issue
was left to fester: the Sauks retained the right of occupancy until
the Americans served notice that they would take possession of the
land. Indeed, all of the unresolved issues between the Indians and
their new American "allies" simmered beneath a patina of tranquility that promised to break if subjected to excessive pressure at any
given point.

# 3

## A Mounting Storm

In 1816, an American shipper named John Shaw ascended the Mississippi River from St. Louis, bound for a mining camp on the Fever River at the future site of Galena, Illinois—the heart of the Indian lead-mining country in southwestern Wisconsin and northwestern Illinois. Various Native groups had mined this country for over four thousand years, and the present occupants—Sauks, Mesquakies, and Ho Chunks—relied on lead exports as a significant component of their economy.[1] These same tribes, however, remained suspicious of the Americans, and they barred Shaw's passage to the Indian mining camp, declaring that "the Americans must not see their lead mines." Speaking impeccable French and commanding a boat manned entirely by French crewmen, Shaw assumed the nationality favored by the indigenous population and thus won the right to pass. At the camp, Shaw and the genuine Frenchmen filled their boat with galena, the valuable ore that yields lead and that furnished the name of the Anglo-American settlement that grew on the Fever River over the ensuing decade—during which the Americans took possession of the mines, the minerals within, and the lands about.[2]

This denouement was neither obvious to the Indians nor assured in 1816. For all of their blustering, the American soldiers who established posts in the Old Northwest were committed to preserving peace on the frontier, whether by intervening in intertribal disputes or running off white violators of the trade and intercourse acts. Although the Indians resented the Americans' prohibition of intertribal war, they regarded American officials as evenhanded. Reciprocity, it appeared, continued to characterize the politics of the *pays d'en haut.* This began to change, however, as the lead country of northwestern Illinois and southwestern Wisconsin drew white miners to the country in ever-increasing numbers. Illinois, made a state in 1818, became a magnet for roughneck opportunists in the mid-1820s. Backed by Illinois politicos, the miners showed no regard for Indian rights and in fact caused a war in 1827. Once willing to flout local white interests to enforce the law, federal officials discovered that the miners enjoyed the sympathies of the nations' highest leaders, who now advocated the removal of all Indians residing east of the Mississippi.

Meanwhile, competition over diminishing peltry spurred intertribal conflict between the Dakotas and their neighbors: the Ojibwas to the northeast and the Sauks and Mesquakies to the south. Although powerless to defend the Indians from white encroachment, Indian agents continued to meddle in intertribal affairs. By the end of the 1820s, the Sauks, Mesquakies, and Ho Chunks entertained no illusions regarding the Great Father's commitment to reciprocity. The Ho Chunks actually took up arms against the Americans to protest their perfidy. In defeat, however, the Ho Chunks developed a modicum of resentful respect for the Americans; their complicated behavior during the Black Hawk War was very much a product of their experience during this tumultuous decade.

For years the Americans had been aware of the mineral wealth of the Upper Mississippi. Following the French and Indian War,

Frenchmen hauled immense quantities of the ore down the Mississippi to New Orleans in twenty-ton river boats, and Julien Dubuque's mining operation in present-day Iowa provided conspicuous testimony to the economic potential of the region.[3] The United States staked its claim to this territory in 1803 with the Louisiana Purchase, which secured the west side of the Mississippi, and in 1804 through a treaty with the Sauks and Mesquakies, which ostensibly secured the eastern shore above the mouth of the Rock River.[4] Hoping to parlay these acquisitions into federal revenue, Congress reserved the mineral lands from sale and resolved to grant leases in terms of three or five years.[5] The Sauks and Mesquakies disputed the legitimacy of the 1804 treaty, however, and the Ho Chunks had not at that point surrendered any of their lands to the Americans. These Indians therefore regarded early American efforts to mine their lands with ill humor, chasing off those bold enough to make the attempt.[6] Treating from a position of strength after the War of 1812, the Americans compelled the Sauks and Mesquakies to confirm their cessions of 1804, although they neglected to consider the Ho Chunks, who occupied a significant portion of these lands.[7]

Despite their apparent concession, the Sauks and Mesquakies continued to resist American encroachment, preferring to deal with their habitual French Canadian trading partners. Aside from a handful of smugglers, the first persistent efforts to draw wealth from the Indian mines began in 1819 or 1820, when James Johnson first established an illegal mining operation on the Fever River.[8] A veteran of the War of 1812 who continued to affect his former station as a colonel, Johnson cajoled the Sauks and Mesquakies into accepting his presence. Johnson flourished, and by 1822 the government deemed the Illinois country stable enough to award leases.[9] On 5 July 1822, Johnson established the first legal American mining camp on the banks of the Fever River. Anticipating trouble from the Indians, Johnson called on Colonel Willoughby Morgan, commander of Fort Crawford and illegitimate son of Revolutionary War hero Daniel Morgan, to furnish "a force sufficient to overawe the Indians." Morgan assented, dispatching forces from Forts Edwards, Armstrong, and Crawford to cow the Sauks and Mesquakies.[10]

The government's policy toward the lead region offered some of the most compelling evidence that the Great Father was not Onontio. Under the French regime, the Indians mined the lead on their own lands and traded the ore to Frenchmen or other Indians in exchange for goods or furs.[11] The Americans, in contrast, intended to deprive the Indians of both their land and their place in the chain of production. In fairness, American officials believed that they were exercising their legal rights in lands ceded to them by formal treaty. In calling on the army to protect these rights, however, the government placed the officers and agents of the War Department in an untenable position. At once charged with implementing a benign Indian policy and with facilitating the exploitation of contested lands, these men behaved in a manner that the Indians could only interpret as duplicitous. Perceptions did not improve in 1824, when the War Department appointed Lieutenant Martin Thomas to serve as the "Superintendent of the United States Lead Mines," a post designed to optimize government revenue derived from the mines.[12] Whereas the agents of the Indian Office and most army officers at least endeavored to balance their divergent obligations, Lieutenant Thomas pursued his more proscribed duties with myopic diligence. Interpreting the Indian cessions of 1804 and 1816 broadly and entirely disregarding the provisions of an 1825 treaty that confirmed Ho Chunk holdings, Thomas issued mining permits for lands well within the country of the Ho Chunks.[13] Initially, the Ho Chunks simply ran off the intruders.[14] When the miners asked Thomas how to respond to such confrontations with the Indians, he reportedly replied, "you must remain there untill blood is spilled, & something will be done."[15] Offered in July 1827, Thomas's advice yielded the desired results within a month.

At first white miners came in only a trickle. Although St. Louis newspapers brimmed with notices "concerning the wealth of the Lead Mines of the Upper Mississippi" in 1822, when the government first decided to issue leases to the land, the terms of the government program were beyond most men's means.[16] Any man wishing to work the land had to post a $10,000 bond and pay the government "one-tenth of all the lead made."[17] Few could afford this sum, but ambitious men of means assembled bodies of ambitious men in want to form the first white mining camps in the region. When they arrived on the Fever River, they took station beside French and Indian mining camps and an American Fur Company trading post.[18] Later, Americans would justify the annexation of Indian mining country by the principle of eminent domain and the supposition that the Indians could not make full use of the minerals bestowed upon them by Providence. Early American miners could not subscribe to this convenient fiction, however, as "The Indian women proved themselves to be the best as well as the shrewdest miners."[19] Still outnumbered by the Indians and their French allies, the white miners worked beside the Indians in relative harmony. As late as July 1825, only 100 white miners inhabited the Fever River camps. Over the next year this number more than quadrupled, to 453. More ominously for the Indians, the white miners had discovered that the government was incapable of limiting the mining operation to leaseholders, and scores of illegal camps spread through the more distant reaches of the mining region.[20] By 1826, the trickle had swollen to a torrent.

Grabbing whatever land they could find, the miners overwhelmed the Indians. From Prairie du Chien, Subagent John Marsh reported that "multitudes of men are flocking here from every part of America and Europe."[21] From Rock Island, a dismayed Thomas Forsyth, agent for the Sauks and Mesquakies, predicted that illegal intrusions onto Ho Chunk lands would incite a war with that tribe.[22] Marsh concurred. "You may easily believe," he wrote his father, "that men, stimulated by such prospects of gain, would not pay that much regard to the rights of the Indians who own the valuable part of the mineral country."[23] Indeed, the miners reveled in their reputations as hard-bitten Indian fighters. Embracing norms of social advancement not entirely dissimilar from those of the Indians, the miner's principal means to become a man of consequence was to offer demonstrations of strength and bravado. Among James Johnson's party worked a "noted bruiser" named "Kentuck" Anderson, who would later participate as a militia volunteer during the Black Hawk War. Anderson was reputed to have engaged in fisticuffs thirteen times in a single day in the town of Mineral Point.[24] Because the miners held up such men as paragons of manly virtue while occupying mining camps as they saw fit, conflict with the Indians was all but inevitable. On a Sunday in the spring of 1826 or 1827, three of Moses Meeker's men went to James Johnson's camp and got drunk. On their way home, they entered an Indian lodge and abused the occupants. One of the Indians grabbed his gun in an effort to ward off the intruders, but the intoxicated miners wrested the weapon away and proceeded to beat the poor man to a pulp—breaking the gun over his head and shoulders. Not contented, the miners "then beat his aged father shamefully."[25]

Fearing retribution, Meeker compensated the victims with gifts, but few Americans went to such lengths.[26] Rightly fearing for the safety of their women and children, the Indian victims—principally Ho Chunks—demonstrated considerable forbearance, enduring further insults rather than retaliating and subjecting their villages to the wrath of men like "Kentuck" Anderson. Already among the most disaffected Indian groups, the Ho Chunks of the mining region found little succor from the Great Father, who was at least as interested in tapping the mineral wealth of the Ho Chunk country as he was in attending to their needs. The army was not a willing party to the defrauding of the Ho Chunks; early miners complained of the army's control of river traffic and attempts to arrest illegal lead miners, as well as "the despotism under which we lived"—but the military proved as ineffectual at protecting the Indians as it was at policing the miners.[27] Years later, a Ho Chunk named Spoon Decorah recalled that the Great Father responded to their pleas for help by saying, "I want this land and will have my own people to work it, and whenever you go out hunting come by this way, and you will be supplied with lead." But the Great Father reneged, and "Never was a bar of lead or a bag of shot presented to us."[28] Instead, white miners took over the Indian mines and exhausted the region's timber to smelt the lead.[29] Had the miners been more perceptive, they would have realized that they were also exhausting Ho Chunk patience. In the autumn of 1826, the Ho Chunks sent a war pipe to the Mesquakies, requesting their aid should the whites attack the Indians.[30]

Just to the west, economic competition between Indians likewise

seemed destined to foment an environmental crisis or a war. Increasingly dependent on manufactured goods and encouraged by
the American Fur Company, which enjoyed a monopoly on the fur
trade following the discontinuation of the factory system, Sauks,
Mesquakies, Dakotas, and Ojibwas overhunted their lands in the
1820s, effecting a precipitous decline in game animals throughout
the region. Only in two areas, the contested zones along the Des
Moines and Chippewa River Valleys, did ample game remain.[31] In
the latter, the Dakotas and Ojibwas resurrected their traditional
animosity for one another. To the south, the Sauks and Mesquakies, who were simultaneously driven from many of their mines by
the Americans, became increasingly belligerent and imperialistic toward their neighboring tribes, piquing the ire of not only the Dakotas, but their Menominee and Ho Chunk allies as well.[32] In 1822,
nearly one hundred casualties resulted from engagements between
the Dakotas and their Sauk and Mesquakie enemies, prompting
the War Department to ask Congress for authority to use troops to
stop the violence. When Congress denied the request, Lawrence
Taliaferro resorted to diplomatic measures. In 1824, Taliaferro took
Dakota delegates to Washington to awe them with the grandeur of
the Great Father's capitol. Few Indians joined the group, however,
and the Sauks and Mesquakies killed the Wahpekute Chief Cloud
on the return voyage. Despite the inauspicious beginning to American mediation, Taliaferro convinced Secretary of War John C. Calhoun to hold a large council the next summer at Prairie du Chien.[33]

In 1825, Superintendent for Indian Affairs William Clark, brother
of George Rogers Clark, convened a treaty council to resolve the
conflict at Prairie du Chien, which, according to British practice,
was a neutral gathering place for the Indians.[34] Although none of
them was eager to submit the disputes to American mediation, Da-

kotas, Sauks, Mesquakies, Ojibwas, Menominees, and Ho Chunks attended the council. The treaty commissioners seemed to effect a compromise between the Dakotas and Ojibwas, roughly splitting the disputed territory down the middle. The dispute between the Dakotas and the Sauk-Mesquakie confederation was less easily resolved. Considerable blood had been shed, and the disputed territory amounted to the northern half of Iowa; the depth of the dispute seemed to exceed the government's capacity to adjudicate. In the end, the Sauks and Mesquakies were pleased with the boundary set by the commissioners while the Dakotas were not—conditions that augured poorly for what was intended to be a compromise settlement. In a further bad omen, many of the Indian delegates became sick and some died on the way home.[35] The treaty accomplished little because Congress never allocated funds to demark the agreed-upon boundaries and the Indians had little incentive to set aside their differences.[36] The fragile peace was short-lived; the Dakotas led a war party against the Ojibwas the following year, resurrecting the retaliatory war.[37]

Meanwhile, in the spring of 1826, the Ho Chunks killed a French-Canadian family that had been harvesting maple sugar about twelve miles above Prairie du Chien on the western side of the Mississippi. Although no evidence suggests that the Indians had a particular vendetta against Monsieur Methode, his wife, five children, and pet dog, their charred bodies provided shocking testimony to the extent of Ho Chunk disaffection. The disaffection became greater yet when the soldiers at Fort Crawford seized the perpetrators and (following their escape) proxy hostages. Rumors circulated that the Ho Chunks intended to sack the American post and liberate their kinsmen, prompting Colonel Josiah Snelling, commander of the Fifth Infantry, to reinforce Fort Crawford temporarily with three infantry companies from Fort Snelling.[38] The paranoia passed, but Ho Chunk resentment remained. Subagent John Marsh traced it to the government's inability to protect the Indians from white encroachment. "The agents of the Government have not been able to control the miners," he complained, "and nothing but a strong force can control them."[39] Hoping to defuse the mounting Dakota-Ojibwa war, however, Snelling concentrated his Fifth Infantry at Fort Snelling in the autumn of 1826, leaving Fort Crawford entirely unoccupied—a movement that some Ho Chunks interpreted as a sign of American weakness.[40] Among those who made the voyage to Fort Snelling were two of the Methode family's killers, whom the Ho Chunks had surrendered to gain the release of their hostages. Anticipating that they would be tried and executed, Marsh feared that American justice would spark a war with the Ho Chunks that would result in their destruction. "This is now, has been, and I fear ever will be the fate of the redman when he comes into contact with the white strangers," he lamented.[41] Marsh came close to accurately predicting the future but, ironically, it was Indian rather than white justice that helped incite the war.

In May 1827, the Dakotas brazenly attacked an Ojibwa party encamped in the shadows of Fort Crawford, compelling Colonel Snelling to assert the futility of treaty negotiations so long as the army retained a defensive posture.[42] Snelling, who felt powerless to enforce the provisions of the 1825 treaty, demonstrated his pragmatic accommodation with Indian modes of dispute resolution by delivering four of the Dakota murderers to their victims' aggrieved kinsmen. Snelling took some precautions to distance the government from the affair, dictating that the condemned be given a fair chance to escape and that the Ojibwas dispense their justice beyond the view of the fort. Pursued by picked runners, the Dakotas did not have a chance, and word soon spread of their fate. By the time the story reached the Ho Chunks, however, it represented that Snelling had delivered Methode's killers to the Ojibwas for execution.[43] At about the same time, the Ho Chunks received the probably specious news that riverboat crews had molested Ho Chunk women along the banks of the Mississippi.[44] If the Americans could not conduct themselves as allies, the time had come to punish them as enemies.

The Ho Chunks began by breaking off diplomacy. They informed their subagent on the Fever River that "they could put no faith in any act of the Government Agents" due to the violations of the Treaty of 1825 and that this was the last time they would complain.[45] Shortly thereafter, the Ho Chunks backed out of a planned council at Butte des Morts, where Michigan Territory Governor Lewis Cass and Superintendent of Indian Affairs Thomas McKenney waited for envoys in vain.[46] Fearful that their absence portended violence, Cass set out for Prairie du Chien, where his fears were vindicated. On 27 June 1827, the respected Ho Chunk war captain Waunigsootshkau (Red Bird) and his accomplices Wekau (Sun) and Chickhonsic (Little Buffalo) had incited a panic by murdering a métis family that had been on friendly terms with the Indians.[47] In the absence of the army, white inhabitants stockaded themselves within Fort Crawford and helped themselves to the post's provisions.[48] Meanwhile, Red Bird's followers terrorized the frontier settlements and attacked two army keelboats on the Mississippi.[49] While Snelling tried to recover from his mistakes by sending four companies of the Fifth Infantry back down the Mississippi, Governor Lewis Cass tried to mobilize the militia, and Brigadier General Henry Atkinson deployed from Jefferson Barracks, Missouri, with an additional regiment of regulars.[50] The Ho

Chunks encountered only modest success in their efforts to enlist the aid of their neighbors, the Potawatomis and the Dakotas. While these tribes certainly sympathized with the Ho Chunks, the Potawatomis and Dakotas did not share the Ho Chunk "determination never to suffer themselves to be surrounded by the white settlements, but . . . [to] perish first, men, women, and children."[51] Cognizant of the risks associated with allying against the United States, most Native communities distanced themselves from the Ho Chunk "uprising." Still, rumors of a broader Indian war ran rampant, kindling a paranoia that had not been seen in the area since the Potawatomi betrayal of the garrison of Fort Dearborn during the War of 1812, when Potawatomis attacked a retreating American garrison they had pledged to protect. Perhaps aware that the Ho Chunks had sent war wampum among the Potawatomis and certainly recalling their earlier treachery, many Americans assumed Potawatomi complicity.[52]

Yet the Ho Chunks acted independently, and indeed many of their tribesmen disassociated themselves from Red Bird's actions. Spoon Decorah, who resided between the Portage and Lake Winnebago, recalled that Red Bird was a "bad Indian" and that most Ho Chunks desired to remain at peace with the Americans.[53] Yet Spoon's people were well removed from the crisis in the lead country, and the Winnebago War revealed significant divisions within Ho Chunk society. Although the Ho Chunks nominally recognized a paramount, hereditary chief, their expansion and dispersion over the preceding century had dissipated the authority of his office. By the time of the Winnebago War, real authority resided with the civil and war chiefs of the individual villages, who pursued policies fitted to their unique circumstances.[54] Hoping to distance themselves from the actions of their southern brethren, Ho Chunks from the Lake Winnebago area joined a force of 101 regulars, 23 militiamen, and a band of friendly Menominees that marched to the Portage to make a show of united Indian-American force.

Reaching the Portage on 1 September 1827, the contingent, accompanied by Thomas McKenney and John Marsh, learned that Red Bird and Wekau intended to surrender themselves. In a regal processional, the two Indians marched into the Portage on 3 September, accompanied by 114 Ho Chunk warriors. Clad in white leather with a scarlet cloth adorning his breast and carrying a calumet decorated with feathers and green paint—the color of peace—Red Bird was, according to Indian agent John Kinzie, "certainly the best looking Indian in the nation."[55] Perhaps not as handsome, Carymaunee the Lame (Walking Turtle) and Waukon Decorah wielded considerably more influence among the Ho Chunk people, albeit in evolving, divergent fashions. Heir to his tribe's paramount chieftainship, Carymaunee manifested traditional but waning conceptions of Ho Chunk authority, while Waukon Decorah represented a Ho Chunk variant of the "alliance chief." Descended from a French officer and the daughter of a Ho Chunk chief, members of the Decorah family acquired prominence as orators and diplomats, which they parlayed into increased political power under the American regime. Both leaders if not chiefs, Carymaunee and Waukon had repaired to the Portage and offered speeches to soften the Great Father's rage at Red Bird, whom they depicted as a misguided but honorable warrior. Offering nine horses in return for a promise that the Americans would treat the prisoners fairly, the chiefs also requested that McKenney take possession of the prisoners rather than the military commander, Major William Whistler. This preference reflected American negotiating practices, in which Indian agents and the army officers represented the Great Father's benevolent and disciplinary sides, respectively. In this particular case, the Ho Chunks might have detected the depth of McKenney's empathy. Terming Red Bird's surrender "heroic," McKenney acknowledged that the Ho Chunks had only enforced Indian law when American justice had left them wanting.[56] Although McKenney turned the prisoners over to the army, he assured them that John Marsh would accompany them to Prairie du Chien. This appeared to comfort the Indians.[57]

The Ho Chunks were less comforted by the news that Brigadier General Henry Atkinson was approaching with thirteen companies of infantry. "The nation is alarmed much," Kinzie related. "They don't know what to make of this."[58] In talks with the Ho Chunks at the Portage and Prairie du Chien, Atkinson allayed Ho Chunk fears with his diplomatic bearing and assurances that the government would investigate white abuses in the lead region.[59] Subsequently, it became apparent that the Ho Chunks were less alarmed by the seven hundred regulars under Atkinson, whom the Indians respectfully referred to as the "White Beaver," than they were by the militia troops called up by Illinois Governor Ninian Edwards.[60] Perhaps no other factor called into question the Great Father's justice and wisdom more than his dependence on the militia, which was made up of many of the Indians' most bitter antagonists. While the president punished the Indians who took up arms to redress their own grievances, he rewarded the white instigators for doing the very same. To some Ho Chunks at least, it appeared the Great Father held his red and white children to different standards.

Although troubled by the militia, the Ho Chunks do not appear to have been alarmed by the Americans' Indian allies, who numbered as many as 250 and consisted of Menominees, Stockbridges, and Oneidas.[61] Relations between the Ho Chunks and the Menomi-

nees remained friendly, and it seems likely that the latter's participation represented nothing more than a demonstration of allegiance to the United States—and that the Ho Chunks understood
this. Almost unique among the tribes, the Menominees were depicted by both contemporary and modern observers as ardent
friends of the white man, whether French, English, or American.
Historian Patricia Ourada has written, "The Menominees professed
a loyalty to the French that surpassed that of any other nation in
the West."[62] For their part, the French regarded Menominee women
as "rather pretty, and more gentle than those of the neighboring
tribes."[63] The French affinity for Menominee women likely served
the tribe well by facilitating the formation of kinship bonds between the powerful French and a tribe struggling to survive. These
bonds in turn provided the French with allies who compensated for
their lack of numbers by their fidelity. According to his grandson,
the famous French captain Charles Langlade considered the Menominees "the most peaceful, brave, and faithful of all the tribes
who ever served under him."[64] Following the French and Indian
War, the Menominees extended similar loyalty to the British. After
their defeat at the Battle of the Thames in 1813, Robert Dickson
commented of the Menominees, "it is fortunate for us there are
such Indians in such times."[65] Even among American frontiersmen,
who lost little love on any Indians, the Menominees developed a
reputation for fidelity and friendliness. In the words of one, "they
were neither treacherous nor belligerent. Always friendly to the
whites, they gained the friendship and confidence of the latter."[66]
Given such praise, it is easy to imagine the Menominees as devoted
"friends of the white man," but they were hardly his pawns. Out of
the Beaver Wars, the Menominees had learned to embrace the prevailing white power as a means of sustaining their vulnerable peo-

ple through troubling times, such as those that visited Wisconsin in 1827.

While the Winnebago War presented the Menominees with an opportunity to strengthen their attachment to the Americans, it placed the tribes in closer contact with the white frontier in a precarious position. Nothing struck fear in the hearts of white settlers like the prospect of a general Indian uprising, and violence on the part of a few Indians invariably elicited allegations against all Indians, particularly those closest at hand. Occupying approximately fifty villages centered on the southern end of Lake Michigan and with nearly four thousand people living within the boundaries of Indiana and Illinois, the Potawatomis endured more than their share of suspicion.[67] As Secretary of War John Eaton observed in 1829, "The States will not consent for their limits to be occupied by a people possessed of savage habits, and who claim to exercise the rights of government independent of any control but their own."[68] For the Potawatomis, the Winnebago War was something of a dress rehearsal for the Black Hawk War. In each case, the Indians in conflict with the United States proposed alliance with the Potawatomis, and in both instances were rejected. In both wars, the Potawatomis sympathized with the belligerent tribes—some going so far as to kill American livestock during the Winnebago War—but chiefs and elders refused to endorse opposition to the United States, fearing costs too great to bear.[69] As their agent, Alexander Wolcott realized that the Potawatomi leaders appreciated "the power of the American People, and must dread to encounter it. Being nearest to the settlements, they know that the blow would first fall on them."[70] Nonetheless, Wolcott recognized that young warriors and disgruntled chieftains sympathized with the Ho Chunks and shared their antipathy for the miners. Leaving nothing to chance,

Wolcott dispatched three men from the Chicago area to ride among the more remote Potawatomi settlements to dissuade their kinsmen from joining the hostile Ho Chunks.[71] Five years later, these same men—Billy Caldwell, Alexander Robinson, and Shaubena—would play a prominent role in preventing a Potawatomi alliance with Black Hawk. Finally, in each conflict the Potawatomis had to contend with exaggerated or specious allegations of collaboration with the belligerent bands. In the Winnebago War, the Potawatomis handled this problem with pledges of fidelity. In the Black Hawk War, words alone would not be enough.

Nor had words proven sufficient to maintain peace between the Indians and the whites in 1827, so the government resolved to strengthen its frontier defenses. Both Michigan Territory governor Lewis Cass and Potawatomi agent Wolcott recommended the immediate reoccupation of Fort Dearborn in Chicago, which had lain empty since 1823.[72] Even the usually beneficent McKenney was "of the opinion in regard to the defense of the frontier . . . that a show of Military force would be exceedingly judicious, as would be the occupation of the Portage, and Chicago."[73] Aware that the Winnebago War had revealed only a meager portion of the discontent brewing among the Indians who were in close contact with the whites, McKenney doubted that "until these two positions are taken whether there will be any positive security from the acts of violence which the Winnebagoes and Potawatimies are at all times ready to commit, and which nothing but fear can effectually restrain."[74] Subject to Cass's and McKenney's recommendations, the Fifth Infantry Regiment established headquarters at Fort Howard, Green Bay, which it garrisoned with four companies; reoccupied Fort Dearborn with two companies; and positioned another two each at Michilimackinac and Sault Ste. Marie. The war also provided the impetus to construct Fort Winnebago at the Portage, where two companies of the First Infantry Regiment settled while four each garrisoned Forts Snelling and Crawford.[75]

Even so, the reinforcements were not intended solely to quiet the Ho Chunks and their supposed friends. In the aftermath of the Winnebago War, vindictive white miners resumed their invasion of unceded Indian lands. A distraught Joseph Street reported that they had mutilated the face of a respected Menominee woman before killing her by caving her head in with the heel of a boot. "The Indians are not so stupid, or astounded at late events, as to let these things pass unnoticed," he informed Secretary of War James Barbour. "I am not without serious apprehensions," he continued, "if a more vigilant eye is not kept upon the heterogeneous mass of population, which *Europe* and the United States have furnished at the mines." Although Street's xenophobia was misplaced, he correctly predicted that the miners would not honor Atkinson's promises to the Indians.[76]

Thomas McKenney shared Street's anxiety. He wrote to General Alexander Macomb, Commanding General of the U.S. Army, and urged him to furnish whatever military aid William Clark might deem necessary to evict trespassing white miners from Indian lands.[77] McKenney also enjoined his agents to "execute the law spiritedly upon all those who encroach upon Indian rights. The miners, as reported in a former letter in the fever river country, should be ferreted out, and punished as the law provides."[78] The agents of the Indian Office did their best to adhere to McKenney's directions, but they soon discovered that the resolve of the miners matched that of their superintendent and that the miners' reinforcements dwarfed those of the army.

Deserted during the Winnebago War, the lead country was now

overrun by opportunistic whites hoping to cash in on the Indians' misfortune, thereby compounding it. According to one early chronicler, the reports made by the officers and men of Atkinson's force "first drew public attention to the unbounded fertility and exhaustless resources of south-western Wisconsin—and their return was followed by a large immigration to the lead region."[79] By January 1828, Subagent John Marsh estimated that ten thousand white miners were illegally working Indian lands.[80] Among the offenders was Henry Dodge, the man destined to become the American hero of the Black Hawk War and Wisconsin's first governor. Dodge established his camp with fifty armed men in the winter of 1827–28, compelling Carymaunee to complain to Joseph Street in Prairie du Chien that "the hills are covered, more are coming and shoving us off our lands to make the lead. We want our Father to stop this before blood may be shed."[81] Street dispatched John Marsh to "Dodge's Diggings" in the bitter January cold with an eviction notice penned by Street. At Dodge's camp, Marsh discovered approximately 130 well-armed men, none of whom seemed particularly awed by the Harvard graduate wielding a piece of paper. Dodge sent Marsh on his way with some assurance that he would move his camp when it was practicable, but Dodge subsequently constructed a stockade and boasted to his men that the regular army could try to evict them if it wished. Learning of Dodge's intransigence, Street called upon Major John Fowle at Fort Crawford to send 180 troops to evict the trespassers. The major responded that he had only 130 men fit for such duty and, in a statement reflecting the prevailing sentiment in Washington, that it was beyond his power to comply with that request.[82] In St. Louis an anxious William Clark commissioned an investigation to resolve the dispute. Conveniently, the investigating officers found that Dodge's Diggings were within U.S.

territory, and an appreciative Henry Dodge retroactively filed for a lease to his claim and paid outstanding royalties due the government.[83] Afterward, Dodge and another illegal miner, Alexander Hamilton's son William, further ingratiated themselves to the government by—paradoxically—offering to help Lieutenant Martin Thomas remove illegal miners from Indian lands.[84] Without recourse, the Ho Chunks formally ceded their title to Dodge's Diggings on 25 August 1828.[85]

Although the Sauks and Mesquakies had surrendered their Illinois lands nearly a quarter-century earlier—and confirmed the cession in 1825—they continued to occupy their villages on the Rock River. Beginning in the spring of 1827, white squatters took possession of Saukenauk, the principal Sauk village, and mercilessly abused the Indians when they returned from their winter hunt.[86] This pattern repeated itself in subsequent years and, although the Indians were clearly the aggrieved party, it provided Illinois governor Ninian Edwards the leverage he needed to agitate for their permanent removal. If the federal government would not do it, he threatened William Clark, he would see to it himself, "and that very promptly."[87] No doubt aware of the dreadful consequences an Illinois-effected removal would hold for their people, most of the Sauks and Mesquakies drew close to their Great Father through their agent, Thomas Forsyth, and pledged their peaceful intentions. Not all of the Sauks and Mesquakies concurred with this course, however, and a renegade faction developed that rejected the accommodationist spirit of the councils. In council with Forsyth, these Indians vowed "that they would not move from the place where the bones of their ancestors lay, and that they would defend themselves against any power that might be sent to drive them from their permanent villages."[88] This faction gained a measure of support in the spring of 1829, when the Rock River Indians returned from their winter hunts in Iowa to find that white squatters, anticipating the public sale of these lands in October, had laid claim to the Indian cornfields and destroyed the Indians' lodges.[89] Forsyth found himself in an impossible position, attempting at once to assuage two constituencies with mutually exclusive interests. On 16 May 1829, he advised the Sauks and Mesquakies to leave their Illinois lands.[90]

In response, the Sauk "Peace Party" under the chief Keokuk and the renegade faction decided on irreconcilable courses. While Keokuk vowed to abide by the 1804 land cession and remain west of the Mississippi, the more recalcitrant members of the tribes proposed resistance. Within this group, a fiery war captain rose in prominence. His name was Ma-Ka-Tai-Me-She-Kia-Kiak, or Black (Sparrow) Hawk, and those who followed him garnered the epithet of "British Band" on account of their idle hope that the British would aid them in a war against the Americans and their display of the Union Jack as a deliberate snub of the U.S. government. In 1827, Sauk civil chiefs had frustrated Black Hawk's designs to mount a campaign against the Dakotas; the current impasse with the Americans offered him a new outlet to vent his martial ambitions.[91] On 20 May 1829, three members of the British Band visited their agent, Thomas Forsyth, and "spoke very fiercely on the subject" of the land cession. In no uncertain terms, they repudiated the treaty and vowed to resist removal—with force if necessary. To add bite to their rhetoric, the Sauks assured Forsyth "that they had formed an alliance with the Chippeways, Ottaways, Pottowatomies, Kickapoos & Menomonies who were ready to assist them at any time in defending their country against any force whatever."[92] Forsyth had no reason to doubt the existence of such a coalition; upon questioning, "a number of" Ojibwas, Ottawas, and Potawatomis affirmed their solidarity with the aggrieved Sauks.[93] In all likelihood, however, the Indians Forsyth interviewed were already adopted members of the British Band and in no way representatives of their respective tribes.

A legitimate delegation from these tribes, loosely confederated as the "Three Fires," gathered in Prairie du Chien in the summer of 1829 at the request of their Great Father, who wished to complete the extermination of the Indian title to the mineral country.[94] Unsatisfied with the extent of the Ho Chunk cessions from the previous year, the Great Father also beckoned the now-compliant Ho Chunks. Although the government compensated the Indians for the title to their lands, the terms were hardly equitable. In return for perpetual annuities of $16,000 and $18,000 to the Three Fires and Ho Chunks respectively, the United States gained possession of 8-10 million acres "of Land of as great fertility as any in our country, A large proportion of which contain the richest Lead mines perhaps in the world."[95] Secretary of War John Eaton was optimistic that, by ridding the lead country of "claimants who can never work the mines with any advantage to themselves," the United States had quieted "the agitations of that frontier by leaving the title to its occupancy by our citizens free from the collisions which have heretofore so often disturbed the peace of that frontier."[96]

To further ensure this tranquility, the Americans had sent a Ho Chunk delegation to Washington the previous winter "with the view of impressing upon them opinions of our power which they have never had the means of forming; and which it is believed may tend to quiet their restlessness, and tame their ferocity."[97] From October to December 1828, the Rock River chief White Crow and more than a dozen other head men of the Ho Chunks toured the eastern

United States, where they witnessed diplomatic theater. Although feted and treated to shows, the Indians also observed a purposeful demonstration of the manifest power of the United States. Teeming cities, serried ranks of mustered militia (who were in truth far better fitted for parades than for campaigns), and the firing of gunboat cannon all served to demonstrate to the Ho Chunks the folly of further resistance. An article in the *Washington Intelligencer* explained, "The humane design {of bringing them East} is to introduce in their minds a conviction that it is ruin to contend against us."[98] Thomas McKenney concurred: "This mode of conquering these people is merciful, and it is cheap, in comparison to what a war with them would cost, to say nothing of the loss of Human life."[99] A more cynical correspondent from the *Washington Telegram* had a different interpretation of the impressive display made to the Indians: "This is all to get a better contract for their lands."[100]

During the Ho Chunk visit, President John Quincy Adams prudently pardoned Wekau and Chickhonsic, Red Bird's accomplices in inciting the Winnebago War.[101] Red Bird had died in prison the preceding February, and the Indian agent in Chicago had reported the likelihood of another Indian war should the Americans decide to execute the surviving Ho Chunk prisoners (as a Green Bay judge in fact decreed).[102] Thus, the government hoped at once to awe the Ho Chunks with American might and assuage them with the Great Father's mercy—but the Americans could not offer any real protection from further encroachments. Without resort to more effective devices, the Ho Chunks blazed the trees along the new line that demarked their country, but, as one wag observed, it was "a prohibition about as effectual as the whistling of the wind."[103]

Had they listened closely during their visit to Washington, the Ho Chunks might have discerned a momentous wind of change regarding the Great Father's attitude toward their people. His Secretary of War, Peter Buell Porter, appeared perplexed to discover that the United States had developed a relationship with the Indians that exceeded the simple "relations of war" that had characterized the early years of the Republic. "We have been entering into treaties with them, not of peace merely," Porter exclaimed, "but of property, of intercourse, and trade; and have actually contracted between them and ourselves most of the complicated relations which appertain to the municipal state."[104] A matter of sound diplomacy in 1816, the fostering of these relations burdened the Adams administration with a political yoke in 1828. In the interim, white settlers had enveloped Indian communities in various quarters of the frontier, and state and territorial governments chafed at the presence within their boundaries of Indian groups that considered themselves sovereign allies of the United States. Fortunately for John Quincy Adams, the Winnebago War had helped discredit the idea that the Indians could be assimilated into the mainstream white society, and this called for a reassessment of government's policy toward the Indians. Addressing Congress on 2 December 1828, Adams signaled a new direction in American Indian policy by proclaiming the failure of the civilization experiment and asserting that the only rational and humane alternative was to isolate the Indians west of the Mississippi, beyond the reach of the whites.[105]

Adams's proclamation caught few by surprise. Thomas Jefferson and James Monroe had each considered Indian removal inevitable but left the unhappy business to their successors. Always the pet project of eastern intellectuals and evangelicals, the civilization program was never popular in frontier states, and the failure of the factory system in 1822 seemed to offer further evidence that assimilation was impossible. In that same year, Congress attempted to eliminate federal funding for the civilization program, and by 1826 McKenney was aware that many of his own agents were working to undermine the program. When questioned by Congress in 1830, McKenney had to admit that the program was a failure.[106] During the 1820s, McKenney and other proponents of the civilization program came to the conclusion that the Indians could never assimilate while subjected to the insidious influence of white traders and the "ardent spirits" they often distributed among the Indians. Believing that the Indians' salvation depended on it, in 1827 McKenney began to urge Congress to pass legislation providing for the voluntary removal of Indians to the trans-Mississippi west.

Removal proved to be a divisive issue within the humanitarian-missionary community that labored to "civilize" the Indians, estranging McKenney from many former comrades and, ironically, aligning him with the western, anti-Indian lobby. Although Indian removal always enjoyed the support of men like McKenney, who sincerely believed the policy best served Indian interests, the driving impulse behind removal was the discontentment of America's frontier population, which regarded the Indian population as a savage menace and lobbied their state and territorial representatives for relief. An Adams partisan, McKenney was stunned by the 1828 election of Andrew Jackson, who employed humanitarian rhetoric to justify Indian removal but clearly represented a constituency unconcerned with Indian welfare.[107] Alarmed by the new administration's priorities, McKenney issued a circular to his agents in February 1829, blaming frontier instability on white intruders and placing on the president responsibility to extirpate "The evil of their presence."[108] In addition to enjoining his agents to screen carefully all supplicants seeking entry into the Indian country, he directed the application of military force to evict unlawful or disruptive whites. Provocatively, he suggested that, if U.S. military forces were not at hand, the agents should employ Indian warriors to enforce this law.[109]

Accurately reading the prevailing political climate, none of McKenney's agents took such drastic measures. Indeed, even the employment of federal troops for such purposes was becoming infeasible. Although the army chased illegal miners from the Dubuque Mines in the unorganized territory west of the Mississippi, army commanders and officials within the War Department grew increasingly reluctant to use federal troops to defend tribal sovereignty within the defined boundaries of states and territories.[110] Hence, Major Fowle denied Joseph Street's request to march troops against Dodge's Diggings in 1828, and by 1830 Secretary of War John Eaton concluded that the provision of the 1802 Trade and Intercourse Act allowing the use of military force to evict white squatters was unconstitutional.[111] The following year, Eaton's successor, Lewis Cass (formerly governor of Michigan Territory and one of the most vocal advocates of removal), went so far as to contend that the trade and intercourse acts no longer held sway within the states and organized territories.[112] Gradually, then, the legal foundation on which America had dealt with the Native peoples of the Old Northwest had eroded under the pressure of white settlers until, by 1831, it had disintegrated altogether. Unbeknownst to many Indians on the periphery of his domain, the Great Father was no longer interested in making allies of the Indians; instead, he wished to see them removed.

Before they could be removed, however, the Indians would have to set aside their internecine squabbles and accept peace.[113] The Menominees, Dakotas, and Ho Chunks were never satisfied with the 1825 treaty; they considered the Sauks and Mesquakies the ag-

gressors in the ongoing conflict and sought an opportunity to exact revenge for a growing catalog of Sauk and Mesquakie insults.[114]
In November 1828, a Mesquakie band abducted the child and preg-
nant wife of a prominent Dakota chief, and the following year a
Sauk and Mesquakie war party decapitated a Dakota woman.[115]
In another sensational slaying, a Menominee man died with a Mesquakie blade in his throat. Although the Mesquakies later claimed
that this event was a tragic case of mistaken identity, they availed
themselves of the opportunity to take possession of the Menominee's scalp—a gesture reserved for enemies.[116] Joseph Street, the
Indian agent at Prairie du Chien and self-described "novice in Indian affairs," suggested constructing buffer zones in the disputed
areas by filling them with Ho Chunks who had recently been defeated in the 1827 Winnebago War.[117] Secretary of War John Eaton
liked this idea and, in 1829, authorized William Clark to organize
a council to implement such a policy.[118] In May 1830, Wynkoop
Warner, subagent on the Fever River, invited Mesquakie and Dakota delegations to the council at Prairie du Chien.[119] The Mesquakies would send diplomats; the vengeful Dakotas and Menominees would send warriors.

To many Indians, the 1820s revealed the limits of the
Great Father's commitment to his allies. Although pledging justice
and beneficence to all of his children, white and red, his conduct regarding the lead country suggested partiality toward the former.
During the Winnebago War, Ho Chunks lashed out to teach the
Americans the errors of their ways, but the Indians came away with
the most salient lessons. The Great Father did not uphold his obligations to his red children, it was true, but he was too powerful to

oppose by force of arms. Observing the Winnebago War from a distance, the Sauks and Mesquakies concurred on the first point, but militant members of both tribes were willing to test the latter. The Dakotas and Menominees exhibited little concern for the plight of their neighbors in the lead country. Instead, they remained fixated on the escalating conflict between themselves and the Sauks and Mesquakies over the fur-rich Des Moines River Valley. By the end of the decade, each Indian group had mounting cause to regard the American officials as interlopers rather than allies. Incapable of preventing white encroachment on Indian lands, Indian agents and army officers discovered in 1830 that they were no more capable of preventing Indians from killing one another.

# 4

## CRISIS ON THE UPPER MISSISSIPPI

In the evening twilight of 5 May 1830, three or four Mesquakie canoes came ashore just south of Prairie du Chien. Summoned to a treaty council at Prairie du Chien by Subagent Wynkoop Warner, the party of approximately twenty Indians that disembarked included several Mesquakie chiefs and one woman. Hungry from their journey and well within the neutral grounds of Prairie du Chien, the Mesquakies retrieved from their canoes only what they needed to prepare a meal, leaving their guns and war clubs in the birch-bark vessels. In the shadows, a war party of fifty Menominees and Dakotas waited patiently for their prey. Made aware of the Mesquakies' voyage by a report from their friend John Marsh, the former Prairie du Chien subagent, they had anticipated the Mesquakie landing site. Now they seized the opportunity presented to them and attacked their helpless foes. The Mesquakie woman and at least fifteen of her companions died in the melee. The Menominees and Dakotas briefly took a single prisoner—by some accounts the lone survivor—but they released him so that he could bear news of the attack back to his people.[1]

Whatever may be said of the circumstances of the attack, the Menominees and Dakotas were unashamed, and they wanted the Sauks and Mesquakies to know who was responsible. Afterward, the blood-smeared victors paraded through Prairie du Chien to the accompaniment of a drum and rattle, proudly displaying their trophies of war, which included not only the standard scalp poles but sundry dismembered body parts and a head at the end of a stick.[2] To the evident dismay of one of the very few American women in that town, the Dakota and Menominee warriors also "danced the war-dance and scalp dance, ending with yells characteristic of incarnate devils." As if this was not spectacle enough, the victors roasted the heart of a Mesquakie chief in plain view, divided it among several warriors, and ate it.[3] This proved too much even for the commander of Fort Crawford, who compelled the Indians to take their celebration to islands in the river.[4]

From their own perspective, the attackers had just evened the score. Their sanguinary celebration attested to the fact that they believed they had done no wrong and indeed had only obtained justice. The Mesquakies begged to differ, and efforts by William Clark and Thomas Forsyth to make amends failed to assuage Mesquakie grief. On 7 July, Colonel Willoughby Morgan, commander of the First Infantry Regiment at Fort Crawford, tried to use threats to secure peace: "Your Great Father the President commands me to say to you, if you continue your wars he will march an army into your country, and take side with those who regard his admonitions, and chastise those who refuse to regard his council." To drive home the now evident point that the Great Father did not love all of his subjects equally, Morgan added, "and more especially will he do this, if in your wars your young men should kill any of his white children."[5] Although Morgan could not know it, his blustering would prove prescient.

The burgeoning conflict between the Sauks and Mesquakies and their Dakota and Menominee foes was no mere sideshow on the road to the Black Hawk War. Indeed, the army's initial orders in the spring of 1832 made no mention of Black Hawk, who had not yet conducted his fateful "invasion" of Illinois. Instead, federal officials hoped to intervene in an intertribal conflagration that threatened to engulf the frontier. As far as the Menominees and Dakotas were concerned, the "Black Hawk War" had nothing to do with the Sauk war leader or Illinois land disputes. Their participation in the conflict is best understood as the brief convergence of two wars: the American campaign to remove the Sauks and Mesquakies from Illinois and the enduring intertribal contest for control of hunting grounds in the Upper Mississippi watershed.

Although their inability to protect the Indians from white encroachment contributed to the first conflict, federal officers persisted in their efforts to stem the second. They were not helped by the Andrew Jackson administration, which gutted the Indian Office of qualified agents, replacing them with loyal party men. Not surprisingly, federal officials struggled to defuse both conflicts in the two years before the Black Hawk War. Increasingly, Illinoisans regarded all Indians as a mortal threat. This forced the Potawatomis and Ho Chunks into a conundrum in which the stakes were clear but the proper responses were not. Hoping to simply ride out the storm, most of these tribes advocated neutrality; but their environment left no room for such a policy. By 1832—after two years of federal efforts to preserve the peace—the entire region was primed for war.

In July 1830, Colonel Morgan convened a council at Prairie du Chien. Originally intended to implement Joseph Street's "buffer zone" scheme, the meeting now aimed at nothing more than restoring peace among the tribes. Morgan began by singling out those tribes who had kept to "the good road of peace"—Omahas, Ioways, Ottoes, and Ho Chunks.[6] He reserved special praise for the

Ho Chunks, who complained of five injustices at the hands of the Sauks and Mesquakies and yet remained at peace: "Your conduct will merit the high approbation of your Father the President of the United States."[7] On the second day of the council, William Clark patronized the remaining tribes, who were active parties to the present conflict: "You are losers by a war among yourselves: you lose your bravest men and neglect the cultivation of the Earth, which compels your women to work harder for your support."[8] Despite decades among the Indians, Clark had apparently not yet grasped that the Indians regarded farming as women's work in the first place, and by commanding them to lay down the hatchet and take up the plow he was requiring them to surrender their masculinity. Clark waited for some response from the head men of the Menominees and Dakotas, but none was forthcoming. Finally, an exasperated Keokuk, the accommodationist Sauk chief, interjected that it was incumbent on the agents of the Great Father to redress the Mesquakie grievance. Regarding any blood debts owed the Dakotas, Keokuk insisted that "their bodies have been paid for, and all arranged," but that the Dakotas had persisted in seeking vengeance.[9] Keokuk concluded by holding Warner responsible for the deaths of his delegates two months earlier and, consequently, for arranging compensation from the Dakotas.[10]

For their part, the Dakotas were now satisfied, and the Dakota chief Wabasha expressed eagerness "before these white people to make peace with you, and forget it all."[11] That Wabasha saw fit to articulate this desire "before these white people" is significant. So long as the Great Father persisted in his attempts to mediate this conflict, it benefited the Dakotas to even the balance sheet in the presence of his agents. In the likely event that the Mesquakies attempted retaliation, it would be they who garnered the ire of the

Great Father. The Sauks and Mesquakies, too, recognized the Great Father's self-mandated prerogative to maintain peace among the Indians, but they were less than certain of his sincerity or effectiveness. On the third day of the council proceedings, the Mesquakie chief Wapello reported to the treaty commissioners that the Mesquakies and Menominees had made peace. Rather than seeking the endorsement of the U.S. government, however, Wapello sardonically commented, "and I hope you the white people will not meddle in our peace."[12] Keokuk pledged to observe this peace, but also managed a swipe at the peacekeeping skills of the government. Referring to the disaster occasioned by Warner's invitation earlier that year, Keokuk quipped, "we hope you will see that your Agents and Sub Agents observe it like-wise, and not make themselves too busy."[13]

This exchange at Prairie du Chien illustrates two persistent themes in Indian-U.S. relations in the Old Northwest. First, the Indians acknowledged the U.S. government's role as a peacekeeping agency, but they typically did so only to achieve some relative advantage over their antagonists. The Dakotas, having achieved satisfaction in their recent attack, were more than willing to enlist the gratis assistance of the U.S. Army in preventing a reprisal. It is therefore not surprising that a Dakota, Little Crow, expressed a steadfast desire for peace and confidence that the United States would fairly settle the boundary dispute.[14] Based on the government's prior performance, Little Crow's trust was misplaced, but his was likely a disingenuous gesture designed to effect a de facto alliance with the United States. Second, tribes and their assigned agents often formed affiliations with each other that transcended nationality. Keokuk's aspersion against Wynkoop Warner was less an indictment of the Indian agents as a body than an attack on those agents who were aligned with the enemies of the Sauks and Mesquakies, which were many. The Sauks and Mesquakies enjoyed the ardent support of their own agent, Thomas Forsyth, until June 1830, when "public policy and the public service combine[d] to make it advisable to appoint another person in his place."[15]

Ostensibly relieved because he frequently absented himself from his place of duty, Forsyth was both one of the most capable Indian agents in the region and a vocal critic of Jacksonian Indian policy, and his dismissal no doubt contributed to the Sauk and Mesquakie sense of disenfranchisement. Having served as a fur trader in the region since 1804 and a U.S. Indian agent since 1812, Forsyth believed his services to have been indispensable to the government, and his dismissal appears to have caught him off guard.[16] He inquired of friends in Washington to learn the cause and discovered that complaints of supposed "negligence and laziness" had surfaced in Washington and that politicos there used the opportunity to lobby for his relief—and the appointment of one of their friends in his place. William Clark, who had not helped Forsyth's case, expressed regret when he learned that he would lose the former agent's services.[17] In his place, the government appointed Felix St. Vrain, whose inexperience did not bode well at this critical juncture in U.S. relations with the Sauks and Mesquakies. With good reason, the sagacious nineteenth-century historian Lyman Copeland Draper later opined that, had Forsyth "been continued over them, it is believed, the Sauk war of 1832 would never have occurred."[18]

Unfortunately, Forsyth's dismissal was not exceptional. Shortly after succumbing to the pressure to relieve this important agent, Superintendent of Indian Affairs Thomas McKenney was likewise excused from federal service. Despite his patronizing ethnocentrism, McKenney had been a tireless advocate for a humane Indian policy through four presidential administrations. Jackson peremptorily dismissed him in 1830. When McKenney enquired of Acting Secretary of War Philip Randolph the reason for the dismissal, Randolph responded that "General Jackson has long been satisfied that you are not in harmony with him, in his views in regard to the Indians."[19]

Treating the office of Indian agent as little more than a sinecure, Jackson dispensed appointments as a form of patronage with little regard for qualifications. The previous year, the talented John Marsh lost his post as subagent in Prairie du Chien because he had grown too close to the Dakotas.[20] The government replaced Marsh with Thomas Burnett, whose only commending quality was that he was "one of Gen. Jackson's early friends and firm supporters."[21] Although this was sufficient to earn him "favorable notice and fraternal feelings" among Jackson cronies, it did not prepare him for the job he was to undertake; upon arriving in Prairie du Chien in June 1830, Burnett discovered that, according to his father-in-law, his duties "did not exactly suit his taste, or meet the pre-conceived idea he had formed of it."[22] To compound matters, Burnett worked for the equally unqualified Joseph Street, who marginalized his own influence over the Indians by his overbearing manner. The injured Forsyth took refuge in St. Louis, where he attacked the administration in anonymous newspaper articles, but the Indians disadvantaged by Jacksonian patronage could only retire to their villages. Of the twenty agents and thirty-six subagents who held office when Jackson assumed the presidency in March 1829, fully half of the agents and nineteen of the subagents failed to retain their posts through September 1831.[23] Between Prairie du Chien and Rock Island—perhaps the most important 150-mile span on the American frontier—the Great Father had replaced the agents of alliance with paragons of political loyalty.[24]

Without Forsyth's counsel at Prairie du Chien in July 1830, the Sauks and Mesquakies brooded. Not only had the Mesquakies suffered the affront of their murdered delegation, but they also had to endure the Great Father's enjoinments to bury the hatchet and to leave justice to his hands. History suggested, however, that white justice was intolerably slow and rarely gratifying. The government secured a treaty of nonhostility and further land cessions from the concerned tribes on 15 July, but only the latter provisions stuck. Almost wistfully, the text of the treaty began, "The said Tribes being anxious to remove all causes which may hereafter create any unfriendly feeling between them . . ."[25] This passage failed to convey the true sentiments of the signatories, though, least of all the Sauks and Mesquakies. As Keokuk would latter claim, "we did not wish to make peace, but we did make peace for fear of the Americans, we acted from fear like whipped children."[26] Soon, they would act from vengeance as ferocious warriors.

The peace accord of July 1830 was no more successful than that of 1825. The Dakotas renewed their attacks against the Ojibwas within weeks of signing the treaty.[27] The Ojibwas responded with blows against the Dakotas and their Menominee allies as well—killing two women of the latter tribe in the autumn of 1830.[28] Winter brought with it an abatement in the violence, although the Ojibwas killed a young Menominee man in his winter hunting grounds.[29] On 2 February 1831, the Menominees implored Joseph Street to uphold the government's pledge to keep the peace. Their losses compelled the Menominees to reappraise the wisdom of conceding the right of peacekeeping to the United States at Prairie du Chien the previous summer. At that time, the Menominees had (to their minds) evened the score with their enemies and were more than willing to let the U.S. Army enforce a peace that would work to their benefit. Having conceded to their Great Father the responsibility for adjudicating intertribal disputes, however, the Menominees could consider taking revenge now only at the risk of incurring his wrath. Consequently, the western bands of Menominees around Prairie du Chien appealed to Street to deliver justice. A Menominee spokesman explained that "the Chippewas [Ojibwas] believe we do not revenge because we are afraid" and rhetorically asked, "Shall we sit still in our lodges with folded arms till the Chippewas kill more of us?"[30] Although Street was sympathetic to the Menominees and admitted to Secretary of War John Eaton that Ojibwa "speeches shew much caution, and want of candour," he could not tell the Menominees anything they wanted to hear.[31] Citing a refrain that would become tired over the next year and a half, Street directed the Menominees to leave matters to their Great Father. As the winter months passed, however, the Menominees received no satisfaction.

Appreciating the depth of discontent among the competing Indian groups, Street warned the War Department of "the probability of a War between them in the Spring if not anticipated by some earlier movement on the part of the Government."[32] The first indication of this war arrived in May 1831, when the Dakota chief Wabasha arrived in Prairie du Chien to complain that the Sauks and Mesquakies had violated the agreed-upon boundary and killed at least three of his people. Realizing that they were, at least for the present, in the good graces of the Americans, both the Dakotas and the Menominees reluctantly pledged to remain at peace while they waited for the Americans to dispense justice.[33] The Sauks and Mesquakies moved more quickly than the Great Father.

In April 1831, Black Hawk crossed the Mississippi in defiance of the United States and returned to his summer village of Saukenauk, by this time the private property of American settlers. If

Black Hawk entertained ideas of retaking these lands by force, he reconsidered upon learning that Major General Edmund P. Gaines, Commander of the Western Department of the U.S. Army, was en route with six companies of regulars from Jefferson Barracks, Missouri, and—more ominously—that Illinois governor John Reynolds had called up seven hundred militiamen.[34] Black Hawk resolved to die in his village rather than give it up, and he was encouraged by an influential shaman, who dreamed that the approaching American force would do the Sauks no harm.[35] Not all of Black Hawk's followers shared his determination, however, and approximately fifty families defected to Keokuk's peace party by retiring to the west side of the Mississippi.[36] Convinced that Gaines, a "great war chief" of the Americans, would not harm the Sauks as long as they remained at peace, Black Hawk remained defiant.[37] The arrival of Reynolds's militiamen finally induced Black Hawk to surrender his designs of reclaiming Saukenauk. "I would have remained and been taken prisoner by the *regulars,*" he later explained, "but was afraid of the multitude of *pale faces,* who were on horseback, as they were under no restraint of their chiefs."[38] Although the dialogue between Black Hawk and Gaines was often heated, the general impressed Black Hawk with his "manly conduct and soldierly deportment." Empathetic to the plight of the Sauks and eager to avert bloodshed, Gaines offered to compensate the Sauks for their corn crops if they would peaceably quit their fields and return to Iowa.[39] Reluctantly, Black Hawk agreed to abandon Saukenauk—much to the chagrin of the bellicose militiamen, who mocked Gaines's "corn treaty."[40]

Animated by Black Hawk's movements, the Illinois volunteers now turned their attention to the state's other indigenous tribes. From the outset of this "crisis," the citizens of Illinois labeled the

Potawatomis and Ho Chunks accomplices of Black Hawk's British Band. Responding to a crescendo of complaints, General Gaines assured Governor Reynolds, "If I find this to be true, I shall gladly avail myself of my present visit to see them well punished."[41] The previous summer, Black Hawk had in fact engaged the Potawatomis of the Peoria area in talks but had come away frustrated. Black Hawk had ample reason to expect support, or at least sympathy, from these Potawatomis: they too had been subject to insult and injury from white trespassers, and they considered themselves disenfranchised by the 1829 treaty, in which Potawatomis from the Chicago area took it upon themselves to cede land belonging to their western brethren.[42] Senachewine, principal chief of one of the Peoria-area bands, saw no benefit in allying with Black Hawk against the United States, and he impressed this view on his people.[43]

The Potawatomis, however, were not bound to follow their chief's lead. By the nature of his office, Senachawine could withhold support for ventures he considered deleterious to the best interests of the band or tribe, but he could not coerce compliance. This dynamic of Potawatomi politics was understood—and shared—by their neighboring tribes, but not the white residents of Illinois. Consequently, Senachawine's success in persuading *most* of his people to forswear allegiance with Black Hawk would be seen by many whites as a failure of the Potawatomis to ensure absolute fidelity to the United States. Like the Winnebago War, Black Hawk's abortive "invasion" of 1831 followed a discernible pattern: the belligerent band courted the Potawatomis, they refused, rumors of the courtship implicated them nonetheless, and the Potawatomis labored to distance themselves from the belligerent band. Although they had done so successfully in 1827 and 1831, the Potawatomis were becoming something of a usual suspect. It was therefore not surprising that their loyalty to the United States would come into question the next time frontier whites feared an Indian "uprising."

Memories of the Ho Chunks' "treachery" were even fresher in white minds, and they were likewise presumed guilty by association. In fact, the Ho Chunks' relationship with the Sauks and Mesquakies was complex and often ambiguous. In the Prairie du Chien area, Ho Chunks frequently fell victim to Sauk and Mesquakie raiding parties, fueling century-old enmity and deterring Ho Chunks on the Wisconsin from traveling toward the Mississippi.[44] At the Prairie du Chien council in the summer of 1830, Carymaunee complained of injuries endured at the hands of the Sauks and Mesquakies and proclaimed union with their archenemies: "With the Sioux and Menominies, we are as one; our hands have never been stained in each others blood." He closed his talk by reemphasizing, "The Sacs and Foxes have hurt us."[45] Ho Chunk orator Waukon Decorah's daughter, married to a Dakota man, had been slain in the autumn of 1829.[46] In 1830, Waukon agreed to let the Americans bring his daughter's killers to justice, but a year had passed without satisfaction, and Waukon's patience was growing thin.[47]

Yet while many Ho Chunks continued to regard the Sauks and Mesquakies as their mortal enemies, those residing on the Rock River gradually achieved détente with their Indian neighbors. Early American miner Moses Meeker observed that, when the Ho Chunks came to trade with the Americans, the Sauks and Mesquakies relocated to the west side of the Mississippi until the Ho Chunks departed. A Sauk named Mock-to-back-sa-gum (Black Tobacco) explained "that they were friends, and that it was better to keep it so."[48] Throughout the 1820s, shared adversity and a common enemy in the American miners facilitated a rapprochement between the Ho Chunks and the Sauks. Although the treaty of 1828 formally secured peace between the Unites States and the Ho Chunks, the assault on Indian lands and liberties continued. White miners continued to take liberties with Ho Chunk mines and with Indian women along the Rock River.[49] Having learned the folly of seeking redress from their agents, many of the Rock River Indians turned inward for guidance.

Half Sauk and half Ho Chunk, the "Winnebago Prophet" Wabokieshiek provided disillusioned Sauks, Ho Chunks, Kickapoos, and Potawatomis with an alternative vision of alliance—one that fulfilled their needs far better than that offered by the Great Father. Approximately fifty miles up the Rock River from Saukenauk, Wabokieshiek's village, "Prophetstown," developed into a gathering place for the disaffected of every tribe.[50] Although later demonized as an instigator of the Black Hawk War—one historian called him the "evil genius" behind it—Wabokieshiek actually discouraged his followers from resorting to armed conflict with the whites.[51] His vision that the U.S. Army would not harm the British Band had stiffened Black Hawk's resolve in the summer of 1831, and subsequent visions of a Sauk-British alliance would encourage the Sauk to return to Illinois in the coming year. Even then, Wabokieshiek envisioned a peaceful resolution of the conflict with the Americans, believing that the American army officers would not dare attack the Sauks so long as they behaved peaceably.[52] Interestingly, Wabokieshiek's visions were partly vindicated by subsequent events: the army posed no threat to the British Band—even after reentering Illinois—while the Sauks abstained from violence. Wabokieshiek erred catastrophically, however, in failing to account for the Illinois militia, which adjudged any movement by the Sauks to be hostile.

Rightly fearing that this militia would not discriminate between the obstructionist Indians of Prophetstown and the Great Father's loyal followers, Ho Chunk chiefs appealed to William Clark "to break up Prophets Town, which is considered by them as composed of renegadoes from their own nation, as well as from other Tribes."[53] Feasible or not, the Americans never acted on this request; more pressing concerns demanded their attention.

On 31 July 1831, thirty to forty Menominee men, women, and children encamped a mile and a half above Fort Crawford. The men may have been drunk, and very few were armed.[54] Similar circumstances had provided the Menominees with an enticing target fifteen months earlier; now the Menominees were the vulnerable ones. Just before dawn, under the cover of darkness, as many as one hundred Sauks and Mesquakies neared the camp.[55] They approached the thresholds of the Menominee wigwams with impunity, leveled their weapons, and opened fire. A young Menominee warrior named Me-she-nau-tau-wa (Great Rattle Snake) later claimed to see the attackers approach but lamented, "we had no guns or axes to defend ourselves." After the initial volley, which did not appear to harm anyone, "they then attacked us with spears and knives."[56] At least one of the Menominees was armed; he returned fire and killed two assailants but fled after seeing his family killed.[57] Wounded in the foot himself, Me-she-nau-tau-wa had no means to defend his family, and his wife sustained a serious wound.[58] They were among the lucky. When the smoke cleared and the sun rose, ten men, four women, and nine children lay dead. Another eight were wounded, at least two mortally.[59] The loss of the women and children were particularly objectionable to the Menominees. They did not subscribe to the (often breached) Western morals that regard women and children as immune from war, but they valued women as producers of food, mothers of children, and keepers of the hearth; and children represented the future of their people. The death of wife and child incurred not only emotional anguish, but a considerable loss to the clan, band, and tribe as well.

Their grievous losses exhausted the patience of the Menominees, who sent envoys among their allies to coordinate a counterattack. That same day, runners carried red wampum belts to the Dakotas, who had suffered two killed by the Sauks and Mesquakies as recently as 25 July, and to the Menominees of Green Bay.[60] On 1 August, the Menominees made their first attempt to enlist the aid of the United States. In council with Joseph Street, the western Menominees pleaded, "We hope you, our Father will take pitty on us all and help us;—and we will wait a little while to see what our G. F. [Great Father] will do for us."[61] The Menominees were still smarting from the murder of some of their people at the hands of the Ojibwas the preceding winter—murders that had gone unpunished by the United States. They were looking for any sign of good faith on the part of their allies.[62]

Street urged forbearance and issued clothing to the Menominees as a sign of goodwill, but he could do little more.[63] Sympathetic to the plight of the Menominees, he recognized the gravity of the situation. "If something is not speedily done," Street warned Secretary of War John Eaton, "the whole of this frontier will in all probability be involved in a cruel, retaliatory Indian War."[64] Even within the city of Prairie du Chien, a fight seemed to be brewing. Although Street sought to see them leave, the wounded Menominee victims— two of them near death—remained in the village to agitate against their foes, getting into altercations with the Sauk and Mesquakie wives of French traders.[65] Individual Menominees continued to approach Street, both in search of help and to level accusations:

Now at your own land, and near to your Fort, I had a
wife and brother and children at night. I laid down &
slept; in the night the Saukies & Foxes came into my
lodge, and in the morning I was alone. They murdered all
my family—And I have no wife nor brother nor child:
Who will revenge me? Your Chief of the Soldiers is gone.
I see no person going against the murderers. You do not
even promise that I shall have help to revenge my people
& my family.[66]

Unable to give succor and unsure what to do, Street appealed to his
superior for guidance: "For myself I feel much at a loss how & what
to assure them, and will be obliged by your instructions."[67]

By 15 August, a Menominee envoy had reached Green Bay. In
council, Great Rattle Snake related the events of 31 July to the U.S.
agent and then sat. Kaush-kau-nau-nieu (Grizzly Bear), a respected
orator and war leader of the Green Bay Menominees, then addressed Acting Agent Samuel C. Stambaugh: "Now, my father, you
have heard the mournful story of our children's murder, and we ask
you to help us to make war against our enemies." To give weight to
his words, Grizzly Bear presented Stambaugh with three strings of
red wampum and three plugs of red-painted tobacco. Grizzly Bear
also informed Stambaugh that he had dispatched runners to other
Menominee bands in northeastern Wisconsin to deliver similar in-
vitations to war. Bound by instructions, however, Stambaugh refused to accept the wampum and tobacco, and he enjoined the assembled Menominees to exercise patience. Distraught, Grizzly Bear
motioned to a picture of President Andrew Jackson on the wall of
the agency building. Recalling a meeting with the president the
previous winter, Grizzly Bear protested, "He told me that he would

help our nation when we got into trouble, & we now want his assistance." Although the Sauks and Mesquakies considered the recent attack just retribution, the Menominees felt otherwise. Grizzly Bear opined that the attack on the Mesquakie camp in 1830 had evened the score and that, prior to this injury, the Menominees had no grief with the Sauks and Mesquakies.[68]

Stambaugh, in whom the Indians vested considerable trust, continued to preach patience and to promise that the government would provide redress, but he also believed that the Menominees had every right to seek revenge. In addition to satisfying the wants of an ally, such a course promised to solve the problem of Sauk and Mesquakie intransigence once and for all. "The Menominies are much excited," he wrote the new secretary of war, Lewis Cass, "and, although one of the most peaceable and Friendly Tribes on this Frontier, when they become roused by frequent insults and aggressions, a sanguinary war terminating only in the total overthrow and destruction of one of the contending parties, is sure to be the Consequence."[69] Unlike Street, Stambaugh told the Menominees much they wanted to hear. In the company of influential Green Bay citizens and the officers of Fort Howard, Stambaugh resolved the necessity of punishing the murderers: "Justice, humanity, the *peace* of this frontier demands it . . . the *honor* of the government demands it." Further, he could report that even the Great Father himself, President Jackson, was "much grieved to hear of this aggression" and pledged a delivery of justice.[70] Satisfied with what he had heard, Grizzly Bear reluctantly pledged to obey, but cautioned that the Menominees could not be expected to exercise unlimited patience: "we have been promised redress so often that we almost tired [of] waiting."[71]

By winter, Menominee patience was exhausted. The War Department continued to forbid them from taking matters into their own hands without demonstrating the alacrity seemingly promised by the Great Father.[72] Colonel Morgan leaned on the Sauks and Mesquakies to deliver up ten of the Indians involved in the attack on the Menominees, but most of the perpetrators had taken refuge in the British Band and were beyond the reach of the chiefs who maintained diplomatic relations with the United States.[73] Only the tactful diplomacy of Agent Stambaugh, whom the Menominees regarded as an ally, maintained the peace. The western bands did not place such confidence in Agent Street at Prairie du Chien, and they spent the winter of 1831–32 forming a coalition army to punish the Sauks and Mesquakies for their aggression, sending strings of war wampum among the Dakotas, Ojibwas, Ottawas, and Potawatomis to solicit their aid.[74] In January 1832, western Menominee warriors began to gather at a rendezvous site on the Black River.[75] By March, Indian agents in Wisconsin were detecting rumors of a Dakota and Menominee coalition that was plotting a spring offensive.[76] In April, Street learned that the Menominees intended to strike the Sauks and Mesquakies when the *"grass would be half leg high."*[77]

To avert the impending conflict, Commanding General of the U.S. Army Alexander Macomb ordered the Western Department of the U.S. Army to deploy the "efficient force now at Jefferson Barracks," Missouri, with the object of seizing hostages involved in the previous summer's attack and thereby averting an Indian war that threatened to consume the northwestern frontier.[78] With Edmund Gaines recovering from influenza and rheumatism in Memphis, command of the expedition fell to Brigadier General Henry Atkinson, who had acquitted himself as a skilled peacekeeper and Indian diplomat during the Winnebago War of 1827. In the eyes of the Jackson administration, however, Atkinson's most redeeming quality was simply that he was not Edmund Gaines, who had fallen out of favor with the president over Indian removal, which the general regarded as immoral.[79] Patient, cautious, and conscientious, Atkinson was destined to similarly disappoint the president. On 3 April, Atkinson informed Commanding General Alexander Macomb that he would soon depart for Rock Island, Illinois, where he intended to call the Sauks and Mesquakies to council and compel the surrender of the Menominee killers. Optimistically, Atkinson ventured to Macomb, "I am persuaded that I shall be able to carry your views into effect without much difficulty." Presciently, he added, "In this however I may be mistaken."[80]

While Atkinson assembled six companies of infantry and the Menominees prepared for war, Black Hawk attempted to form his own coalition against the Americans. In February 1832, the Sauk war captain invited the Ho Chunks and Potawatomis to form a united front against the settlers of Illinois.[81] Although sympathetic, the response from the Potawatomi and Ho Chunk chiefs was tepid —the risk of making an enemy of the United States was too great. Despite the failure of this council, Black Hawk remained optimistic, thanks to the assurances of his advisors: Neapope, the principal hereditary chief of the British Band; and the "Winnebago Prophet" Wabokieshiek, who had invited the British Band to plant corn at his Rock River village in the coming summer.[82] Claiming to secure the allegiance of some Potawatomi villages on the Rock River and in Wisconsin, Neapope and Wabokieshiek also promised support from the British in Canada and all of the other Illinois tribes.[83] Whether they believed such support to be forthcoming or they were practitioners of wishful thinking is unclear. In either case, it was all Black Hawk needed to hear. On 5 April 1832, his British Band crossed the Mississippi into Illinois for the final time.

Possibly unaware of Black Hawk's movements, a Ho Chunk war party departed Prairie du Chien under the cover of darkness on 8 April. Led by Waukon Decorah and accompanied by the Menominee chief Carron, the party hoped to settle old and new scores with the Sauks and Mesquakies. Two and a half years had passed since Sauk and Mesquakie raiders had killed Waukon's daughter in Iowa, but it had been only eight months since Carron had lost his entire family in the Mesquakie attack near Prairie du Chien. Each of the chiefs had endured Joseph Street's admonitions to remain at peace and to permit the Great Father to dispense justice, but the government's inactivity compelled the disgusted leaders to seek justice themselves.[84] Learning of the foray the next day, Street called on the army to pursue the war party and compel its return. Assisted by former subagent John Marsh, a thirty-man force succeeded in performing this mission, but it did little to placate Waukon Decorah and Carron.[85] The Menominee chief in particular bided the American's interference but seethed with indignation, though he took a measure of consolation in the news that the Great Father had finally deployed the army to bring the Menominee killers to justice.

On 13 April, Atkinson convened a council with the principal Sauk and Mesquakie chiefs at Rock Island, Illinois. Believing the British Band to field as many as five hundred warriors and noting that it had yet to evince a hostile disposition, Atkinson resolved to avoid provocative movements and to seek a diplomatic solution. At Rock Island he learned that about half of the Menominee killers—fifty or sixty warriors, including the "principal persons engaged in that affair"—had taken shelter with the British Band.[86] Undeterred, Atkinson demanded hostages, who would remain in U.S. custody until the murderers were apprehended.[87] Less than a week later, the

Mesquakie chief Wapello surrendered three of the murderers from his tribe. Estranged from the British Band, Keokuk could offer none of the Sauk offenders, but he hoped that this offering would suffice to cover the debt. Although hoping to imprison four murderers from each tribe, Atkinson was satisfied with the effort and pledged that he would seize the remainder from the British Band.[88] "Up to this time," one of Atkinson's officers recalled, "it appeared to have been the general belief of the officers of the army . . . that the Indians . . . would under the forbearing, dignified and determined course pursued by the General, be brought to a sense of their conduct and situation, and induced to comply with the demands of the Government."[89]

The Menominees were less enthusiastic. On 21 April, Menominees at the Wisconsin Portage indicated a willingness to let the government arbitrate, but those near Prairie du Chien remained disgruntled.[90] Although dismissed from federal service, John Marsh remained indispensable to his government, which dispatched him up the Mississippi to gauge the sentiments of the western Menominees. On the morning of 17 April, Marsh met with them at the mouth of the Black River and found their mood dour. His reputation among the Menominees diminished on account of his role in turning back the Decorah-Carron war party, a despondent Marsh reported to Street that "they are resolved to fight the Foxes at all hazards: that though they are few and feeble they have resolved to fight until they are killed to a man or until they have *subdued* the Foxes."[91] Disgusted with their Great Father's inactivity, the Menominees also informed Marsh that they would no longer visit Prairie du Chien. Hence, when Street called the Menominees to a council several days later, only thirteen warriors attended. Covering tired ground, Street again admonished the Menominees to remain at peace. The warriors replied that they were not chiefs, that the chiefs had stayed away because they had no wish to be treated like children, but that they would convey the message.[92] Although several chiefs, including Carron, remained obdurate and refused to accept any presents, Street—aided by the news that Wapello had turned over three of the killers—ultimately convinced the western bands to stand down.[93] In Green Bay, the Menominees appealed to Stambaugh "to redeem the promise I made them last Summer, that if the murderers of their people were not punished last fall or very early this Spring, that I would permit them to take up the hatchet, and would myself accompany them." Stambaugh, however, induced the chiefs to sign a pledge to remain at peace for an additional three months.[94] The prospects for peace, however, were fleeting.

This was not evident to Henry Atkinson. By early May 1832, he had reason to hope that the situation was under his control; the British Band remained peaceable, the Mesquakies had surrendered hostages, and the Menominees had agreed to stand down. In fact, Atkinson had achieved not peace but a respite, during which he hoped to negotiate the British Band's withdrawal from Illinois. Moreover, Atkinson had no control over the white citizenry of Illinois, which lacked the general's forbearance. So long as it remained in Illinois, the British Band destabilized the region, eliciting panic, ambition, hope, or fear in each of its societies—often simultaneously within the same society. Discerning opportunity, those with much to gain yearned for war. Others, threatened with the loss of everything they had, hoped for peace. Any other denouement threatened to refigure the region for all time.

# 5

## EVERYTHING TO LOSE

On 8 April 1832, Billy Caldwell anxiously wrote to U.S. Indian agent Thomas Forsyth, his former employer, to solicit advice on behalf of his Potawatomi associates. Caldwell, a man of European and Indian descent, acted as an intermediary between the Potawatomis and their government-assigned agents, serving as what ethnohistorians term a "cultural broker."[1] Versed in both cultures, Caldwell moved comfortably between his roles as white bureaucrat and Indian diplomat, but he increasingly identified with his Native comrades as the Potawatomis came under pressure from white settlers, and the well-informed Caldwell understood that the Indians' days in the Old Northwest were numbered. After morbidly inquiring about western tracts of land like a terminally ill man picking out his own headstone, Caldwell observed, "the thunderstorm looks black to us."[2]

The cloud seemed blacker still when Caldwell learned of Black Hawk's crossing, which the roughly 200,000 white inhabitants of Illinois regarded as an invasion.[3] The British Band's movements placed the Potawatomis and Ho Chunks of Illinois in a very awkward situation. Over the preceding decade, each tribe had endured abuse from white miners and settlers, and many members of each tribe sympathized with the Sauks and Mesquakies. Others, more familiar with the scope of American power, urged caution. With the assistance of Caldwell and other cultural brokers, the Potawatomis mitigated divisions within their tribe to promulgate a remarkable, multiband neutrality policy. Geographical dispersion and divergent experiences precluded such unity for the Ho Chunks, whose various bands developed independent policies as the situation developed. Like Henry Atkinson, a majority of both tribes hoped for a peaceful settlement to the standoff with the British Band; like Henry Atkinson, they were destined for disappointment.

On 14 May 1832, imprudent militiamen attacked Sauk envoys and shattered the prospects of nonviolent resolution. Discerning opportunity in Black Hawk's tactical victory at the "Battle of Stillman's Run," disaffected Ho Chunks and Potawatomis lashed out at their American tormentors. Gratifying to a few, the attacks vindicated white claims of Potawatomi and Ho Chunk perfidy. Hoping to disguise their role, some Ho Chunks resorted to duplicity. Alarmed Potawatomi leaders, realizing that the actions of a few indicted the entire tribe, reacted more decisively. Considering alliance with Black Hawk foolhardy and neutrality impossible, the Potawatomis offered their military services to the United States Army. Under normal circumstances, Henry Atkinson likely would not have accepted such support. In late May 1832, Henry Atkinson did not enjoy normal circumstances.

Although the Potawatomis had carved out a peaceful coexistence with the whites around French and métis-dominated Chicago, they were less appreciated elsewhere. Three generations following the collapse of New France, the influence of French traders in the Old Northwest had finally reached its nadir, and the good feelings of the métis population of Chicago mattered far less than the loathing of Anglo-Americans in Peoria and Galena. Possessing valuable land along the shores of Lake Michigan and having betrayed the garrison of Fort Dearborn during the War of 1812, the Potawatomis excited more than their just share of jealousy and anxiety among the white populations of Illinois and Indiana, who assumed the worst about their neighbors when Indian troubles arose in 1827 and 1831. On both of those occasions, the Potawatomis had been assailed by rumors of conspiracy with the "hostile" Indians. Now, with Black Hawk's crossing, the Potawatomis soon found themselves again disparaged in the press and threatened with violence on their own hunting grounds. If Potawatomi removal appeared likely in April 1832, it had nearly become a foregone conclusion by the end of May.

However awkward the Potawatomi position was following Black Hawk's crossing, the Ho Chunks were at an even greater disadvantage. Having only five years earlier made war against the United States, the Ho Chunks were always the subject of fear and loathing. Moreover, they had limited means at their disposal to ameliorate white sentiments. Unlike the Potawatomis, who enjoyed the services of Billy Caldwell and other métis brokers in Chicago, the Illinois Ho Chunks had relatively few voices among the Americans. Reluctant to intermarry with whites, the Ho Chunks could not turn to influential métis relatives for advice, and the experience of the previous decade had induced many Ho Chunks in Illinois to withdraw from their assigned government agents.[4] Yet perhaps the greatest disadvantage under which the Ho Chunks labored was their relative lack of unity. Numbering close to six thousand souls in villages ranging from Green Bay to Rock Island, the Ho Chunks now vested real political authority in local chiefs, who developed policies based upon their own experience and the perceived interest of their people.

Not surprisingly, the Ho Chunks of the Rock River—many of

whom were intermarried with the Sauks—exhibited considerable sympathy for Black Hawk. Like the Sauks and Mesquakies, they had endured dispossession and abuse by the whites. While
the denouement of the "Winnebago War" cowed the Ho Chunks,
many shared Black Hawk's aspirations to evict the Americans
with a pan-Indian confederacy. Here, the single Ho Chunk voice
that rose above the din of 1831 and 1832 was that of Wabokieshiek, the "Winnebago Prophet," who encouraged Black Hawk to
recross the Mississippi and whose followers regarded the United
States with hostility.

Elsewhere, the Ho Chunks wanted nothing to do with Black
Hawk. Beyond the reach of American settlers and abuse, the Ho
Chunks of Wisconsin did not bear the same vendetta nursed by
their southern brothers. To these Indians, the Winnebago War represented a costly folly rather than unfinished business. It had disrupted the fur trade and attenuated important relationships with
whites. At the Portage, the Ho Chunks were divided. Some favored
joining the Americans, while others sympathized with the British
Band—or feared its vengeance.[5] In several villages, however, family
ties compelled involvement in the Black Hawk War. In the vicinity
of Green Bay and Prairie la Crosse (approximately sixty miles north
of Prairie du Chien on the eastern shore of the Mississippi), Ho
Chunks were intermarried with Dakotas and Menominees, and the
bonds of kinship proved strong enough to draw young men into
the conflict. For the Decorah family of Ho Chunks, the animosity
was more personal, and Waukon Decorah called on his followers
and those of his brothers to join the war against Black Hawk and
thereby avenge his daughter. Among the Ho Chunks, ties of blood
and community mattered more than a more diffuse conception of
the Ho Chunk people as a tribe.

To complicate matters, the Ho Chunks reported to no fewer than three different Indian agents, and the three rarely offered complementary advice. Following the Winnebago War, the government established new subagencies at the Portage and on the Rock River to better attend to the tribe, but their appearance only reinforced existing divisions among both the Ho Chunks and the agents of the Indian Office.[6] Ostensibly the sole agent for the Ho Chunks prior to 1828, Joseph Street resented this intrusion on his authority and questioned the wisdom of establishing agencies in areas where the government hoped to extinguish the title to Indian lands.[7] Although himself the beneficiary of patronage, Street decried the political appointments of Henry Gratiot and John H. Kinzie to the Rock River and Fort Winnebago subagencies, respectively. Son of two of the most influential French trading families on the American frontier and brother to the chief engineer of the U.S. Army, Henry Gratiot seemed ideally suited to Indian diplomacy. But Gratiot's principal motive was commercial, and he had gained his familiarity with the Ho Chunks of the Rock River by trespassing on their lands to establish his own mining camp. Called to account by the Indians, Gratiot compensated the Ho Chunks and appears to have enjoyed amicable relations with them subsequently, but it was not without reason that Street complained that the Jackson administration had created the Rock River subagency for the good of the Gratiots rather than the furtherance of U.S. Indian policy.[8]

Street was even less fond of John H. Kinzie, whose father had traded among the Indians of the Old Northwest since 1804 and who had himself clerked for the American Fur Company since he was fifteen.[9] In a lifetime of service to the fur company, Kinzie mastered the Ho Chunk language and developed a deserved reputation for fair dealing among the Indians. Indeed, one biographer has claimed that "John Kinzie was a white man gone Indian."[10] For this reason—and for Kinzie's ties to the American Fur Company—Street loathed Shaw-nee-aw-kee, as the Indians called Kinzie. Whereas Street advocated civilization and removal, Kinzie obstructed both, hoping to preserve the Old Northwest as an Indian hunting ground protected from the encroachment of white settlement and even culture. In this endeavor, Kinzie found a willing ally in Schachip-kaka, or "Old Decorah," a cousin of Waukon Decorah and prominent chief among the Portage Ho Chunks. When presented with a proposal for the education of his people in 1830, Schachipkaka responded that "if the Great Spirit had wished us to be like the whites, he would have made us so. As he has not seen fit to do so, we believe he would be displeased with us, to try and make ourselves different from what he thought good."[11] To Street's chagrin, Kinzie refused to push the issue, and an animosity developed between the two men. Hence, while the Potawatomis at least enjoyed the leadership of a man determined to stake out a coherent course, different engines within and without Ho Chunk society were pulling it in different directions and, ultimately, apart.

Although the majority of both the Ho Chunks and the Potawatomis favored neutrality, such a policy proved impossible to maintain in the face of Black Hawk's "invasion." With a few enlightened exceptions, most Americans failed either to understand or to accept the divided, diffuse authority of the "tribe" as a political entity. Divergent courses by bands of the same tribe suggested duplicity, and any activity hostile to the United States furnished a pretext for punishing the tribe as a whole.[12] Hence, allegations of complicity with the British Band posed a grave threat to all the Ho Chunks and Potawatomis. Such charges—some substantiated but most baseless—surfaced the moment Black Hawk set foot in Illinois, and they gained in volume and intensity in the weeks that followed. Eventually, the cacophony of calls for the removal or extermination of the Ho Chunks and Potawatomis swelled into a torrent that outlasted the war and carried both tribes west of the Mississippi.

The initial reports of Black Hawk's movements indicted nearly every tribe that lived in the region. On 9 April, John Bliss, commander of Fort Armstrong, reported Black Hawk's crossing to Brigadier General Henry Atkinson and subsequently indicated that the British Band comprised six hundred warriors augmented by some one hundred Potawatomis and Kickapoos and an unspecified number of Ho Chunk and Menominee allies. Significantly, these "allies"—if present at all—were adopted members of the British Band, independent of their respective tribes (otherwise they would have had no need to cross the Mississippi with Black Hawk—they would have already lived in Illinois). This distinction was lost on Bliss, however, and Atkinson had no reason to question the report, corroborated by influential fur trader George Davenport. Consequently, Atkinson listed "a few Pottawattamies" among the belligerents in his report to Commanding General of the Army Alexander Macomb and Illinois governor John Reynolds.[13] As for Wabokieshiek's Ho Chunks, Atkinson reported that they "have assumed a hostile attitude, at least One of defiance."[14]

Such reports alarmed Indian agent Henry Gratiot, who operated from Gratiot's Grove, his mining camp in southern Wisconsin. Of Wabokieshiek's warm feelings for Black Hawk there was little doubt, but Gratiot rightly feared for the security of the neutral Ho Chunk villages along the Illinois-Wisconsin border. In mid-April, he visited such a community on Turtle Creek, where he was reassured by its leaders. Three times Black Hawk had sent them red wampum, an invitation to join them in war, and three times they had sent it back. The Ho Chunks avowed their desire to remain at peace, but they were alarmed that their brothers from the Rock River had not distanced themselves from the British Band. They asked Gratiot to accompany twenty-six of them to Wabokieskiek's village to win its residents over to a policy of neutrality.[15]

It was very nearly the last trip Henry Gratiot ever made. Upon arriving at Wabokieshiek's village, the Turtle Creek Ho Chunks found that Black Hawk and his followers had taken up residence there, and none evinced much goodwill toward the agent. Fearing for his life, the Turtle Creek Ho Chunks raised a white flag over Gratiot's tent and stood guard. The Sauks replaced it with the Union Jack—as much a symbol of their antipathy for the United States as for their affinity for the British—and danced a war dance around the tent. The tension abated, however, and a perplexed Gratiot was permitted to continue on to Rock Island. Black Hawk later claimed that the Turtle Creek Ho Chunks had deceived Gratiot into making this trip, and that they had told Black Hawk that he enjoyed considerable support among the upper Rock River Indians. Although grateful for this intelligence, Black Hawk considered Gratiot "a good man" and placed a guard on his tent to prevent anyone from harming him.[16] Gratiot, however, remained ignorant of any intercession by Black Hawk on his behalf. When he arrived at Rock Island, his Ho Chunk escorts claimed to have ransomed the lives of Gratiot and another white companion with great difficulty and at great cost.[17] Whether duped or not, Gratiot remained convinced of the fidelity of the Ho Chunks of his agency, and he became an outspoken advocate of their interests throughout the war.

The Potawatomis had an advocate of their own: Billy Caldwell, the son of a British officer and his Mohawk consort. Unlike most children of such unions, Billy received an excellent education and an English upbringing.[18] Groomed for service in the colonial administration of British Canada, young Billy considered himself "a true Briton."[19] The subject of much Chicago folklore, Caldwell fought for Great Britain during the War of 1812 and, after a failed career in the British Indian Department in Canada, found a niche as a middleman between the Chicago Indian Agency and the Potawatomis.[20] Married to the daughter of Nee-scot-nee-meg, an important Potawatomi chief, the charismatic and learned Caldwell gained influence among the Potawatomis, who adopted him as their representative, counselor, and (by some accounts) leader.[21] His value to the Potawatomis is captured in his adopted Indian name, Sau-ga-nash, which meant, very simply, "Briton."[22] Conversant in two worlds, Caldwell provided the Potawatomis a cultural bridge that they desperately needed.

Like Henry Gratiot, Caldwell recognized the threat Black Hawk posed to the fragile neutrality of the Indians of Illinois. Upon learning of Black Hawk's crossing, he assembled a team of riders from the village of Shaubena, a chief who, although Ottawa by birth, had married and risen to prominence among the Potawatomis. Caldwell and Shaubena rode among the Potawatomi villages in Illinois and urged them to abstain from joining Black Hawk. Likely unaware that unkind words about their adopted tribesmen were circulating in official correspondence, Caldwell and Shaubena probably made this journey because they recognized the existence of disaffected bands and individuals among the Potawatomis, and they endeavored to ensure that sympathies toward Black Hawk remained latent. Although "perfectly satisfied" that the Potawatomis wished to remain at peace with the whites, Caldwell could only cover so much ground. After canvassing the countryside, Caldwell and Shaubena traveled to Chicago, where they determined to convene a formal council of the Potawatomis on 1 May, at which, they hoped, the Potawatomis would adopt a peace policy.[23]

In the meantime, the Potawatomis and Ho Chunks found their fidelity assailed from all quarters. Atkinson, who was in the process of deploying from Jefferson Barracks, Missouri, to deal with the crisis, feared that he would soon face "at least a thousand desperate Indians, and should the Winnebagoes and Pottawattamies join, a much larger number." On 18 April, the novice agent for the Sauks and Mesquakies, Felix St. Vrain, reported that some Potawatomis in the British Band rudely rebuffed peace overtures from Keokuk's band, knocking the hat off Keokuk's interpreter and confirming Potawatomi representation in Black Hawk's ranks. The reports of these officials reflected the incomplete intelligence with which they operated, but the popular press indicted the Potawatomis with more conviction. On 26 April, the *Sangamo Journal* of Springfield, Illinois, printed a letter in which several prominent citizens appealed to Governor Reynolds for aid in the face of an imminent onslaught by "the hostile Sacs, and the Pottawattomies . . . who, it is pretty certain, will join them." The authors closed with a melodramatic flourish: "WAR IS CERTAIN—and the inhabitants here entirely at the mercy of the savages." These same writers informed Governor Reynolds directly that "we regard it as entirely certain that the pottawattimes will join the Sacs." Reynolds seems to have accepted this assertion as gospel, echoing it throughout the war and making it an article of faith for the residents of Illinois.[24]

No one knew exactly what Black Hawk intended to do. His own followers entertained divergent thoughts about their captain's designs, ranging from the reoccupation of their old village at Saukenauk to waging a pan-Indian war against the United States with British backing. In all likelihood, Black Hawk was looking for an opportunity to restore some modicum of Sauk sovereignty, first by simply reentering Illinois and later by planting corn or making war as the circumstances allowed. Although Atkinson had bragged at Rock Island that the British Band could be as easily crushed as a "piece of dirt," he regarded Black Hawk's military capability with some anxiety.[25] As of 27 April, Atkinson reasonably estimated that the Indians could field 486 warriors against his own 320 regulars, and he feared that area tribes would join Black Hawk, swelling his ranks to over one thousand warriors.[26] Leery of his prospects, Atkinson made an ill-advised appeal for help.

On the same day he met with the Sauk and Mesquakie chiefs at Rock Island, Atkinson informed Governor Reynolds that "I think the frontier is in great danger." Unauthorized to mobilize the Illinois militia on his own, Atkinson left it to the governor "to judge of the proper course to be pursued."[27] Atkinson dropped another thinly veiled suggestion to the governor several days later, but Reynolds had already jumped at the opportunity presented to him. The governor was up for reelection, and nothing promised political capital like leading the citizen-soldiers of Illinois in a campaign to rid their state of the Indian scourge.[28] On 16 April, Reynolds informed Atkinson that he had called up the state militia.[29] Hoping to avert an Indian war, Atkinson instead made it inevitable.

Unwittingly setting the stage for a contest of arms between the citizenry of Illinois and the British Band, Atkinson then returned his attention to the task of preventing a war between Indians. He fired off a series of messages to the military officers and Indian agents at posts throughout the region, authorizing the use of force to prevent the Dakotas, Menominees, Ho Chunks, and Potawatomis from entering the fight for or against the Sauks and Mesquakies.[30] On 8 May, Atkinson ordered Brigadier General Hugh Brady, recently arrived from Detroit, to station himself at Fort Winnebago "to admonish the Winnebagoes against joining the hostile Indians at their peril, and advise the Menominies to be quiet till measures are taken to bring the Sacs and Foxes to an account for their outrage against their tribe." Atkinson specifically addressed the Potawatomis on 18 May when he requested their Chicago agent, Thomas J. V. Owen, to "advise the Indians of your Agency to remain quiet, and take no part in the present difficulties."[31]

Meanwhile, Ho Chunk and Potawatomi leaders were taking measures to retain control of their respective fates. On 28 April, Ho Chunk chiefs White Crow and Whirling Thunder visited Atkinson at Rock Island. Representing Ho Chunk villages from the upper reaches of the Rock River, White Crow and Whirling Thunder sympathized with Black Hawk but hoped to insulate their people from the brewing conflict. White Crow claimed that the purpose of his visit was to recall the members of his band then residing in Wabokieshiek's village. Asserting that Black Hawk had sent him war wampum, White Crow assured Atkinson, "We want nothing to do with these bad birds."[32] Aware that extensive intermarriage between the Rock River Ho Chunks and the Sauks complicated his efforts to disassociate the two groups, White Crow publicly disavowed any Ho Chunks who remained with the British Band. In truth, the bonds of kinship were not so easily severed, and subsequent events revealed that White Crow was unprepared to abandon his own flesh and blood.

Among the Potawatomis, the situation was no less complex. On 1 May, Billy Caldwell and other Potawatomi leaders from southern Wisconsin and northern Illinois gathered outside of Chicago to promulgate a multiband response to the British Band's activities. The tone of the council was acrimonious at times, owing largely to young warriors who wished to join Black Hawk so that they could make a name for themselves in battle. When calmer minds prevailed, the assembled bands passed a resolution declaring any Potawatomi who supported Black Hawk a traitor to his tribe.[33] Following this council, white attitudes toward the Potawatomis cleaved fairly neatly along federal-state lines, with army officers and Indian agents trusting the tribe and state politicians, settlers, and militiamen convinced of their nefarious scheming. Even as Atkinson and St. Louis Superintendent of Indian Affairs William Clark informed their superiors of the Potawatomis' refusal to aid Black Hawk, Reynolds's subordinates continued to indict the tribe.[34]

By this time, well-informed members of the Potawatomi, Ojibwa, and Ottawa tribes, known collectively as the Three Fires or United Tribes, recognized the gravity of their position. On 12 May, they sent a deputation to Agent Thomas J. V. Owen to express the understandable concern that the Illinois militia would mistake them for hostile Indians. Owen held a council with the worried chiefs, and in it they pledged their fidelity to the United States and expressed apprehension that the British Band might intentionally mingle with their population, exposing them to indiscriminant violence at the hands of the militia. In response, Owen dispatched Subagent Gholson Kercheval, Billy Caldwell, and Alexander Robinson (another métis broker) to urge the vulnerable Indians to move toward Chicago and "out of the reach of the exasperated militia." Owen also recommended to Governor Reynolds the propriety of guarding against acts of indiscriminant violence by the militia, admonishing him that it would be "productive of the worst of consequences should any of them unfortunately fall a sacrifice to the Militia under your command."[35] The United Tribes and Owen had good reason to be concerned. The next day, Henry Dodge wrote a note to Governor Reynolds in which he likewise observed that Reynolds's vanguard would be hard-pressed "to discriminate between frinds and Enimies in the present state of our Indian Relations." Confident that Potawatomi and Ho Chunk sympathies rested with Black Hawk anyway, Dodge urged not caution but alacrity.[36]

Black Hawk made his last bid for Potawatomi support on 13 and 14 May 1832. Moving up the Rock River after his crossing, he found that his ostensible Ho Chunk allies, who by this time were alarmed by the extent of American agitation, lacked enthusiasm for collective action. Accompanied by Wabokieshiek, Black Hawk continued northeast into Potawatomi country, in search of safe harbor from the pursuing militia under Reynolds and regulars under Atkinson. Black Hawk met a deputation from the Potawatomis on 13 May, but was disappointed to find his questions met with "unsatisfactory answers." Finally realizing "that the Winnebagoes and Pottowatomies were not disposed to render us any assistance," Black Hawk resolved to accept whatever terms Atkinson would offer. The following day, Black Hawk graciously prepared a feast for the Potawatomis who had denied him succor, but the feast was interrupted by advancing cavalrymen, who did not fancy dog on a spit. It was not Atkinson who first encountered the British Band, but Isaiah Stillman's militia battalion. Unlike Atkinson or Edmund Pendelton Gaines before him, the Illinois militia offered no terms for Black Hawk to accept.[37]

Upon learning of the militia's approach, Black Hawk dispatched a delegation under a white flag of peace. A nervous militiaman answered on Stillman's behalf—with ball and powder. The ensuing fight seemed to confirm one U.S. Army officer's characterization of the militia as "that prosopopœia of weakness, waste, and confusion."[38] Fleeing the battlefield in a panicked rout, Stillman's battalion suffered at least eleven men killed, while Black Hawk lost only three.[39] Much to the chagrin of Isaiah Stillman, the fight garnered the moniker "Stillman's Run." Although the battle was a tactical victory for Black Hawk, it was a strategic disaster for the British Band. With few friends or provisions and hundreds of miles from sanctuary, the British Band was now on the warpath but at the end of its rope.

Stillman's Run placed the Potawatomis and Ho Chunks in an extremely awkward position. After the fight, most United Tribes villages evacuated to Chicago, abandoning their corn crop for the safety of Fort Dearborn. Concurrently, Governor Reynolds issued a proclamation of profound consequences. Contrary to available evidence, Reynolds announced that he was "of the opinion that the Pottawotamies and winnebagoes have Joined the hostile Sacs and all may be considered as waging war against the United States."[40] The Potawatomi leadership and its Indian agent were taken aback by this invalid allegation by the state's chief executive. The fallout was immediate and widespread, extending to neighboring Indiana, where the Indian agent for the Potawatomis feared for the lives of his charges and had them call in their hunting parties. On 17 May, Caldwell and Robinson arrived at Atkinson's headquarters and assured him of the peaceful intentions of their tribe. They also pledged to encourage the Ho Chunks to pursue a similar policy. Meanwhile, Owen received a dispatch from his charges, recounting their unsuccessful attempts to dissuade the British Band from continuing their belligerence following the Battle of Stillman's Run. Owen was "much pleased to see that the Indians of this Agency have fully evinced their determination to render no aid to the Sacs whatever in this matter" and that they were relocating to Chicago for their safety.[41]

Not all Illinois Indians responded to Stillman's Run with trepidation. To the contrary, Black Hawk's victory animated latent animosities borne by several Ho Chunk and Potawatomi communities that had endured insult and injury from the Americans. After the fight with Stillman's men, Black Hawk determined to seek sanctuary in the dense swamps at the head of the Rock River. As they passed the head of Kishwaukee River, the British Band encountered a band of Ho Chunks who were heartened by Black Hawk's recent success. They offered to join him and guide his party to a safe haven. First, however, Black Hawk sent out a number of war parties to cover the movement of his main body.[42]

Subsequently, Black Hawk enjoyed aid from the various Ho Chunk bands of the upper Rock River, which furnished guides, corn, and warriors.[43] On 19 May, Ho Chunks killed a courier named William Durley and delivered his scalp to Black Hawk. Five days later, a party of white messengers found Durley's mutilated body, unaware that four of them would shortly meet the same fate. Led by Sauk and Mesquakie agent Felix St. Vrain, the seven Americans encountered approximately nine mounted Ho Chunks about thirty-five miles southeast of Galena, near Kellogg's Grove. The parties neared to within a hundred yards of each other, then the Ho Chunks gave chase, picking off four Americans—including St. Vrain—while the remaining three made good their escape. Ultimately, as many as thirty Ho Chunks may have joined in the attack, which newspapers initially attributed to the Sauks.[44]

Although no doubt significant to their victims, Ho Chunk contributions to Black Hawk's war paled in comparison to those of the Potawatomis. On Indian Creek lay a small Potawatomi village comprising about twenty lodges and seventy or eighty inhabitants who relied upon the fish of Indian Creek for sustenance. In the spring of

1832, a white settler named William Davis built a dam across Indian Creek about six miles below the Indian village. In addition to providing power for his mill, the dam prevented spawning fish from reaching the village. The principal chief of the village, Meau-eus, protested to Davis but was rudely rebuffed. In early May, Davis caught a Potawatomi named Keewassee, who was attempting to dismantle the dam, and severely flogged him. In the face of this indignity, Meau-eus's village stood ready to retaliate, but Shaubena and fellow Potawatomi chief Wabaunsee counseled moderation. Although Meau-eus heeded this advice, he and his people seethed quietly, awaiting their opportunity for revenge.[45]

Stillman's Run provided just such an opportunity; it made Black Hawk look strong and the Illinois militia appear weak. Eager for justice, opportunity beckoned to Meau-eus and his people. To Shaubena, who gauged their sentiments, it must have seemed as if Reynolds's unwarranted proclamation had become a self-fulfilling prophecy. Realizing that he could not divert his aggrieved tribesmen from their intended course, he resolved at least to remove potential victims from its path. After learning of the Battle of Stillman's Run, Shaubena sent his son and nephew to the Fox River and Holderman's Grove settlements to warn white settlers to evacuate the area. Shaubena himself went first to the settlement on Bureau Creek, then to Indian Creek, where Davis lived. While everyone on the Bureau heeded his warning, those at Indian Creek were not so wise.[46] According to one of the settlers, "Indian rumors were so common, and some of our neighbors did not sufficiently credit this old Indian."[47]

Initially, members of the Hall family followed Shaubena's advice, packing their valuables and heading for the safety of Ottawa, Illinois. During their journey, however, they encountered Davis, who

convinced them that a mounted company from that town had rid-
den out to find the enemy and would provide ample warning if
there was any danger. The Halls stopped at Davis's house, where
they joined the Davis and Pettigrew families, a Mr. Howard and
son, John H. Henderson, and two of Davis's hired hands, Robert
Morris and Henry George. Complacently assuming their safety in
numbers, most of the men were working in the fields when the
Potawatomis struck.[48] On 20 May, as many as eighty of Meau-eus's
disaffected warriors fell upon the Davis homestead, leaving fifteen
men, women, and children dead and mutilated.[49] The war party
also took prisoner the teenage Hall girls, Sylvia and Rachel, and
Davis's seven-year-old son, killing him shortly thereafter.[50]

Potawatomi participation in what became known as the "Indian
Creek Massacre" was not immediately evident to the whites. Shaubena, Caldwell, and others who had labored so hard to distance the
tribe from Black Hawk, however, must have considered it an embar-
rassing failure in their multiband policy. The Potawatomi leadership now found itself at a critical crossroads. After the Indian victory at Stillman's Run, young Potawatomi warriors, eager to prove
their mettle in battle, agitated for participation in the conflict on
Black Hawk's behalf. Nearly twenty years had passed since Potawatomi men were able to win reputations for themselves as warriors,
stagnating social advancement for males not born into the hereditary offices of civil chiefs or shamans. Young men, therefore, clam-
ored for the opportunity to prove themselves in battle—and elders
often complained of their inability to restrain their young men.[51]

Not surprisingly, talk of joining Black Hawk alarmed Caldwell
and the architects of the Potawatomi peace policy, who convened
another council at Chicago to resurrect their tattered resolutions.
Thomas J. V. Owen attended this conference, at which some chiefs

vociferously protested past abuses at the hands of the whites and implied that an opportunity to seek justice now presented itself. To this, Caldwell, Robinson, and Owen responded with impassioned oratories. Their words now lost, these speeches succeeded in carrying the issue among the other chiefs, who afterward offered their hands to Owen and pledged their friendship.[52]

With the public yet unaware of Potawatomi involvement in the Indian Creek Massacre and most local villagers voluntarily quarantined at Chicago, the Potawatomis could have tried to ride out the storm and hope for the best. Caldwell was too shrewd, however, to assume that the whites would take Potawatomi loyalty for granted, even in the absence of further depredations. After all, just a week earlier the Illinois governor proclaimed the Potawatomis to be enemies of the state, and even the shoddiest inquiry would eventually implicate Meau-eus's village in the Indian Creek attack. Indications, both real and imagined, of Potawatomi involvement began to surface on 21 May, when an army officer incorrectly reported that Big Foot's band of southern Wisconsin Potawatomis had joined Black Hawk.[53] Shortly thereafter, Governor Reynolds received a secondhand report that the Potawatomis had held a war dance in preparation for joining Black Hawk. On 26 May, Colonel Zachary Taylor discovered what he assumed to be scalps from the settlers on Indian Creek in what appeared to be Potawatomi villages. The next day, Illinois militia commander Samuel Whiteside wrote Atkinson to assert the likelihood of Potawatomi cooperation with Black Hawk, citing the construction of a new wigwam village as evidence that the Potawatomis intended to shelter the British Band. Among the citizens (and governor) of Illinois, paranoia prevailed, compelling one James Strode to write directly to the secretary of war and claim, "This Section of the State is invaded by powerful detach-

ments of Indian Warriors of the Sac, Fox, Winebago & Potawatamie & part of the Kickapoo Nations." Although the veracity of
these reports was by no means assured, they had a cumulative
effect, and by the end of the month William Clark reported the
probability of Potawatomi involvement to the secretary of war. It
became increasingly imperative that the Potawatomis make a convincing demonstration of their loyalty to the United States or suffer the consequences.[54]

Critical to Potawatomi knowledge of reports against them
were their intercultural brokers, principally Billy Caldwell, without whom legitimate village leaders would have been unable to
gauge popular sentiment. While his understanding of Native society made him useful to the government, his standing in white society now made Caldwell an asset to the Potawatomis. Through
Caldwell and their agent, Thomas J. V. Owen, the Potawatomis attempted to clear their name. Owen wrote to the superintendent of
Indian affairs at Detroit on 24 May, reporting, "I have had several
Councils with my Chiefs and Headmen, and feel fully assured of
their friendship and sincerity." But Potawatomi chiefs acted under
their own auspices, too. To dispose of the source of their agitation
speedily, the band chief Big Foot sent a string of peace wampum to
the British Band, requesting that they leave Potawatomi territory
(to which the band replied that they would do so upon drying their
meat and in the absence of white interference). While most Illinois
citizens harbored more than a little ill will toward the Potawatomis
even during happier days, the citizens of Chicago enjoyed good relations with the Potawatomis and offered the tribe a collective vote
of confidence in a petition dated 29 May. Petitions and the good
word of agent Owen would prove insufficient to clear the Potawatomi name, however; the time had come to make a more profound

avowal of the tribe's disposition. To cement their alliances with whites in the past, the Potawatomis had offered two marketable commodities to their European associates, furs and warriors—and this was no time to set a trap line.[55]

Still, the offer of military service to the United States faced obstacles. Before and after the Black Hawk War, the United States generally adhered to a policy of maintaining the neutrality of Native American groups. Although the colonial era provided ample precedent for Anglo-Indian military cooperation, it was usually the product of military weakness on the part of the colonists, who regarded their would-be allies with some uneasiness. In the years before King Philip's War (1675–76), New England Puritans considered themselves sufficiently secure to dispense with reliance on Indians, excluding them from the colonial militia. The unprecedented scale of this conflict, however, in which Indians destroyed a quarter of all New England villages and killed five percent of the colonial population, finally compelled the employment of Indian troops. Even then, public outcry compelled the discharge of Christian "Praying Indians," who had enlisted in the Puritan cause in July 1675. Only the repeated defeat of white militia units rendered Indian aid acceptable, and Mohegans, Pequots, and Niantics soon swelled the Puritan ranks. Afterward, the English colonists regarded their Indian allies with considerable distrust, imprisoning many of them on an exposed island, where many died of exposure and privation. By the end of the war, roughly forty percent of New England's Indians were dead.[56]

Reluctance to enter and maintain interracial military alliances reflected more than simple racism on the part of the supplicants, although it certainly was a factor in European dealings with the Indians. Rather, it was more the logical result of the recognition of a

dilemma inherent in alliances with potential enemies. While mili
tary weakness demanded a search for allies, the very search adver-
tised this weakness, often to those most likely to exploit it. Thus,
solicitation of military aid suggested an inverse corollary to the
cliché "if you can't beat them, join them": in this case, if they want
to join you, beat them. Once established, interracial military alliances often remained fragile and tempered by mutual suspicion.
Even in victory, Indian and European allies regarded the conduct
and methods of their allies with ambiguity. During King Philip's
War, for example, Indian auxiliaries present at the Great Swamp
Fight were appalled by the devastation and inhumanity wrought
upon an Indian village.[57] Here, precious few degrees separated victims from allies. To the colonists, conversely, Indian methods of
warfare seemed only to confirm their savagery and ungodliness.

This view tempered the Americans' enthusiasm for fielding Indian warriors during the Revolutionary War. Although the Continental Congress authorized George Washington to recruit two
thousand Indian auxiliaries in 1776, recruitment of Indians was as
much a means of depriving the British of allies as it was an integral
part of American military policy.[58] The dilemma of alliance figured
prominently, and the Americans made it clear that alliance offered
an opportunity for Indians to show where they stood, but that the
Patriots did not need Indian aid to win. Even before the conclusion
of the American Revolution, George Washington began to turn
away Indians willing to assist the Patriot cause.[59] Similarly, George
Rogers Clark refused the offer of Chief Young Tobacco to furnish
about one hundred Kickapoos and Piankashaws because he wanted
to demonstrate that the Americans did not require Indian assistance.[60]

Following the Revolution, the United States slashed its defense establishment, and commanders charged with conquering the Ohio country in the early 1790s could not afford to be so particular. By offering the Indians an opportunity to strike their traditional enemies, the Americans induced Chickasaws and (later) Choctaws to accompany the commands of Arthur St. Clair and Anthony Wayne.[61] Military weakness persisted into the War of 1812, during which American commanders—including Andrew Jackson—fielded Cherokee and allied Creek warriors against enemy "Red Stick" Creeks. With assistance from Native allies, Jackson broke Indian power in the South. To ensure it would not recover, he punished his allies as harshly as his enemies at the Treaty of Fort Jackson.[62]

Not surprisingly, few opportunities for interracial alliance arose in the years following the War of 1812. As the states became more secure through the nineteenth century, a reluctance to employ Indians returned. When military necessity—usually a lack of familiarity with terrain or a simple lack of strength—mandated, the Americans continued to solicit Indian allies, as in the First Seminole War in 1818 and the Arikara campaign of 1823, in which the Sioux participated. In each of these instances, however, appeals to Indians for assistance represented the initiative of individual commanders rather than a sanctioned military practice.[63] The Arikara campaign, moreover, seemed to justify the worst fears of those wary of allying with the Indians. Disgusted by Colonel Henry Leavenworth's leniency against their common foes, the Sioux developed, according to historian Richard White, "a low estimation of the ability of white soldiers that would last for years."[64]

Certainly this estimation lasted up to and beyond 1832, when political considerations further militated against the formation of American-Indian alliances. For over a decade and a half, the government had labored to pacify and "civilize" the Native populations of the Old Northwest; arming Indian groups to fight against one another seemed contrary to the very foundation of federal Indian policy. As the frontier white population grew, so too did popular aversion to permitting—let alone condoning—intertribal warfare, which threatened to disrupt commerce and engulf white settlements. Although Edmund Gaines, the commander of the Western Department of the U.S. Army, may have liked the idea of training and fielding Indian soldiers, the associated political consequences were potentially severe.

The Battle of Stillman's Run, however, had changed everything in two important ways. First, Henry Atkinson was no longer a third-party arbitrator trying to prevent a general Indian war; he was now a field commander trying to win an Indian war. Second, the rout of Stillman's battalion and subsequent attacks on civilian settlements had an unnerving effect on the Illinois militiamen, many of whom deserted or demanded discharge.[65] Governor Reynolds relented, retaining enough men to form just six companies of volunteers until he could muster another militia army. Atkinson deemed this interim force, combined with his 300 regulars, insufficient for the task at hand, especially now that Black Hawk had demonstrated a determination to fight.[66] Although Atkinson called for reinforcements from Fort Leavenworth, the regulars lacked horses and stood little chance of overtaking the British Band.[67] Reynolds had called for 3,000 mounted volunteers following the debacle at Stillman's Run and the dissolution of his first army, but the new force would not be available until mid-June. Regardless, the performance of the militia to date was far from awe inspiring. Capturing the common assessment of the regular officers, Colonel Zachary Taylor complained, "The more I see of the militia the less confidence I have in their effecting any thing of importance; & therefore tremble not only for the safety of the frontiers, but for the reputation of those who command them."[68] His own reputation and the outcome of the war in the balance, Atkinson looked elsewhere for a solution.

By the end of May, Henry Atkinson had much in common with the Potawatomis and Ho Chunks of Illinois. Victims of circumstance all, they were powerless to avert a war from which they stood little to gain and much to lose. Cool minds among them sought a peaceful resolution to the crisis, but passionate elements within each society lobbied for war. The Illinois militia's defeat on 14 May placed both tribes and the American commander in very awkward situations. Learning of Black Hawk's victory, militant Ho Chunks and Potawatomis attacked isolated Americans along the frontier, confirming the suspicions of Illinois's paranoid citizenry. Assisted by capable métis counselors like Billy Caldwell, the Potawatomis realized that their neutrality policy had failed and grasped the likely consequences. With Caldwell's guidance, the Potawatomis moved decisively to control their own fate, offering military service to the United States. Serendipitously for the Potawatomis, Henry Atkinson needed their help, as well as that of other Indians. Demanding their discharge following the debacle at Stillman's Run, the Illinois militiamen sapped Atkinson of combat power at a critical juncture. Traditionally, the Americans turned to Indian allies only in moments of dire need. Twelve days after the Battle of Stillman's Run, Atkinson judged himself in such a situation.

# 6

## WARPATH

On 26 May 1832, Brigadier General Henry Atkinson requested the Menominees and Dakotas from the area of Prairie du Chien to fight "in conjunction with the troops against the Sac and Fox Indians."[1] The following day, Atkinson ordered more rations for his army in anticipation of swelling his ranks with three hundred to five hundred Indians, all "Very necessary in such a Warfare as I am engaged in."[2] Apparently, Atkinson arrived at the decision to solicit Indian aid on his own; he informed Commanding General Alexander Macomb of the decision after the fact, venturing, "I thought the state of things justified the measure and would receive your approbation."[3] Whatever Macomb thought of Atkinson's decision, the Menominees were ecstatic. Atkinson's request reached them on 30 May and, according to Joseph Street, the Menominees were "greatly rejoiced that they would be permitted to go to war."[4]

The Menominees' jubilance gave way to frustration in the following weeks. Compelled to accept the services of Indian allies by the aftermath of Stillman's Run, Henry Atkinson did not plan carefully for their employment, and he condemned those most interested in the war to serve under Billy Hamilton, the pretentious and unqualified son of Alexander Hamilton. Meanwhile, hundreds more warriors languished in Green Bay, awaiting a call to arms that only came when the war was almost over. Ironically, the Indians afforded the most immediate and meaningful role in the conflict were those least concerned with defeating Black Hawk. The Ho Chunks and Potawatomis had no desire to abet the Americans in the British Band's demise, but they needed to make a convincing—albeit insincere—display of fidelity to their Great Father to avert their own destruction. Hence, they guided (and perhaps misguided) Atkinson on Black Hawk's trail, pledging allegiance without finding or engaging the "enemy" main force until 21 July. If the first two months of U.S.-Indian collaboration left Atkinson wanting, they also indicated that his Indian allies cooperated for their own reasons and in their own ways.

Upon receiving Atkinson's request for Indian assistance, Joseph Street again called upon his former subagent, John Marsh, to travel up the Mississippi and extend the general's invitation to the Dakotas. Familiar with Marsh's facility with the Sioux language and people, Atkinson specifically requested that Marsh accompany the Dakota warriors. Relieved from his office because he had endeavored to foment the sort of war that Atkinson now endorsed, Marsh was the right man to effect an alliance with his Dakota in-laws. Unbeknownst to Atkinson or Street, Marsh—now a private trader—had already illicitly furnished his kinsmen with arms and ammunition.[5] On 30 May, Marsh left Prairie du Chien in the company of his replacement, Thomas P. Burnett, who knew nothing about Indians but was more accountable to Street.[6]

Better able to gauge Indian sentiments than most Americans in the region, Marsh exceeded the letter of his instructions and stopped by the Ho Chunk village at Prairie la Crosse while ascending the Mississippi. Recognizing the latent animosity the Ho Chunks harbored toward the Americans, Marsh attempted to secure their allegiance to the American cause lest they instead join Black Hawk.[7] The Ho Chunk chief Winneshiek was not interested. The brother-in-law of Wabokieshiek (the "Winnebago Prophet"), Winneshiek had migrated to Prairie la Crosse from northern Illinois in the wake of the Winnebago War, and he judged his people best served by a strict policy of neutrality.[8] Already he had twice rejected entreaties from Black Hawk, and he gave Marsh the same response.[9] Others in the village were more sympathetic. Owing largely to location, intermarriage between the Prairie la Crosse Ho Chunks and neighboring Dakotas and Menominees was common, providing a kinship-based antipathy for the Sauks and Mesquakies.[10] Perhaps more important, Prairie la Crosse was home to One-Eyed Decorah, an influential orator and brother to Waukon Decorah.[11] If the interests of the village dictated neutrality, the bonds of family militated against it; One-Eyed Decorah and his followers pledged to join Marsh upon his return from the Dakota villages upstream.[12] Winneshiek's own family replicated the division of his tribe and village in microcosm. One of his sons was at that very time a member of the British Band, while his other son rode with One-Eyed Decorah against that same party.[13]

On 1 June, Marsh and Burnett arrived at Prairie aux Ailes (present-day Winona, Minnesota), where Marsh presented his Dakota friends with red wampum in accordance with their own protocol for forming military alliances.[14] Dakota headmen Wabasha and L'Arc enthusiastically agreed to join the expedition, claiming that they were already planning to go to war with or without American invitation.[15] While independent action would have entailed chastisement by the U.S. government, Atkinson promised pay and provisions for Dakota warriors operating under American aegis.[16] Sioux experience in the 1823 Arikara War fiasco notwithstanding, this invitation proved too good to refuse. After two days of preparation, Wabasha, L'Arc, and eighty Dakota warriors descended the Mississippi to make war on their enemies.[17]

During Marsh and Burnett's recruiting drive, Waukon Decorah visited the Americans in Prairie du Chien and requested permission to assemble the Ho Chunks of Lake Winnebago, Green Bay, the Fox River, the Four Lakes, and Green Lakes to join the war against the British Band. The Sauks and Foxes, he reminded Street, had killed his daughter at Red Cedar, and he was yet eager for revenge. Years later, Waukon recalled that his "soldier father" (probably Colonel Zachary Taylor) responded by presenting him with an American flag and a military uniform and enjoining him and his people to "dig up the tomahawk, and use it against the Sacs, side by side with the white soldiers."[18] Thus commissioned, Waukon left Prairie du Chien on 4 June to assemble his warriors.[19]

The following day, Marsh returned to Prairie du Chien in the company of Wabasha's Dakotas and twenty to forty Ho Chunk warriors from Prairie la Crosse.[20] Here, they joined forty-one Menominees of singular intent who had busied themselves by escorting fresh horses to American units in the field while awaiting Marsh's return.[21] On 6 June, Street reported that a composite force of about two hundred Indians had assembled and enthusiastically engaged in war dances "nearly all the time since their arrival." The force might have been considerably bigger if not for the delay occasioned by Marsh's recruiting mission. During his absence, perhaps as many as 160 Dakotas waited impatiently for three days, then returned to their villages disgusted by their inaction.[22] Despite the enthusiasm of those remaining, over half of them lacked serviceable firearms, and Street purchased 126 weapons from local traders at a cost of $1,792 to the government.[23]

Atkinson's decision to equip and feed his Native allies worked to their mutual benefit, but his decision to place William S. Hamilton in command of the Prairie du Chien Indian contingent virtually assured that only a handful of these guns would actually see service against Black Hawk. Politician, lead miner, and son of Alexander Hamilton, the ambitious "Billy" Hamilton volunteered his services to Atkinson, who—perhaps because Hamilton had been a colonel during the War of 1812—granted him command of the Indians assembling at Prairie du Chien.[24] One of Atkinson's officers later recalled that Hamilton "was of much use to us from his knowledge of the Indian character and of the country," but it seems likely that Hamilton overstated his expertise on both counts.[25] The Indians subjected to Hamilton's "command" were thoroughly unimpressed by both his pedigree and his assumed qualifications. Well served by their own leaders, the Indians showed little disposition to subordinate themselves to a white miner with whom they were unfamiliar. This much may have become evident to Joseph Street, who referred to Hamilton as nothing more than a "messenger" when the force of 225 Indians departed by canoe for Galena, Illinois, at midday on 7 June.[26]

While Street took measures to bring the Dakotas, Menominees, and Ho Chunks into the conflict, Fort Winnebago subagent John Kinzie preferred that the Ho Chunks stay out of the fight altogether. After learning that Atkinson had called upon the Dakotas and Menominees, Kinzie informed Michigan Territory governor George Porter, "I hope he will not invite the Winnebagoes, as they are perfectly neutral, and have a desire to remain quiet."[27] In fact, Kinzie overstated the unanimity of the central Wisconsin Ho

Chunks. Although convinced that their civil chiefs, women, and older men wished to stay out of the war, Kinzie was aware "that there existed in the breasts of too many of the young savages a desire to distinguish themselves by 'taking some white scalps.'"[28] To Kinzie's wife, the sentiment was entirely justified.

> They did not love the Americans—why should they? By them they had been gradually dispossessed of the broad and beautiful domains of their forefathers, and hunted from place to place, and the only equivalent they had received in exchange had been a few thousands annually in silver and presents, together with the pernicious example, the debasing influence, and the positive ill treatment of too many of the new settlers upon their lands.[29]

Yet the Indians of whom Juliette Kinzie wrote did not regard the Americans monolithically. Although hopelessly outnumbered by avaricious miners and settlers, men like John Kinzie offered the Ho Chunks hope that they could preserve their land and lifestyle. Consequently, fifty lodges of Ho Chunks from northern Illinois and southern Wisconsin relocated to the Portage after Black Hawk's crossing. In so doing, the Ho Chunks hoped not only to distance themselves from the war but to seek refuge from an Indian agent who continued to treat the Ho Chunks as allies even as his countrymen called for their eradication. The latter outcome was likely, Kinzie knew, were the young Ho Chunk warriors to join with Black Hawk. Consequently, Kinzie joined the Ho Chunk civil chiefs in successfully imploring the warriors to set aside their personal ambitions for the good of their people. With varying degrees of success, the Ho Chunks gathered at the Portage thereafter attempted to promulgate a multiband policy of neutrality.

On the same day Atkinson issued his call for Indian allies, the Ho Chunks of Four Lakes convened a council with Rock River sub-agent Henry Gratiot and Henry Dodge, who now commanded a mounted militia battalion of miners from the lead country. Here, Ho Chunk leaders, proclaiming their neutrality, requested that Gratiot furnish the Indians with a piece of paper testifying to their peaceful disposition as a guard against indiscriminant whites in search of Indians to kill.[30] The Portage bands, meanwhile, sent two runners to Prairie du Chien to dissuade (unsuccessfully) the western Ho Chunks from joining the U.S.-allied party assembling there.[31] With the assistance of Kinzie, the Portage Ho Chunks also drafted a letter to their Rock River kinsmen, pleading, "if you love your brother in this section of country, you will immediately leave the Sacs & Foxes, and come among us. We wish to avoid giving suspicion to our friends the whites, or having any thing to do with either party." They also communicated to the Rock River Ho Chunks their intent to kill any Sauks or Mesquakies who entered their part of the country.[32]

Other Ho Chunks were not so committed to neutrality, however. Two days after their council at Four Lakes, Henry Gratiot and Henry Dodge convened another council with Ho Chunk leaders from further down the Wisconsin River. Allies to the Dakotas and Menominees, Ho Chunks in this quarter had become embroiled in the war against the Sauks and Mesquakies, whom the Ho Chunks suspected were responsible for the disappearance of two lodges that never returned from their winter hunt. Although they had sent many of their people to the Portage to avoid the war, the men who remained in their villages on the lower Wisconsin were willing to abandon neutrality altogether. "The tomahawk has been raised four times against us[;] seven of our people have been killed by the

Sacks," their chief, Waukaunkaw (Snake) proclaimed. "My tomahawk is not raised, But just say the word, and it will soon be
raised."[33] Two weeks later, Waukaunkaw made good on this pledge.

While the Ho Chunks from the lower Wisconsin were eager to
join the Americans against the British Band, those on the upper
Rock River weighed the consequences of overtly supporting Black
Hawk. Led by White Crow, who had previously traveled to Rock Island to avow his people's neutrality to Henry Atkinson, the Rock
River Ho Chunks were torn. Only slightly removed from the heart
of the lead-mining country and aware that their own displacement
could only be a matter of time, White Crow and his people viewed
Black Hawk's campaign with uneasy enthusiasm. Nothing would
have pleased them more than for Black Hawk to drive their mutual
white enemies from the region, but White Crow recognized both
the precariousness of the Ho Chunk situation and the likely outcome of the campaign. Realizing that any sign of Ho Chunk complicity could be disastrous to the fortunes of his people, White
Crow decided that it would be imprudent to assist the Sauk leader
openly. At the same time, Ho Chunk sympathies and kinship ties
would not permit an absolute breach with the British Band, so
White Crow resigned himself and his people to the dangerous path
of duplicity. Over the ensuing weeks, White Crow's followers furnished Black Hawk with guides and provisions while simultaneously giving the Americans demonstrations of fidelity.

In the latter venture, the Ho Chunks were abetted by the capture
of the Hall girls by the Potawatomis and their subsequent delivery
to the British Band. Anxious to recover the women, Henry Gratiot
"sent a runner to White Crow & Little Priest with a promise of the
highest reward that should be offered if they would bring me those
women unhurt."[34] Offered both a reward and an opportunity to

evince goodwill toward the Americans, White Crow assented. Accompanied by Little Priest, Whirling Thunder, and another companion, White Crow traveled to the Sauk camp and, after much cajoling, ransomed the captives on 28 May.[35] Following a three-day journey to the Blue Mounds of southern Wisconsin, where settlers had erected a stockade, the harrowing ordeal of Rachel and Sylvia Hall finally reached its end. Henry Gratiot was not present to proffer the promised reward, so the Ho Chunks reluctantly turned the girls over to Henry Dodge and his militiamen.

Joined by at least two dozen Ho Chunks during their journey, White Crow and his followers eyed Dodge's troopers warily. Although both groups proclaimed loyalty to the Great Father, Dodge's command consisted entirely of miners from the lead region, and the Ho Chunks had ample reason to regard them as enemies. The militiamen shared similar sentiments and had in fact erected the blockhouse at the Blue Mounds for the express purpose of defending themselves against Ho Chunks.[36] While the Americans bedded down for the evening, White Crow and his followers convened in the woods, where the chief disparaged the fighting qualities of Americans in general and Dodge in particular. Learning of the gathering and convinced that Dodge and his men would be massacred, a militia officer awoke Dodge, who arrested White Crow and nearly twenty others, including five principal chiefs. In the morning, Dodge marched his prisoners to Morrison's Grove, where they met Henry Gratiot.[37] Gratiot did his best to salvage what was shaping up to be a disastrous situation. He convinced Dodge to release fifteen of his hostages and to remand the other five to Gratiot's custody. In spite of his timely intervention, the detained chiefs could "scarcely brook the indignity with which they consider themselves treated." Over a week later, Gratiot was still attempting to assuage their humiliation "with presents and promises."[38] Many of Dodge's officers considered White Crow's indignation feigned, however, and they remained convinced that the Ho Chunk chief had been plotting an attack on the Americans.[39]

On 3 June, White Crow opened a council with Dodge and Gratiot by enumerating the many ways in which he had demonstrated his loyalty to the Americans: withdrawing his people from Wabokie-shiek's village, ostensibly saving Henry Gratiot from death during his visit to the same, enjoining the British Band to leave the Ho Chunk country, and—most recently—delivering the Hall girls from their captors. White Crow, whom one of the militiamen regarded as "a Cicero among Indians for his powers of oratory and [e]loquence," made an impressive case, and Dodge conceded that the chief had rendered outstanding service in liberating the Hall sisters.[40] At the same time, Dodge chided the Indians for selling horses to the Sauks and permitting them to encamp on Ho Chunk lands. Perhaps sensing that Dodge remained unconvinced of the Ho Chunks' allegiance, White Crow offered to betray the British Band to the Americans by offering them a sanctuary and then revealing its location to Dodge. Dodge countered by encouraging the Ho Chunks to join with the allied Indians then assembling at Prairie du Chien and to "kill and plunder" the British Band "to remunirate yourselves for the losses you have sustained by the Sauks." Now convinced that circumstances demanded a more strident expression of Ho Chunk loyalty, White Crow met the challenge: "If you give liberty we will raise the Tomahawk and join the redskins and we think that the skins should attack them on one side & the Americans on the other & have the Sacks between us, & all strike at one time, & we will shew you whether we are soldiers or not."[41]

Dodge's troopers did not doubt Ho Chunk martial prowess, but they continued to entertain doubts as to the Indians' true allegiance. According to one of Dodge's officers, "it was generally believed that all their able bodied and efficient young men were with the Sauks in both feeling and action."[42] Accordingly, Dodge convinced Gratiot to retain four chiefs and a warrior as hostages to guarantee the Indians' continued faithfulness. Gratiot escorted Whirling Thunder, Spotted Arm, Big Man, and the sons of White Crow and Broken Arm to his mining camp, where they remained in custody until 14 June. On that day, Henry Dodge arrived at Gratiot's Grove and offered the Ho Chunks liberty in exchange for service as scouts. The Indians assented, and Gratiot "gave them five horses five guns and other presents as a propitiation for their detention and to ensure their fidelity for the future."[43] Their fidelity proved as uneven as the treatment afforded them by the Americans, but Ho Chunk allies accompanied American forces for the remainder of the war.

Potawatomi collaboration with the Americans began under similarly inauspicious circumstances. Many Potawatomis of northeast Illinois continued to cower in the shadow of Fort Dearborn, forced to seek shelter under the big guns of their Great Father lest his other white children murder them in their villages. Although his people were safe from harm at Fort Dearborn, Billy Caldwell realized that the Potawatomis could not sit passively while events transpired that would have a grave influence on the tribe's future. On the morning of 31 May 1832, Caldwell arrived at Atkinson's headquarters and proclaimed that the Potawatomis were willing to take the field against the British Band on behalf of the United States. Atkinson was delighted, proclaiming that "they could hardly do otherwise than take sides and it is altogether important we should Know which." Atkinson directed Chicago Indian agent Thomas

J. V. Owen to raise a force of Potawatomi warriors to be ready to rendezvous at Ottawa, Illinois, on or about 15 June. Valuing their extensive knowledge of the country, Atkinson intended to use the Potawatomis as scouts and guides, but he intimated to Zachary Taylor that his pact with the Potawatomis was more diplomatic than military. He wanted their aid, he informed the future president, "not so much on account of their strength, but to make them a party in the war."[44] As compensation, Atkinson promised only to provision this force.[45]

Unbeknownst to Atkinson, provisions were high on the list of Potawatomi priorities. After fleeing their villages and leaving crops in the field unattended, the Potawatomis found themselves desperate for food, which Owen obligingly provided at government expense. After a two-day council with the Potawatomi chiefs on 2 and 3 June, Owen depicted the tribe as fairly paralyzed by privation but reported, "About 20 young men headed by Mr Robinson . . . will be ready to engage in any service you may desire." Still, Owen remained skeptical that the Potawatomis would be able to muster much of a force. "It is my opinion that you cannot with safety depend on more than 300 of these Indians, although the utmost reliance may be placed upon the sincerity of their friendly professions," Owen notified Atkinson. He explained that "many of them are not inclined to change their present mode of living in peace and quiet, for the toils and difficulties attending a war-like expedition."[46] Caldwell, at least, realized what Owen did not: that the Potawatomis' present mode of living depended on submitting to such difficulties for its very existence. Caldwell's compatriot, Alexander Robinson, seems to have impressed this fact on Atkinson, who promptly sent the métis leader back to Chicago to raise another eighty warriors.[47]

By this time, Owen was already using the service of the Potawatomis to rebut claims—particularly Governor John Reynolds's proclamation of 15 May—that they were in league with the enemy. In addition to chastising the governor for his loose tongue, Owen defended the tribe's conduct during the crisis and assured the people of Illinois that the Potawatomis had "evinced the most ardent desire to join us against" the British Band. As evidence, Owen pointed out that fifty Potawatomis had already taken the field as scouts and that Shaubena had offered a force of a hundred warriors at the outset of the conflict (although Illinois militia officers had rebuffed this overture and perhaps threatened Shaubena's life).[48] Atkinson considered the tribe redeemed to the extent that they had nothing to fear from truculent militiamen, and he authorized the Potawatomis to return to their crops. Just to be sure, however, Atkinson ordered the commander of nearby Fort Hennepin to keep a tight rein on his new levies to minimize the possibility of fratricide.[49]

Atkinson was naïve to believe that public sentiment had substantially changed. When Indians attacked a militia blockhouse outside of Chicago on 16 June, killing one, the commander threatened to kill the first Indian his men saw, "whether friendly or otherwise."[50] On 21 June, Owen informed Elbert Herring, Thomas McKenney's replacement as superintendent of Indian affairs, that he had countermanded Atkinson's authorization for the Potawatomis to return to their villages: "Such is the prejudice of the whites against even the friendly Indians, that their safety requires that they should convene . . . [near] this place." Because popular sentiment remained so inimical to the Potawatomis, "they have been compelled to abandon their villages, fields, & hunting grounds, for the present, and have no means of subsistence."[51] Owen also informed George B. Porter, his immediate superior in Detroit, that he made no disbursements of provisions between 1 and 21 June because the Indians had returned to their villages after the initial alarm died down, "but it was soon found necessary to recall them, owing to the threats and prejudices of the whites who, were constantly exhibiting towards them feelings of a hostile character, particularly that portion of the militia from the interior unaccustomed to Indians."[52]

The residents of Galena may have considered themselves accustomed to Indians, but they were not a little alarmed by the large force of friendly Indians that descended on their town on 8 June, when the Prairie du Chien contingent of Menominees, Dakotas, and Ho Chunks arrived via canoe. The sight of so many armed warriors unsettled the residents of the city, which by this time was perhaps the most anti-Indian settlement in the United States. Inclined to believe that all Indians were allied with Black Hawk and advocating Indian policies ranging from removal to genocide, the Galenians saw fit to impress their "allies" with a show of martial prowess. Nearly one hundred militiamen of Galena marshaled for a parade, but the intended audience was unimpressed. According to one white observer, the Indians laughed at the pitiful spectacle.[53] That night, the Indians reciprocated the display with their own war dance, although they did so to gain the favor of the spirits rather than that of the Americans.[54]

From Galena, the warriors set out on foot for Dixon's Ferry on the Rock River, where they were to have joined the regular forces under Colonel Zachary Taylor. On 12 June, Hamilton rode into Taylor's camp and received his orders. The warriors were to cut off small parties of the British Band, "take a feamale prisoner if practicable, steal their horses, & distress them in every possible manner."[55]

Auguring poorly for the campaign ahead, Hamilton's first report from the field on 13 June indicated that his command consisted of 170 Indians instead of the 225 originally reported by Joseph Street. He made no mention of any Indians leaving his force, and it is possible that an incorrect tally accounts for the discrepancy, but the first signs of dissension were already evident. With considerable effort and at Atkinson's urging, Street had persuaded John Marsh to accompany Hamilton's contingent. Marsh's facility with the Indians may have unsettled Hamilton, who wrote to Atkinson and requested clarification of his command relationship with Marsh—a polite means of requesting permission to put the trader in his place. Still, Hamilton seemed optimistic: "they are now generally armed and I think maybe relied on to annoy the enemy."[56] Unfortunately for the anxious members of the party, they narrowly missed their opportunity to do so.

On 16 June, Henry Dodge's troops killed seventeen warriors of the British Band on the Pecatonica River in one of the most pitched and celebrated engagements of the war. The Prairie du Chien Indians arrived an hour after the fight and discovered that a composite force of two Wisconsin River Ho Chunk bands under Waukon Decorah and Waukaunkaw had beat them to the scene. Following Dodge's mounted battalion on foot from Blue Mounds, this Ho Chunk contingent—comprising approximately fifty warriors—had likewise arrived late to the battle but managed to exact a measure of retribution from their foes.[57] Discerning that two of the enemy, although wounded, had extracted themselves from the battlefield, the Wisconsin River Ho Chunks tracked these survivors, dispatched them, and collected their scalps.[58] Shortly thereafter, the Prairie du Chien contingent arrived, and the Wisconsin River Ho Chunks invited its members to help themselves to the remaining scalps. The Menominee warriors demurred, however, indicating that the scalps were not theirs to take. Edward Beouchard, who accompanied the Wisconsin River Ho Chunks, later observed that "the Menomonees, were too proud to appropriate and display scalps from enemies whom they had not slain."[59] The Menominees were not too proud but rather determined to reap their own revenge; Indians killed by the Americans might suffice to "cover" the deaths of other Americans, but these deaths did not slake Menominee vengeance. The Dakotas and Ho Chunks of Hamilton's force had no such reservations. Linguistically related, these tribes also shared the practice of granting war honors to the first four warriors to touch the body of a fallen foe.[60] They not only took scalps but also cut the corpses "literally to pieces."[61]

Afterward, the Indian allies celebrated by dancing around the scalps outside nearby "Fort Hamilton," a settler-built stockade named for Billy Hamilton, whose farmstead was nearby. Tragically, a farmer named Spencer, who had barely survived an attack by the now deceased Sauks, was just at this time seeking shelter in the same stockade. As he neared it, a horrific spectacle greeted him: yelping Indian warriors dancing jubilantly around gory human scalps. Supposing the entire garrison to have been massacred, he fled to a homestead some six or seven miles distant. There, he hid himself in a hog pen for ten days, after which he was discovered. The poor man had lost his mind, however, and subsequently wandered off, never to be seen again.[62] Conditioned to regard armed Indians as a mortal threat, Spencer could conceive of them in no other way.

The day after the Battle of Pecatonica, Henry Dodge read aloud a "Talk to the Winebagoes" penned by Atkinson a week earlier in response to White Crow's neutrality pledge at the Porter's Grove council. This policy of neutrality, Atkinson decreed, was no longer an option for the Ho Chunks. "You must take up the Hatchet and join us," he enjoined their leaders. In an odd attempt to exert peer pressure, Atkinson also submitted that "The Sioux, Menomonies and Pottowattomies are our friends. they will go with us against the Sacs."[63] Awkwardly, Dodge delivered this speech to Prairie la Crosse and Wisconsin River Ho Chunk allies, all of whom had already marched to war with the Americans. Still eager to avenge the death of his daughter, Waukon Decorah overlooked this diplomatic gaffe and agreed to assemble warriors for an extended campaign. He planned to return to his village on the Wisconsin, where he would raise a larger force of warriors while their women made them new moccasins and made other preparations for the warpath. He told Dodge that he and other Ho Chunk leaders would reconvene with Gratiot and Dodge at the latter's house within a few days to complete their plans.[64]

Dodge was enthusiastic about the prospect of fielding such a considerable force of Indians. With augmentation from Decorah's band, the Indians would again number over two hundred "who will be urged under their Leaders to ranging the country so as to cover this portion as well as the fort at the [Blue] Mounds."[65] Although Dodge recognized that the Indians served under their own war chiefs and that they had to be "urged" rather than commanded, he was nonetheless disappointed by the course now selected by the Native leaders. It soon became evident that the Ho Chunks from Prairie la Crosse intended to return to Waukon Decorah's village. Upon hearing this, the Dakotas also resolved to return to their villages, vowing to raise more forces but also complaining that Marsh had hurried them from their homes and that they were being misused.[66] The complaint about being hurried was probably exaggerated, as Marsh had given the Dakotas two days to prepare, although this was not sufficient time for the manufacture of moccasins or other durable items that the Dakotas now found lacking. There was more substance, however, to the allegation of misuse. Each of the tribes present was practiced in their own brand of warfare, and it did not involve marching in a column of over two hundred men through American towns. Nor did it involve subjecting venerated warriors such as Wabasha and L'Arc to the pretensions of a man like Billy Hamilton. Over the ensuing week, more Indians abandoned him, and by 24 June he reported, "The inactivity of our service has so disheartened the indians under my command that they have allmost all returned to their homes[;] there are at present only Twenty five menommes remaining."[67] The most animated of the Sauk and Mesquakie enemies, the Menominees were willing to endure Hamilton's supervision further if it promised an opportunity to strike their foes.

To the Americans, the retirement of the Ho Chunks and Dakotas smacked of cowardice and a lack of resolve. Indeed, twenty-six Indians who returned to Galena to collect their canoes were detained as deserters, and one of Dodge's troopers opined that "we were better off without them, as they were a cowardly and treacherous set of miserable fellows."[68] But the Americans failed to understand Indian frustration or motivation. Even the knowledgeable Marsh appears to have been ignorant of the connection between the Prairie la Crosse and Wisconsin River Ho Chunks, who were led by the brothers One-Eyed and Waukon Decorah, respectively. Weary of Hamilton and his methods, the Ho Chunks were understandably enticed by the prospect of uniting their two bands under Native leadership. Interpreting their retirement from the field as reluctance to "engage heartily in the War against the Sacs & Foxes," Joseph Street subsequently told the Decorahs and the western Ho Chunks that "we did not want their assistance" and directed them to move their families to Prairie du Chien and thence to Prairie la Crosse so as to stay clear of the war.[69] As for the Dakotas, L'Arc expressed their sentiments when they returned through Prairie du Chien to be chastised by Street. L'Arc responded that Hamilton was "a little man" and complained that "he did not use us well." The Dakotas objected to both Hamilton's pretension to command their forces and the methods he employed. Walking over hardened wagon trails through abandoned towns, the Dakotas exhausted both their legs and their faith in the Americans, who appeared afraid to fight for themselves.[70] Street later lamented to Atkinson that the Dakotas were placed into service beside the militia and attributed their retirement to "their not being taken where they could have seen a respectable force."[71] None of the Indians had abandoned the war—their war—but most who left Hamilton's Diggings that day would not again fight in concert with the Americans.[72]

Despite the disbandment of the Prairie du Chien force, Henry Dodge still needed Indian messengers, guides, and spies. The two dozen Menominees who remained continued to seek a combat role and were not within their own country, compelling the Americans to seek assistance from White Crow's Ho Chunks. On 14 June, Henry Gratiot sent Whirling Thunder, Spotted Arm, three warriors, and Oliver Emmell (a French trader with a métis spouse) to attempt to locate Black Hawk's camp on the Rock River.[73] On 27 June, the scouting party returned in the company of White Crow and made their report. Emmell, whom the Ho Chunks had disguised as an Indian for his safety, reported that the British Band had encamped near Lake Koshkonong, a body of water surrounded by forbidding swamps and marshes in southern Wisconsin. He also indicated that the scouting party had come across starving Ho Chunk families who, fearing that the Americans meant to obliterate their people, had abandoned their fields and taken to hiding in a swamp. White Crow also spoke, recounting the sacrifices his people had made to obey Atkinson, Dodge, and Gratiot. They had left their crops untended, were displaced repeatedly, and as a consequence now suffered greatly. In addition to requesting provisions, White Crow expressed the fear that Black Hawk would soon make open war against the Ho Chunks and implored the Americans to strike the British Band as soon as possible.[74]

Despite White Crow's adamant pledges of fidelity, the whites continued to doubt his loyalty and that of his people. On 6 June, Indians had attacked the blockhouse at Blue Mounds, killing a man named William Aubrey. A larger war party struck the same post two weeks later, killing militia officers George Force and Emerson Green. Initially suspected only of conducting the first attack, Ho Chunks were actually responsible for both engagements.[75] Whether White Crow was being sincere when he urged the Americans to attack the British Band is subject to speculation. In postwar testimony, a Mesquakie named Ma-kauk identified White Crow as one of the British Band's principal accomplices, and many of Black Hawk's followers identified the Ho Chunk chief as a bellicose rabble-rouser who had urged Black Hawk to make war on the whites and counseled against a peaceful return to Iowa.[76] According to the Sauk chief Neapope, ten lodges of Ho Chunks supported the British Band and brought in American scalps on eight different occasions. Perhaps more significant, the Ho Chunks also sustained Black Hawk's band by trading corn and potatoes for durable goods. Unlike his tribesmen at the Portage, who made a legitimate attempt to distance themselves from the conflict in order to maintain neutrality, White Crow appears to have actively supported both parties while weighing their respective prospects for success. "When the Winnebagoes discovered that the Sacs would be whipped," Neapope later asserted, "they turned their faces and went back, and turned against the Sacs."[77] Precisely when White Crow reached this conclusion is a matter of conjecture, but he had not yet done so when he departed Gratiot's Grove on 29 June to join Dodge's command. The following day, White Crow and at least thirty of his warriors joined Dodge's militia, Henry Gratiot, Billy Hamilton, and the remaining Menominees at First or Kegonsa Lake of the Four Lakes region.[78] Despite lingering doubts about White Crow's loyalty, Dodge entrusted the direction of his battalion to the Rock River chief.

To the south, Henry Atkinson was likewise turning to Indian allies for guidance. And while Atkinson did not doubt the fidelity of Billy Caldwell's Potawatomis, the settlers between Chicago and Atkinson's camp at Dixon's Ferry were not disposed to discriminate between "good" and "bad" Indians. Surrounded by Indian-haters and anxious militiamen—often in the same person—the Potawatomis were perhaps more afraid of their "allies" than of their supposed enemies. To guard against fratricide, the Potawatomis wore white headbands when they sallied forth from Chicago to join their allies on 22 June 1832.[79] The absence of traditional war paint and garb may have been intended to minimize risk, but it also reflected the fact that this was not a traditional Potawatomi war. No evidence suggests that the Potawatomis conducted a ceremonial war dance in preparation for their campaign or that young warriors participated with the hope of making names for themselves. Unlike the Dakotas, Menominees, and some Ho Chunk bands, the Potawatomis had no grievance with the Sauks and Mesquakies, and it was clear from their demeanor that their business was more diplomatic than military. At their helm rode the men responsible for its design: the rolls of this company listed Billy Caldwell as principal chief, Alexander Robinson as "2nd. Chief," and Wabaunsee and Shaw-we-nesse as "War Chief" and "2nd. War chief," respectively. Sixteen chiefs of various bands (including Shaubena) and seventy-five of their warriors were also mustered into federal service.[80] To ensure safe passage through ranging parties of paranoid militiamen, Indian trader and county sheriff George Walker accompanied the party.

Walker, who was married to a Potawatomi and spoke his wife's language, entered Atkinson's camp at Dixon's Ferry on 27 June accompanied by three warriors. Deeming it imprudent to approach the hub of the American war effort with nearly one hundred armed Indians, the Potawatomis elected to encamp at the Kishwaukee River and had sent Walker ahead as an envoy. The Indian trader must have conveyed the Potawatomis' concerns for their security because on 28 June Atkinson ordered Colonel Jacob Fry and his regiment to the Kishwaukee River "to give countenance & protection to the 75 Pottawatamis encamped there."[81] The following day, Fry rendezvoused with the anxious Potawatomis; the rest of Atkinson's main force (comprising approximately 450 regulars under Colonel Zachary Taylor and Brigadier General James Henry's Third Brigade of Illinois militia) joined Fry and the Potawatomis later that evening. According to one militiaman, "The Indians appeared to be highly pleased to think they were honored so far as to take a hand with us against the Sacs."[82] More likely, the Potawatomis were relieved to be operating within the protective fold of the United States Army.

Although "well armed, with both guns and spears," little suggests that the Potawatomis were interested in trading blows with the British Band.[83] Nor, for that matter, did Atkinson envision his Potawatomi allies as surrogate infantry to replenish the ranks of his disheartened militia force. Instead, Atkinson proclaimed himself "desirous . . . to employ the Pottowattomies who Know the Country occupied by the enemy," a service "of very great importance."[84] Yet questions linger whether the Potawatomis rendered this important service in earnest or if they merely intended to demonstrate their loyalty to the Americans while dissuading their own people from joining Black Hawk's cause. In the latter regard, the Potawatomis succeeded admirably, but their accomplishments in the former did not fulfill Henry Atkinson's expectations. As his army ascended the Rock River on the evening of 1 July, the crack of Potawatomi muskets broke the quiet of dusk and raised hopes that the enemy was at hand. Deer rather than Sauks had drawn the Indian fire, however, and the Potawatomis did not fire another shot during the war.[85]

Atkinson's fortunes seemed to fade daily over the ensuing week. Guided by his Potawatomi scouts, Atkinson reached Black Hawk's camp near the foot of Lake Koshkonong on 3 July, only to find it abandoned.[86] Although the camp showed signs of several weeks' use, it had been unoccupied for at least two days. Atkinson halted his march to scout the area and await the arrival of militia units that had been ranging the lead mining region. On 4 July, Milton Alexander's Second Brigade of Illinois militia rejoined the main body, bringing with it eleven Ho Chunk guides and their French liaison, Oliver Emmell, who had fallen in with Alexander's force the day prior.[87] Atkinson's available Indian contingent swelled on 5 July when Dodge's battalion and Alexander Posey's First Brigade of Illinois militia reached the southwest end of Lake Koshkonong in the company of White Crow's Ho Chunks and the remaining Menominees from Prairie du Chien. Any comfort Atkinson might have felt at the concentration of his army eroded that evening with the arrival of a three-week-old dispatch from Acting Secretary of War John Robb, who castigated Atkinson for the glacial pace with which he was prosecuting the war and his failure to communicate with Washington more regularly. "I am directed by the President to say, that he views with utter astonishment, and deep regret, this state of things," Robb wrote.[88] Atkinson further learned that the secretary of war had dispatched Major General Winfield Scott, commander of the Eastern Department of the U.S. Army, and approximately one thousand of his soldiers to assume overall command of the campaign.[89] The order, which had been issued nearly a month earlier, represented a repudiation not only of Atkinson's handling of the war but of the Western Department of the U.S. Army as a whole. Given the theater of the conflict and the soldiers presently engaged in its execution, Edmund Gaines, as Atkinson's immediate superior, should have assumed command if the president or his secretary of war found Atkinson's performance lacking. But the president had grown weary of both Atkinson and Gaines, each of whom seemed overly sensitive to Indian interests and prone to negotiate rather than fight.[90]

Chastened, Atkinson did not immediately share news of his de facto relief with his subordinates. Instead, the general reorganized his army and resumed his march on 6 July. Led by White Crow's Ho Chunks and the Prairie du Chien Menominees, Dodge's battalion and Alexander's brigade moved up the western shore of the Rock River to the head of Lake Koshkonong. To the east, the remainder of Atkinson's army followed Caldwell's Potawatomis and Oliver Emmell's eleven Ho Chunks to the mouth of the Bark River and a nearby, abandoned Ho Chunk village, where it encamped for the night.[91] Dodge's battalion and Alexander's brigade spent the night just above Lake Koshkonong where, one soldier recorded, "The friendly Indians had a war dance."[92] Presumably, Menominees conducted this dance in vain preparation for the battle that continued to elude them. Perhaps to convince the Americans of their mock earnestness, the Rock River Ho Chunks might have danced as well, but they had no illusions of imminent combat: escorted by Ho Chunk guides, Black Hawk had fled the area a week earlier.[93]

Nonetheless, the Ho Chunks guiding Atkinson insisted that the British Band's main camp lay just across the Bark River on an elevated piece of ground in the otherwise boggy morass formed by the confluence of the Rock and Bark Rivers.[94] Although the swampy banks of the Bark River seemed to render this "island" stronghold impenetrable, a handful of Ho Chunks—alleged to have been among Atkinson's guides—managed to make their way to the far bank. From this station, they opened fire on a regular soldier who was fishing the south shore of the Bark, wounding him severely.[95] The identity of the assailants was not immediately known to Atkinson, who continued to rely on his Ho Chunk guides as they subsequently guided the army fifteen miles eastward, up the Bark River in search of a phantom ford. As night approached, these same guides insisted that further movement was senseless, for they were entering a trackless marsh known as the *terre tremblant*, or "trembling grounds." Suspecting by then that "our Winnebago guides had intentionally deceived us," Atkinson's men began to grumble about the reliability of their supposed allies.[96]

West of the Rock River, Dodge's men similarly questioned White Crow's motives. While their relationship with the Ho Chunk chief was never one of trust, White Crow's behavior on 7 July engendered renewed suspicion among the already wary miners. Originally, Atkinson had envisioned a double envelopment of Black Hawk's "island" camp, with Dodge's and Alexander's forces forming the left pincer while Atkinson's main body comprised the right. After the shooting incident on the morning of 7 July, however, Atkinson reconsidered his plans. Sensing that a pitched fight was imminent, Atkinson recalled Dodge and Alexander, ordering them to join the main body directly. While Dodge was "somewhat vexed" at this change of plans, White Crow was decidedly opposed to the new design and insisted that Dodge press on to attack Black Hawk's camp in accordance with the original plan.[97] Only through the use of "severe language" was Dodge able to convince White Crow to accept the new mission. Although White Crow obeyed, Dodge's men speculated that the Indians had intended to lead them into a trap.[98]

Harboring no such suspicions and anxious to find the elusive enemy, Henry Atkinson welcomed White Crow's counsel the following morning. The wily chief insisted that the British Band's camp remained on the "island" near the mouth of the Bark River and volunteered to forfeit his life if proven wrong.[99] Made credulous by desperation, Atkinson heeded White Crow's advice and countermarched his entire force to its earlier camp—much to the chagrin of his soldiers, who suspected that they were being led on a wild goose chase. On the morning of 9 July, Atkinson's spy company and Hamilton's Menominee contingent crossed the Bark River to ascertain the validity of White Crow's report. Within hours, the spy company returned, reporting only evidence of a recent camp. The Menominees were more thorough but returned in the evening only to confirm that the British Band had indeed left the area.[100] Regulars and militiamen alike now grumbled "that there was no dependence to be placed in those treacherous Winnebagoes," and

Dodge's officers convinced themselves that White Crow had intended to lure them into an ambush from the very beginning.[101]
Regardless, Atkinson continued to rely on White Crow's services.
While the general acknowledged that the strength and disposition
of the British Band compelled most of the Indians in southern
Wisconsin to adopt a policy of neutrality, Atkinson remained dependent on these same Indians to guide his army "over a difficult
and almost impassable route" and to locate the enemy.[102] Only after
the war and an examination of Sauk and Mesquakie prisoners did
Atkinson seriously question White Crow's loyalty.

In the meantime, Atkinson was more concerned with the im-
providence of his militiamen than with the purported treachery of
his Ho Chunk guides. By a combination of extravagant consump-
tion and lackadaisical accountability, each of Atkinson's militia brigades was now nearly paralyzed by a lack of supplies. Exasperated,
Atkinson suspended operations and, on 9 July, ordered his militia commanders to provision their forces—sending Posey's brigade
to Hamilton's Diggings while ordering Dodge's battalion and the
other militia brigades to Fort Winnebago. To further alleviate his
supply shortages, Atkinson discharged superfluous militia forces
and released all but thirty of the approximately one hundred sixty
Indians then with his army. On 10 July, after a fruitless month of
campaigning under Billy Hamilton, the Prairie du Chien Menominees returned home, leaving only three of their number—Wekan,
Wahnachco, and Askaiah—to serve as guides and messengers.[103]
Not yet suspected of prevarication by the commanding general,
White Crow and his son stayed with the army and offered to pilot
Dodge's battalion to Fort Winnebago.[104] Sending seventy of the
ninety-five Potawatomis to Chicago with the potential of continued
service with Winfield Scott, Atkinson explained to the senior gen-

eral, "They will be faithful I have no doubt, but they eat highly."[105] For most of the Potawatomis, however, the Black Hawk War was already over. Overwhelmed by cholera during their voyage through the Great Lakes, Scott and his soldiers were in no position to join the war when they arrived in Chicago on 10 July.

Despite his subordinates' misgivings, Atkinson remained convinced of the value of Indian allies, and his decision to dispense with their services at Lake Koshkonong appears to have been predicated entirely on logistical considerations. Albeit belatedly, by mid-July Atkinson had developed a more sophisticated understanding of Indian participation in the war and was willing to tailor his plans to accommodate the disparate motives of each group. Grasping the limited nature of Potawatomi commitment to the war, Atkinson informed Winfield Scott that the Potawatomi scouts "will be of service only as guides, and probably to fight beside of you[;] they will not go alone any distance ahead." Reconciled, if not sympathetic, to the Potawatomis' unenviable position in this conflict, Atkinson added, "I speak, not however in disparagement of them."[106]

Henry Atkinson understood Menominee involvement in the war differently, and he conceived of their potential contributions accordingly. Although a supply crisis had compelled Atkinson to send home most of the Prairie du Chien Menominees, he foresaw a sustained, significant role for these, the most indefatigable of his Indian allies. Suspecting that Black Hawk might follow the Rock River northward and eventually slip into Canada (perhaps by canoeing across Lake Michigan), Atkinson called on the Green Bay

Menominees to intercept this movement. In stark contrast to his advice to Scott regarding the employment of the Potawatomis, A-tkinson's 12 July orders to Green Bay Indian agent George Boyd specified, "I do not wish them to join me, but to act against the Sacs in front."[107] While logistical considerations may have informed this guidance, Atkinson recognized that the Menominees were capable of conducting independent, decisive operations whereas the Potawatomis were not. Atkinson again appointed Billy Hamilton the nominal commander of this new Menominee force, but he prudently granted Boyd the discretion to overturn the appointment.[108] If the general had not yet entirely soured on Billy Hamilton, Atkinson appears to have, by this time, understood that the Indians found him wanting as a liaison and intolerable as a commander.[109]

Relying on White Crow to lead them to Fort Winnebago, Henry Dodge's troops viewed their guide in a similar, pejorative light. On several occasions in the preceding month, they had suspected the Ho Chunk chief of treachery, and they now interpreted every suspicious circumstance as affirming evidence. In guiding Dodge's battalion, White Crow and his son took a circuitous route of approximately sixty miles, claiming that the direct route was littered with swamps. Dodge's men grew more and more convinced that the Ho Chunk chief was deliberately misleading them in order to facilitate Black Hawk's flight, but they safely reached their destination on 12 July.[110] The arrival of Atkinson's provisioning parties struck John Kinzie and the sundry bands of Ho Chunks assembled at the Portage as inopportune. Describing the refugee Indians as "in a state of demi-starvation," Kinzie had been issuing the Ho Chunks provisions from Fort Winnebago to relieve their suffering—a practice brought to an immediate halt by Atkinson's requisition.[111] The militiamen were interested in more than food, however. No longer willing to follow White Crow, they also sought new guides and reliable intelligence.[112]

Pierre Paquette offered both. The subject of considerable Wisconsin folklore, Paquette was born in 1800 to a Frenchman and a Ho Chunk woman (and happened to be White Crow's nephew). Popular remembrances of the métis trader dwell on his size and strength. In 1830, he stood six feet, two inches tall and weighed 240 pounds. According to one early American resident of Wisconsin, "He was the strongest man I ever knew; he would pick up a barrel of pork and throw it into a wagon as easily as a man would a ten gallon keg."[113] Although illiterate, Paquette was fluent in the languages of each of his parents as well as English, which rendered his services indispensable to the Americans and Ho Chunks alike. A man whose strength of character matched the strength of his back, Paquette was revered by both populations. One American described him as "the best specimen of Nature's noble-men I ever met," largely because Paquette possessed "as fine a sense of honor as any gentleman I ever knew; and all who knew him would take his word as soon as any man's bond."[114] Without racial qualification, another American averred that Paquette was "the very best specimen of a man."[115] The Ho Chunks shared this appraisal; Old Decorah's son later recalled Paquette to be "a good man in every way,—very friendly to our people."[116]

Called upon to collect new guides for the army, Paquette sent Naheesanchonka (Man Who Thinks Himself of Importance) into the Ho Chunk camps surrounding the Portage. He told his tribesmen that "if we would go into the war we would make a name for ourselves, and get presents; also win the good opinion of White Beaver, and the Big Father at Washington."[117] Admonished to maintain strict neutrality by John Kinzie and their own chiefs, however, most Ho Chunks rejected Naheesanchonka's pleas. Many of them regarded the Sauks with pity and, although not inclined to fight on their behalf, disdained the idea of fighting against them. Ultimately, only a handful of volunteers came forward, among them Naheesanchonka, Pa-nee-wak-sa-ka (White Pawnee or Pania Blanc), Notsookega (Bear that Breaks up the Brush), Ahmegunka, Tahnichseeka (Smoker), and Rascal Decorah. Although Dodge's men no longer tolerated his service as a guide, White Crow could not risk the diplomatic consequences of withdrawing at this juncture. Accordingly, he advised his son (also named White Pawnee) to join the newly assembled contingent of Portage Ho Chunks.[118] Perhaps to further ingratiate himself to the federal government, White Crow accompanied Alexander's brigade back to Lake Koshkonong, where he again proffered his services to Henry Atkinson.

From the Indians at the Portage, Henry Dodge learned that the British Band was then encamped on the Rock River at Hustis' Rapids.[119] Armed with this intelligence, Dodge convinced militia brigade commander James Henry that they should pursue Black Hawk rather than return to Atkinson's camp with provisions. Departing the Portage on 15 July under Pierre Paquette's guidance, Dodge and Henry reached the rapids three days later. Here, Ho Chunk villagers suggested that the British Band was nearly twenty miles to the north, but couriers en route to Atkinson's headquarters stumbled upon the fresh trail of the British Band and turned back to report their discovery.[120] The news breathed fresh life into a demoralized force that continued to question the loyalty of their Indian guides. According to one of the more skeptical militiamen, "it was apparent that they designed to lead us in a different direction from that in which we should have went in order to find Black

Hawk[.] The soldiers had began to dispair of ever seeing an Indian without a white knapkin on his head and the word good Winebago or Potawatamie in his mouth."[121] With a well-trodden path before them, the militiamen set their own course and speed. This time, Black Hawk's band would not elude them.

Yet unaware of this development, Atkinson's regulars busied themselves constructing a palisade around their Lake Koshkonong camp while Indian and militia scouts continued their futile search for an enemy long since departed. The remaining Potawatomis brought in a Sauk prisoner on 16 July and predicted (correctly) that Black Hawk would attempt to flee westward, across the Mississippi.[122] The following day, White Crow returned to Atkinson's camp in the company of Alexander's brigade and once more offered to guide the army. A regular officer who had already soured on the usefulness of Indian guides noted disapprovingly, "His services were gladly accepted."[123] Unlikely a matter of coincidence, White Crow found forty-one members of his band in Atkinson's camp. Starving, they had arrived two days earlier to await the arrival of their chief and—more importantly—the provisions he escorted from Fort Winnebago. On 19 July, White Crow and sixteen of his followers led Atkinson's troops on a final, fruitless drive up the Bark River. Impeded by a torrential storm, the Americans abandoned their venture when news arrived of Dodge's and Henry's discovery. On 20 July, Atkinson ordered the remaining Potawatomis, two Ho Chunks, and a militia spy company to conduct a final, futile search of Black Hawk's abandoned "island" camp. Now convinced that the British Band was fleeing westward in hopes of recrossing the Mississippi, Atkinson disbanded what remained of the Potawatomi company, retaining only Billy Caldwell, Wabaunsee, Shaubena, and Pierre LeClerc as couriers. With three stalwart Menominees still in his service, Atkinson quit his newly constructed Fort Koshkonong for the Blue Mounds on 21 July.[124]

The same day, after three days of pursuit covering nearly eighty miles, Dodge's and Henry's commands approached the Wisconsin River and began to encounter stragglers from the British Band. Uninterested in taking prisoners, the militiamen dispatched the unfortunate Indians where they found them.[125] The militiamen correctly interpreted the abandonment of invalids as a sign that Black Hawk was desperately trying to make good his escape across the Wisconsin River. Accordingly, Dodge's and Henry's commands surged forward like bloodhounds on a fresh trail.

Detecting the movements of the militiamen, Black Hawk raced to remove his women, children, and elderly to the west side of the Wisconsin. Covering their escape, he deployed the bulk of his warriors along a ridgeline to the east of the river to confront the onrushing militiamen. In the only conventional fight of the war, Dodge's and Henry's troopers dismounted, formed lines, and drove the Indians from their position. Most of the Ho Chunks had no desire to fight the Sauks, let alone to do so in open terrain using European tactics. Hoping merely to catch a glimpse of the action, they took shelter in sinkholes or behind trees. They may have been startled to observe Pierre Paquette and two of their own number fighting beside the Americans. Pa-nee-wak-sa-ka (Pania Blanc or White Pawnee) and White Crow's son had joined Dodge's ranks and "fought uncovered like white men."[126] Together, the Americans and the Ho Chunks killed sixty-eight of Black Hawk's warriors at a cost of only one killed and seven wounded militiamen.[127]

Although White Crow's son may have been eager to establish

himself as a warrior in his own right, it is unlikely that he would have so actively and decidedly cast his lot against Black Hawk without his father's approval. By the Battle of Wisconsin Heights, it seems, the outcome of the war was finally clear to White Crow, and he no longer deemed it necessary to hedge his bets. Although Ho Chunks had helped guide the British Band across the Wisconsin River during the engagement, Black Hawk was stunned by this betrayal.[128] He later confided to an American that he was surprised "that the Americans could, in so brief a period, have assembled so large a force, and still more surprised to find some Indians among them."[129]

The Indians did not remain long at the Heights. Immediately after the battle, they returned to the Portage bearing eleven scalps—grisly testimony to the violation of the Portage bands' neutrality policy.[130] "We feared that Black Hawk, thinking us now to be his enemies, would turn up the river and attack us at Portage," the principal chief's son recalled. "Our sympathies were strongly with the whites. Our trading interests were with them, and we were bound to them by treaties. Yet we did not like to be fighting old neighbors like the Sacs."[131] Ho Chunk leaders now divided, some advocating a withdrawal from the area until the trouble had passed and others favoring an armed defense against Sauk encroachment. Harrowed by the militia and running for their lives, however, Black Hawk's Indians posed no threat to the Ho Chunks. Following the Battle of Wisconsin Heights, a member of the British Band scaled a tree and broke the calm of night by calling out to the Americans' Indian allies. Unaware that the Ho Chunks had already departed, the orator entreated them to tell the whites that Black Hawk was not for war and hoped to leave Wisconsin in peace.[132] He did not get that chance.

Nearly two months after Henry Atkinson had called for their services, the United States' Indian allies had accomplished very little. For the Rock River Ho Chunks and perhaps the Potawatomis, this was partly by design. Sympathetic to Black Hawk but determined to distance themselves from his "hostile" band, these tribes offered symbolic service and avoided direct confrontations with the Sauks and Mesquakies. Meanwhile, the Menominees, Dakotas, and western Ho Chunks sought combat with the British Band but encountered only frustration. Imprudently, Atkinson entrusted them to the incapable Billy Hamilton, who squandered the services of over two hundred Indian allies. Only belatedly did Atkinson develop a better understanding of his allies or avail himself of the three hundred Green Bay Menominee warriors who had waited nearly a year for this opportunity. Hence, by Atkinson's early mismanagement and misunderstanding of his allies, the Indians contributed little to Atkinson's campaign through the Battle of Wisconsin Heights. The Menominees, Dakota, and western Ho Chunks were not prepared to surrender their war to the Americans, however. If denied a meaningful role in its initial phases, they struck its final blows.

# 7

## FINAL BLOWS

Their lackluster performance notwithstanding, Henry Atkinson remained dependent on his Indian allies following the Battle of Wisconsin Heights. Suspecting that Black Hawk would lead his followers either to British Canada or back to Iowa, the general could call only on Indian forces to interdict their movements. Still desirous of striking their foes, the Menominees, Dakotas, and western Ho Chunks remained receptive to Atkinson's appeals for help but insisted on waging war on their own terms. Numbering over three hundred warriors, the Green Bay contingent of Menominees and northeastern Ho Chunks rejected Billy Hamilton as their leader and assented to white and métis liaisons from their trading partners. Even these exerted little influence on the campaign trail, where Menominee war chiefs and spiritual leaders wielded traditional authority—even when it unsettled the accompanying whites. Acknowledging that the Indians' stake in the war was greater than their own, however, the white liaisons did not interfere.

Unfortunately, Atkinson had called on the Green Bay Menominees too late in the contest. Once it became apparent that Black Hawk intended to recross the Mississippi rather than seek refuge in Canada, the Green Bay contingent raced to participate in the fight, while their fellow Indian allies around Prairie du Chien helped intercept their fleeing foes. On 2 August, the American army finally caught up with Black Hawk and fought the "Battle of Bad Axe," which effectively eliminated the British Band as a viable military force but involved neither the Dakotas nor the Green Bay Menominees, who sought their own dénouement to a conflict they considered their own. In the days after this supposedly final battle of the war, the Dakotas and Menominees hunted down and harrowed remnants of the British Band in forlorn corners of Wisconsin and Iowa. Theirs from the outset, the Black Hawk War was the Dakotas' and Menominees' to end.

While Black Hawk traded blows with Henry Dodge and James Henry at Wisconsin Heights, the Menominees of Green Bay bided their time. A year had passed since they had lobbied their Great Father for permission to raise the hatchet against their enemies, which he continued to deny even as Black Hawk recrossed the Mississippi and Henry Atkinson enlisted the aid of Indians from Prairie du Chien and Chicago. Frustrated, the Menominees of Green Bay busied themselves with more meager contributions. In early June, 230 Menominees gathered at the Green Bay Agency after being called in for "the protection of the settlement." Under Samuel Stambaugh's direction, these warriors relieved the local militia of their responsibility for the security of Green Bay (ostensibly so that the militiamen could tend to their crops). The Menominees received provisions, officers agreeable to them, and "assurance . . . that our exertions shall not be wanting in procuring for them a reasonable compensation for their services while in this Employ." More interested in revenge than wages, this body of Menominee warriors no doubt hoped that Black Hawk would be foolish enough to lead his band into the heart of Menominee country. Although this force did little more than drain the stores of Fort Howard while it remained in Green Bay, it also provided the core of the largest Indian contingent to participate in the war.[1]

Samuel Stambaugh shared the Menominees' frustration concerning their inactivity. On 3 June, he surrendered his post to his successor, George Boyd.[2] Having recently consolidated the Sault Ste. Marie and Michilimackinac agencies under Henry Schoolcraft, the War Department reassigned Boyd, who had worked at the latter, to Green Bay, effectively relieving Stambaugh.[3] Unfettered by the constraints of office, Stambaugh expressed his true feelings to Michigan governor George B. Porter on 7 June:

> My orders from the government, you *are aware*, were to
> keep the Indians quiet & on no account suffer them to
> attempt to redress their own wrongs. These instructions I
> implicitly obeyed, althoug I felt convinced, in the prog-
> ress of affairs this Spring, of what was plain to every one
> here, that a contrary course would have saved thousands
> of dollars to the govement. I have no hesitation in saying
> that the Menominees, if armed and backed by the gov-
> ernment sanction would, with the auxiliary force ready to
> join them from other friendly Indian tribes, have ended
> the war long before this time, by the total annihilation of
> the hostile bands now harrassing and murdering our
> frontier settlers. The Menominees have always evinced a
> strong disposition to join in the War, and it requird the
> full exercise of the influence which I have had over them
> that enabled me to restrain them.[4]

Evidently, Stambaugh's influence over the tribe was considerable. Though he placed government interests first and foremost, Stambaugh became something of a champion of the Menominees during a decade-long struggle between the Menominees, the U.S. government, and various tribes of New York State. In about 1820, a congeries of speculators, evangelists, and others produced a plan to relocate Iroquois, Brotherton, Munsee, and Stockbridge Indians from New York State to northeastern Wisconsin. A pair of dubious land "sales" in 1821 and 1822 exchanged millions of acres of Menominee land for goods valued at a few thousand dollars. The government, which had endorsed the sales, spent the next ten years attempting to untangle the mess they helped create. During his tenure as acting agent, Stambaugh vigorously defended the Menominee claim, denounced the government's past actions, and even employed subterfuge to obtain justice for his Menominee charges.[5]

Stambaugh's efforts did not go unnoticed by the Menominees. When Boyd arrived to assume office, Grizzly Bear made a formal appeal that Stambaugh be allowed "to remain with them until their difficulty with the Sac & Fox Indians be settled." Were Atkinson to summon the Green Bay Menominees to join the fight, Grizzly Bear further requested that Stambaugh accompany them in the field.[6] Boyd conceded to these requests.

On 22 June, Grizzly Bear pled once more for permission to strike his enemy. He asked not only for leave to do so, but arms as well: "We have no guns, no arms, or scarcely any implements of War. I wish to go and fight them, at least for a short heat, or two days."[7] Once again, the Menominees exhibited a strong desire to choose their own officers—men who would permit the Menominees to wage war in their own manner. "I have another favor to ask," Grizzly Bear continued. "Here is our friend Colo. Stambaugh—who has been kind to us—and we wish him to stay with us while these troubles last, and head us. Colo. S. who will state to you all our wishes. He knows our wants."[8] Although Boyd had already granted Grizzly

Bear's wish regarding Stambaugh, he withheld permission for the Menominees to join the fray. Grizzly Bear replied that they would return to their crops, but he testily added: "Our Enemies have taken the heads of our men women & children—carried them to their lodges and danced the war dance over them. *We ask revenge.*"[9]

Boyd communicated this request to Henry Atkinson by informing the general that two hundred Menominee warriors stood ready "to repair to your Standard without a moment's unnecessary delay."[10] On 12 July, Atkinson finally delivered the long-awaited call to arms to the Menominees of Green Bay. His orders reflected both a conviction that the Menominees were capable of independent action and a desire to avoid the logistical strain previously imposed by his Potawatomi and Ho Chunk guides: "I do not wish them to join me, but to act against the Sacs in front. [P]arties sent out to annoy the enemy in front, and Pick off their horses would have a salutary effect."[11] Atkinson wanted two to three hundred Menominee warriors in the field as soon as possible, and he ordered the commander of Fort Howard to provide the necessary provisions.

Boyd, receiving these instructions on 18 July, responded promptly by "the usual mode of communicating with the Indians"—sending Indian or métis runners to the Menominee villages.[12] A rough-and-tumble American named Ebenezer Childs claimed that Stambaugh also sent him recruiting: "I collected about three hundred, and brought them to the Bay. We encamped near the Agency; I took charge of them and was appointed commissary. I kept out a scouting party for ten days."[13] Likely much more effective than Childs's pleas were the recruiting efforts of the Menominees themselves. In adherence with traditional diplomatic convention, village headmen invited others to join the warpath by circulating tobacco and red-painted wampum.[14] The bonds of Menominee kinship also served to fill the ranks. According to anthropologist Alanson Skinner, "If a man goes to war his nephew, on either side, or his brother-in-law, must follow him regardless of any hindrance." The nephew's obligation did not end with enlistment: "If the uncle is killed his nephew must get a scalp from the enemy in revenge, or never come home alive."[15] For the Menominees, war was a family affair.

By 20 July, Boyd was able to report that "arrangements are making with all possible expedition to forward to your aid the services of two hundred Menomonies—with a view to arrest the progress of the Enemy towards the Milwalkie Country."[16] Efforts to raise an auxiliary force of New York Indians met only frustration, perhaps because they deemed the enemies of the Menominees to be their friends.[17] This was not the case among the lower Fox River Ho Chunks, however. According to oral traditions, they had always been allies to the Menominees, and they remained allies now. Numbering only twelve warriors, the Ho Chunk party that joined the Menominees in Green Bay was less impressive for its size than for the enduring attachment it represented.

On their way to Green Bay, the Ho Chunks visited a missionary to the Stockbridges, who observed:

> one having a large spear, t[he] blade perhaps a foot & a half long, and the handle covered with red baize, another carried t[he] colors among other things with which it was ornamented was a piece of a Sac Indns. scalp. Some of them were painted red and had horses tales so adjusted upon their heads that the hair all hung down upon their shoulders, and upon the crown of the head was a plume, and another still carried a sort of drum wh[ich] t[he] natives make use of in dancing.[18]

Whether he realized it or not, the accoutrements that drew the reverend's attention reveal much about the party's motives. Inter-married with the Green Bay Menominees and no friends of the Sauks or Mesquakies, these Ho Chunks did not share their south-ern relatives' reservations about making war against the British Band. Like the Chicago Potawatomis, the Ho Chunks who guided Dodge and Atkinson were distinguished only by white headbands worn as guards against fratricide.[19] While the lack of traditional paraphernalia bespoke the limited objectives of the southern Ho Chunks and Potawatomis, the red face paint, headdresses, and war drums of the Lake Winnebago Ho Chunks testified to the earnest-ness of their endeavor.

Arriving in Green Bay, the Ho Chunks discovered that they had been preceded by Billy Hamilton, who had arrived on 18 July bear-ing Atkinson's call to arms. Fully expecting—again—to assume command of the Indians, Hamilton was disappointed by Boyd, who kept his word to Grizzly Bear and named Samuel Stambaugh as the contingent's nominal head. "The feelings of the Menomo-nees," Boyd explained, "as well as of the citizens generally at this place (and most of them allied to this nation of Indians by blood) were so hostile to the pretensions of Col°. Hamilton to command them" that the choice of Stambaugh was unavoidable.[20] Boyd of-fered the position of second-in-command to Billy Hamilton, but, to the relief of all involved, the prideful son of Alexander Hamilton re-fused.[21]

The Menominees influenced the selection of their other officers as well. "They have been selected," Boyd reported to Governor Por-ter, "to meet the wishes of the Indians, as to conciliate public senti-ment." By public sentiment, Boyd was referring to the aspirations of influential Americans in Green Bay. Thus, roughly half of the of-ficers were métis traders respected by the Menominees, while Americans with political aspirations comprised the other half. Augustin Grignon, Sr., and George Johnson served as company commanders immediately beneath Stambaugh. Johnson had been the first sheriff of Brown County and represented white interests. Grignon, conversely, was a métis trader of considerable standing with the Menominees. According to one American observer, "The natives held him in the utmost reverence," largely because he adhered to the principle of reciprocity that governed Indian trade relationships. "Spending much of his time in the Indian country, and speaking but little of the English language, he had but slight connection with civil life, held few public offices; but he was regarded with much respect, as well by his own people, as the Americans and gentlemen of the army."[22] Grignon's wife, Nancy McCrea, was a métis woman related to the famous Menominee chiefs Oshkosh, Tomah, and I-om-e-tah.[23] Grignon himself was the grandson of the famous French-Ottawa soldier Charles Langlade, who had sired métis children at a young age and earned a considerable reputation among the Green Bay Indians.[24] For Grignon, leading Indian auxiliaries was something of a family tradition; Langlade commanded Indian auxiliaries throughout the French and Indian War, most famously in Braddock's defeat.[25] Grignon's son, Charles, and nephew, Robert, served as lieutenants in his company. Another member of the Grignon family, George, served as a volunteer in the ranks.[26]

In Johnson's company, Agent Boyd's son, James, and William Powell filled lieutenant's billets. Powell, who became Robert Grignon's trading partner after the war, was another métis trader who spoke Menominee; his mother was half Menominee and related to the chief Oshkosh.[27] Frustrated in his aspirations of leading a force of New York Indian auxiliaries, Alexander J. Irwin served as commissary, quartermaster, and adjutant for Stambaugh.

The Menominees regarded these métis and white officers more

favorably than they did Hamilton, but they still considered them liaisons rather than battlefield leaders. Native leadership was well represented in the Menominee contingent. In addition to the hereditary chief of the Menominees, Oshkosh, and the tribe's principal orator, I-om-e-tah, band chiefs and war leaders from throughout the Green Bay area assembled with their warriors. War captains of stature, such as Poegonah (Big Soldier), Souligny, and Grizzly Bear, provided all the leadership that the Menominees required. Augustin Grignon later recalled, "indeed all the principal men of the Menomonees, were of the party."[28]

The provisioning of the Menominee contingent, like the selection of its white officers, required sensitivity to the wants of the Menominees and the inhabitants of Green Bay. Although the Americans eventually assimilated or squeezed out the métis traders of this region, they remained an important interest group in 1832. Boyd assured Governor Porter, "Your Exc'y may feel assured that in equipping this Indian force for the field, every œconomy will be used, consistent with the honor and interest of the Country," but he was careful to spread his patronage evenly among his own cronies and influential Menominee relatives.[29] Boyd purchased firearms at government expense from six separate suppliers, including his own son-in-law, Findlay Fisher Hamilton.[30]

For this opportunity to dispense federal largesse, Boyd could thank the deplorable state of Menominee arms, already described by Grizzly Bear. "The Menomonees are most wretchedly armed, or rather not armed at all," Boyd reported, "and I am afraid that with every effort & exertion, not more than 150 of this nation will be able to march efficiently armed." Dismissively, Boyd also observed that the Menominees were constructing spears for the campaign.[31]

The construction of spears did not necessarily indicate a lack of military preparedness on the part of the Menominees. It may have signaled a ritual preparation for warfare. Hunting was still crucial to the Menominee economy, and the tribesmen surely had the implements of bloodshed available. Certain materials, however, were sacred to the Menominees and were proscribed for nonmartial uses. Menominees constructed arrowheads of turtle claws for use only in battle—these arrowheads called upon the magic power of the turtle and could be used for no other purpose. Likewise, the Menominees considered copper arrowheads semi-sacred and appropriate only for war.[32]

Menominee preparation for war was not limited to the construction of spears and arrows. Individual warriors carried a wide range of amulets, often miniatures of war clubs, bows, arrows, or lacrosse sticks in a small packet.[33] Each talisman conveyed spiritual power that either protected its bearer or bequeathed certain skills. George Pamoh's grandfather, for example, wore a rattlesnake belt during the Black Hawk War. A "shade" gave it to him on the fourth day of his vision quest, indicating that it would protect him from harm.[34] Another veteran of the campaign dreamed of eight thunder beings led by a chief dressed in dark blue or black who gave the dreamer a miniature lacrosse stick, a full-sized ball decorated with beads and feathers, a minute bow and arrows, and a "thunderbolt" in the form of a round stone. All but the last were painted black. The chief of the thunder beings said to the dreamer, "Grandson, I give these to you. Whenever you go to war, carry them with you and you will never be hurt." He never was.[35] Other warriors wore bear-claw necklaces to render them invisible, and their women embroidered black panthers on their moccasins to symbolize their ferocity.[36] Snakeskin bestowed "the serpent's power of stealthy approach," while the skin of the swallow "rendered the bearer as difficult to hit as it is that bird in flight." A miniature war club granted its bearer "the ability to strike with the force of the Thunderer."[37]

The most significant of the spiritual accouterments carried to battle was the war bundle or *wapanakian* ("white mat"), one of four sacred bundles known to the Menominees.[38] In Menominee cosmology, the thunderbirds control war, and it was they (together with the morningstar) who presented the first war bundle to the Menominees.[39] The chief thunderer, upon bequeathing it to a warrior named Watakwûna, gave him many instructions. Included were directions to fight at night and strike enemies in their sleep; to feast and sacrifice to the bundle before taking the warpath; to have each warrior carry with him the image of one of the medicine birds and wear a single quill feather in his hair; to smudge with and chew some of the roots within for purification; to lick blood from scalps as a sign of devouring the enemy on behalf of the thunderers; and to hold a ceremony and dance following victory.[40] Menominee warriors adhered to these instructions during the Black Hawk War and afterward.[41]

The Menominees who assembled at Green Bay thus presented an impressive spectacle: faces painted, hair worn in a broad scalp lock and roach, and knives suspended from the neck by a short cord in a leather sheath beautifully ornamented with dyed porcupine quills.[42] On 27 July, Stockbridge missionary Cutting Marsh recorded in his journal this description of the Menominee warriors:

> Their painted faces, ornaments, drums, whistles, war clubs, spears &c. &c. made them appear indeed savage and warlike. Their songs uttered from t[he] throat, consisting in deep gutteral sounds and very loud without distinction in sounds seemed most like the singing of

frogs, and t[he] occasional whoop was calculated to make
one feel that darkness and moral death still broods over
this region, removed at a very considerable distance from
t[he] peaceful abodes of civilization, and peace.[43]

By the time the Menominee contingent left Green Bay on 26 July,
it was evident that Black Hawk was not attempting to escape eastward to Canada, so they set a course for Fort Winnebago.[44] In accordance with traditional Menominee practice, the principal war
chief, or *mikäo*, may have led the procession singing, "The warrior
of the sacred bundle now starts. As he walks he is seeking for
the enemy."[45] Perhaps unwittingly, Lieutenant Powell recorded the
identity of the *mikäo* for this particular campaign: "among the
Menominee chiefs was Ahkamotte . . . selected by the Indians on
this expedition as their prophet, and he held powwows every night
to determine where the enemy were."[46]

On 1 August, the Menominees obliged Stambaugh to halt so that
they could conduct further spiritual preparation.[47] This ceremony
likely entailed the opening of the war bundle, the passing of the
pipe, invocation of the thunderbirds, offerings of meat and tobacco, and a war dance performed with musical accompaniment by
tambourine or water drum.[48] Although Stambaugh found these
ceremonies "fatigueing and sometimes not a little annoying," he
did not interfere.[49] Their salutary effect on Menominee morale was
sufficient cause for toleration, and Stambaugh observed with satisfaction that the warriors were "in excellent Spirits—ready to endure
any hardships that service may require."[50]

The first "hardship" to assail the Green Bay contingent came
from an unexpected quarter. As the Menominees and their Ho
Chunk allies ascended the Fox River, they encountered neutralist

Ho Chunks from the Portage area, who, Stambaugh reported, "attempted at every point we met them, on our route from Green Bay to the Prairie [du Chien], to prevent the Menominees going to war against the Sacs." Dissuaded by John Kinzie from participating in the war and still worried that the British Band would retaliate for the Paquette party's role in the Battle of Wisconsin Heights, some Portage Ho Chunks even asserted that "the americans were enemies of all red-skins, and that the Sacs would yet be victorious."[51] Stambaugh took such threats as evidence that the Portage bands were active accomplices of Black Hawk, but the Menominees and Ho Chunks he accompanied—resolute in their purpose—were undeterred.

Unfortunately for these Indians and their ambitions, the opportunity to meet their enemies in battle was fading fast. After the Battle of Wisconsin Heights, the British Band hurried to recross the Mississippi and avoid further confrontation. Furnished canoes by sympathetic Ho Chunks, Black Hawk sent as many women, children, and elders as possible down the Wisconsin River. Although aware that the soldiers of Fort Crawford guarded the river's mouth, the Indians hoped that the Americans would allow these inoffensive Indians to pass unmolested. Lacking sufficient watercraft, most of the British Band's noncombatants remained with the main body as it made its way overland to a Mississippi River crossing site. Ultimately, neither group escaped their enemies' wrath.

On 27 July, Henry Atkinson sent a Menominee messenger to Prairie du Chien bearing the news of Wisconsin Heights. Discerning Black Hawk's intentions, Atkinson requested that Menominee and Dakota warriors—the same who had suffered under Billy Hamilton—deploy along the eastern shore of the Mississippi to intercept the British Band.[52] At Prairie du Chien, Indian agent Joseph Street

and Fort Howard commander Captain Gustavus Loomis anticipated the general's wishes, dispatching a Menominee screening
force on 26 July and similarly deploying the Wisconsin River Ho
Chunk bands through Carymaunee, Waukon Decorah, and Waukaunkaw. To deny the British Band easy passage of the Mississippi,
Loomis and Street also ordered Ho Chunks up the Mississippi
to bring their canoes to Prairie du Chien (or suffer their con-
fiscation).[53] The divided Ho Chunk community at Prairie la Crosse,
comprising followers of One-Eyed Decorah as well as émigrés from
the Lead Region, greeted the directive with ambivalence but
obeyed. Once assembled at Prairie du Chien, both factions contributed warriors—some reluctant, others enthusiastic—to the search
for Black Hawk.[54]

The first contact occurred on 29 July at the mouth of the Wisconsin River. At approximately 2:00 AM, four canoes attempted to
slip past a detachment of regulars and Ho Chunks guarding the
waterway. At close range, the Americans and their allies poured two
volleys into the canoes, which carried principally women and children. Red Wing, a Ho Chunk warrior, later claimed to have killed
four men in this engagement, and official reports placed the enemy's losses at fifteen killed, but the true number is impossible to
know. Many of the fugitives remained in their canoes after the fu-
sillade, lying low and relying on the river's current to carry them to
freedom.[55] Pursuing Ho Chunks dashed these hopes, delivering
fourteen prisoners to Joseph Street over the next several days.
Street, who had offered amnesty to the British Band's women and
children through the Ho Chunk chief Carymaunee, described his
prisoners as "the most miserable looking poor creatures you can
imagine."[56]

In the four days following the Wisconsin River engagement, the

Menominees and Ho Chunks around Prairie du Chien captured twenty additional prisoners and collected nine scalps at the cost of only one killed.[57] On 2 August, White Pawnee, the Ho Chunk warrior notable for his conspicuous participation in the Battle of Wisconsin Heights, fell into a Sauk ambush while tracking two warriors who had eluded the guards at the mouth of the Wisconsin. Referring to White Pawnee as a "fine warrior," Joseph Street reported his death to William Clark, but White Pawnee's passing drew little notice otherwise.[58] Concurrent with his demise and sixty miles up the Mississippi, the Americans and the bulk of the British Band waged the decisive "battle" of the war.

Two days earlier, Captain Gustavus Loomis had dispatched the steamboat *Warrior* up the Mississippi to alert Wabasha's Dakotas of the British Band's movements. Eager to rejoin their fight, 150 Dakota warriors departed almost immediately, while the *Warrior*'s crew lingered at their village. The following day, on 1 August, the *Warrior* embarked for Prairie du Chien, overtaking the warriors by afternoon. The British Band, the Dakotas reported, were encamped only ten miles below, near the mouth of the Bad Axe River. After cutting more firewood in preparation for action, the *Warrior*'s crew continued down the Mississippi.[59]

At approximately 4:00 PM, the Americans confirmed the Dakotas' information. Near the mouth of the Bad Axe, the ship's crew detected a number of Sauks on the eastern shore, one lofting a white flag of truce. Believing the flag to be part of a ruse, Captain Joseph Throckmorton ordered his crew to commence firing.[60] After the *Warrior* fired three bursts of canister into the Indians, the soldiers on board laid down small arms fire until the approach of nightfall and the exhaustion of the ship's fuel compelled a return to Prairie du Chien. There, the boat took on not only the needed firewood but a number of Menominee warriors. Early the next day, the *Warrior* returned to the mouth of the Bad Axe, emerging from the morning fog to find the panicked remnants of the British Band attempting to cross the Mississippi under intense fire from the bluffs above.

After months of frustration and censure, Henry Atkinson had finally brought the bulk of his combat power to bear on an elusive enemy. For much of the campaign, his officers damned the Ho Chunks for misleading the army and abetting Black Hawk, but Atkinson could thank Ho Chunk guides for this opportunity. After reuniting the various brigades of his army at Helena, Wisconsin, on 27 July, Atkinson winnowed from his force unnecessary baggage, infirm regulars, and disconsolate volunteers, preparing for a pursuit "over the most difficult country imaginable."[61] To navigate his army through a trackless wilderness of thorn bushes and bluffs, Atkinson accepted the services of Nahreechsecochkeshica (Lame Ankle) and Mahheenibahka (Double Knife), two Ho Chunks of the Portage band.[62] Like Atkinson's earlier Potawatomi guides, these Ho Chunks "wore white bands about their heads, to distinguish them from other Indians."[63] The next six days' journey exhausted horses and demoralized men, but, on the morning of 2 August, Atkinson's army reached the Mississippi River. Finally in the presence of the enemy, Atkinson arrayed his regulars and militiamen in line on the high ground, and the arrival of the *Warrior* put Black Hawk's followers between a rock and a very hard place.

Interdicting their escape route, the Menominees and soldiers aboard the steamboat strafed the helpless Indians who were attempting to swim or paddle to the western shore. Observing their fate, other Indians sought refuge in the shallows along the eastern shore, lying still beneath its surface with only noses exposed to draw breath. The crew of the *Warrior* noticed the artifice, however, and drew close to the shore so that its Menominee passengers could pour fire into their unfortunate enemies.[64] Soon, the Menominees and their American allies, out of targets along the bank, turned their attention to clearing the nearby islands of survivors. Philip St. George Cooke observed the *Warrior*'s passengers disgorging on the largest island, his attention drawn to a Menominee warrior named Askaiah, who "ran forward, tomahawk upraised, to obtain the Indian honor of first striking the dead." The next time Cooke saw Askaiah, he lay dead—"shot in the back by a militia friend."[65] Whether this "friend" expressed any remorse is unknown, but Henry Atkinson personally offered the Menominee chiefs his condolences for their loss, and his soldiers buried the warrior beside their own five killed.[66]

To the Menominees, however, the sacrifice of a single slain warrior was well worth the reward. In this single engagement, the British Band suffered approximately 150 killed and ceased to exist as a coherent force.[67] When Atkinson's army entered Prairie du Chien on 5 August, it discovered that the triumphant spirits of the Menominees exceeded their own. Exalting over the scalps of their fallen foes, the Menominee men and women celebrated in song and dance. Special honors were reserved for the Menominee women who had lost relatives in the Sauk and Mesquakie attack of the previous summer. They stood at the center of the dance ring surrounded by their dancing kinfolk. Hoisting their enemies' scalps aloft with long poles, the women compelled their hirsute trophies to join the dance—rising and falling to celebrate the demise of the bodies they had formerly adorned.[68]

Not all Menominees had reason to celebrate. Having learned of the events at Bad Axe, the Green Bay contingent of Menominees continued toward Prairie du Chien with the thin hope that they might yet participate in the war. On 8 August, they crossed paths with homeward-bound Illinois militia brigades and narrowly survived the chance encounter. Marching cross-country to Dixon's Ferry to be mustered out of federal service, the militia nearly opened fire on the Indians when Samuel Stambaugh, the Green Bay contingent's principal white liaison, rode forward to avert tragedy.[69] Each party allied to the U.S. government if not each other, the two forces continued on their separate ways.

The same day, the Green Bay Menominees received disheartening orders from General Atkinson, who no longer deemed their service necessary. "He therefore directs," wrote Atkinson's aide-de-camp, "that those brave and faithful Allies of the U States shall be marched back to their own country, and permitted to return to their homes."[70] The Green Bay Menominees would not, however, abandon their task so easily. Stambaugh realized that the warriors would not respond well to such orders, having "arrived almost within hearing the Warhoop of their antient enemy." Stambaugh determined that—at the very least—the Menominees should move to the front and "receive occular proof that our government had redeemed it's promises that *their* grievances should be redressed."[71] Hoping to salvage a more meaningful role for the Menominees, Stambaugh sent his adjutant ahead to Prairie du Chien, where he lobbied General Winfield Scott—finally arrived at the scene of the war—for a combat mission. The sympathetic Scott consented, much to the gratification of the Menominees, who were beginning to fear that they had missed their war. The army had discovered a trail toward Cassville, Wisconsin, evidently left by fifty to sixty stragglers of the British Band. Through Powell, Scott passed the order to give pursuit. Aware that time was of the essence, Stambaugh left the old men and those hobbled by the lack of moccasins at Brunet's Ferry (six miles above the mouth of the Wisconsin) and, on 9 August, drew three days' rations for the fittest portion of his command. Significantly, not one of the chiefs remained behind. The following morning, a leaner Menominee contingent, 106 strong, sallied forth.[72]

At 11:00 AM on 10 August, the Menominees picked up the Sauk trail, exciting the warriors and accelerating their movement so that "the Officers could scarcely keep pace with them, on horseback."[73] At 6:00 PM that evening, Stambaugh's scouts reported that the Sauk party had encamped in a ravine a mere half mile ahead. The contingent divided into four parties, and Stambaugh enjoined the Indians to take prisoners rather than scalps.[74]

At this critical juncture, the Menominee leadership asserted itself. Through an interpreter, Grizzly Bear responded: "the Great Spirit saw proper to put a switch in the hands of our Sauk and Fox enemies to chastise us last year, which they did at Prairie du Chien, killing a good many of our people. Now he has seen proper to put that same switch into our hands to-day, which I cannot prevent my young warriors from using." He continued, "Since we left Green Bay we have been obedient children to all his commands; but in this matter about not taking scalps, we must be excused if we fail to regard it."[75] Harboring no illusions about the nature of his office, Stambaugh realized he could only resort to hope. Under the guidance of the *mikäo,* Ahkamotte, "The Menomonies prepared themselves *for War* in their own way, by stripping all the clothes from the body, and greasing & painting the skin."[76] Their preparation probably also entailed the passing of the pipe. Just before the assault, the *mikäo* may have sung another sacred war song to the accompaniment of deer-hoof rattles to make the enemy sleep more soundly.

At this point, the war bundle may have been opened again and the medicines within distributed to individual warriors, who bound them to head or body.[77]

Even so, the attack fizzled. Ten to fifteen miles north of Cassville, the Menominees overtook their foes. The "enemy" consisted of no more than ten Indians in what Stambaugh described as a "helpless" condition.[78] Only two of the party were armed, adult warriors. Still, the Menominees made the most of the situation. Ahkamotte commenced the attack with a shrill whistle blow.[79] Poegonah "did not discharge his gun, but rushed among the combatants to show his fearlessness."[80] According to Augustin Grignon, other warriors "fired a volley at the two Sauks, and when they fell, they were riddled with bullets by those coming up, who wished to share in the honor of having participated in the fight."[81] These honors likely included the incantation of a death blow song. For the Sauks, the Menominees reserved a special song: "Skinned and cut up, and sliced to finish!"[82] Another honor was a large wampum belt, offered by Ahkamotte as a reward to the first Menominee to take an enemy scalp. Saunapow (Ribbon) collected this prize.[83]

Much to Stambaugh's relief, the Menominees reserved this grim fate for the two adult warriors; the remaining women and children became prisoners.[84] Tragically, one of the Sauk children was struck by an errant piece of buckshot and died the next morning. Lieutenant Robert Grignon, moreover, imprudently ran in front of friendly fire and got himself wounded.[85] After the fight, Colonel Stambaugh offered congratulatory handshakes to the chiefs. Familiar with the handshake only as a form of greeting or farewell, Grizzly Bear inquired why, since they had seen each other only a few minutes ago, Stambaugh wanted to shake his hand.[86] On a Menominee battlefield in a Menominee war, it seemed an alien gesture.

After the fight, Lieutenant Powell prepared to escort the prisoners to Prairie du Chien. Women of the Menominee band near that town learned of these plans, though, and intercepted the prisoners at Brunet's Ferry. For the Menominees, as for many Native peoples, fighting was a man's business, but warfare was the concern of the entire tribe. Having lost beloved family members at the hands of the Sauks and Mesquakies the previous summer, the western Menominee women desired vengeance not only as Menominees but, more viscerally, as mothers and wives. About twenty Menominee women assembled on the road near Brunet's Ferry, some armed with tomahawks and knives. Once compelled, they relinquished their arms, but the women reaped symbolic vengeance by humiliating their enemies as they passed. Some simply touched the Sauks, others grasped them and shook their bodies.[87] In their war against the Sauks and Mesquakies, those who bore its greatest burden inflicted its final blows.

With the Menominees and Waukon Decorah's Ho Chunks now satisfied that they had obtained their revenge, only the Dakotas retained an unsettled blood vendetta against the British Band—but they, too, were soon satisfied. Although deprived of the leadership of Black Hawk and Wabokieshiek, who remained fugitives east of the Mississippi, the survivors of the British Band who reached the western shore of the Mississippi could not have realized the fleeting nature of the relief they felt. Indeed, many of them had just survived the most harrowing event of their lives. One Sauk woman saved herself and her infant by wrapping her child in a blanket, clenching it in her teeth, and grabbing fast to a horse's tail; at least two other women effected similar escapes.[88] Overwrought by the mixed emotions of euphoria and grief over loved ones less lucky, the survivors of the British Band were unaware that they had crossed from the American frying pan into the Dakota fire.

Following the Battle of Bad Axe, between one hundred and three hundred Dakota warriors—"stripped and painted for war"—presented themselves to Henry Atkinson and requested leave to pursue the survivors.[89] Aware that the request was a diplomatic gesture and that withholding permission might fray U.S.-Dakota relations, Atkinson assented. In only two days, the Dakota warriors covered nearly 120 miles and overtook their prey near the Red Cedar River trading post in Iowa.

Several days after their harrowing ordeal at Bad Axe, the roughly two hundred remaining members of the British Band awoke to the war whoop of the Dakotas. Exhausted, starving, and burdened by women and children, they stood no chance against their attackers. Over the next two hours, the Dakotas made quick, sanguinary work of the Bad Axe survivors while suffering only two killed and seven wounded. The Dakotas eventually claimed to have killed as many as two hundred Sauks and Mesquakies in this single engagement. The actual number was probably much lower, but the Dakotas left the last encampment of the British Band bearing no fewer than sixty-eight scalps, twenty-two prisoners, and thirty-five captured horses.[90]

Afterward, two of the warriors brought news of the "battle" and the scalps to Joseph Street. The Indian agent responded by disingenuously asserting that the Americans had waged this war on behalf of the Dakotas and the Menominees and that the Dakotas were thus obligated to turn their prisoners over to the Americans.[91] Still, Street professed the Dakotas redeemed in the eyes of their Great Father: "You have proved that you are warriors, and I am pleased with the activity and bravery you have displayed against our common enemies the Sacs & Foxes."[92] Not surprisingly, Black Hawk did not share this assessment. "The whites ought not to have permitted such conduct," he argued after the war, "and none but cowards would ever have been guilty of such cruelty—which has always been practiced on our nation by the Sioux."[93] Indeed, even this most recent bloodletting failed to end the feud between the Dakotas and the Sauks and Mesquakies, and they continued to trade blows throughout the coming decade. For the moment, however, the Dakota attack near the Red Cedar signaled the end of combat operations in the Black Hawk War. All that remained was to capture remnants of the British Band who remained in hiding on the eastern shore of the Mississippi—principal among them Black Hawk and Wabokieshiek.

In seeking refuge in Ho Chunk country, these leaders of the British Band provided the Menominees, Potawatomis, and Ho Chunks a final opportunity to demonstrate their fidelity to their powerful ally. Having already satisfied their most important war objectives, Menominee participation in the search for Black Hawk represented tactful diplomacy on the part of their headmen. With their grievance against the Sauks and Mesquakies settled, the imbroglio with the New York Indians assumed renewed importance, and the search for Black Hawk enabled the Menominees to bolster their standing before their Great Father. On 14 August, the Green Bay contingent left Prairie du Chien for Fort Winnebago in two parties. Based on information from a captive Sauk woman, who charged the Ho Chunks with sheltering the British Band, Stambaugh entertained the idea of scouring the Ho Chunk villages around the Four Lakes. A dearth of provisions, however, limited the Menominees to searching a single village, which they found abandoned. Stambaugh did interrogate some Ho Chunks near the Portage and found them "exceedingly anxious to obtain information respecting the reward offered for the apprehension of Black Hawk," further suggesting that the Ho Chunks were aware of the fugitives' whereabouts.[94] Out of supplies but having accomplished their war aims and having placed themselves in good stead with the federal government, the Green Bay Indians abandoned their search and headed home. On 21 August, they reached Butte des Mortes, where Samuel Stambaugh disbanded the force.[95] The Menominees' long war with the Sauks and Mesquakies was at last at an end.

Unlike the Menominees, the Ho Chunks and Potawatomis could not rest on their laurels. Having joined this war with the express purpose of earning the goodwill of their Great Father, the Potawatomis' contributions to this point were modest to say the least. Their uneventful service as guides and couriers seemed insufficient to put them in an advantageous position once land negotiations resumed—especially in light of the "Indian Creek Massacre" and persistent rumors that the Potawatomis had been in league with Black Hawk throughout the conflict. Hence, the Potawatomis were eager to respond when the army again called on their services.

Army officers believed that the fugitives would try to make their way to Canada and directed the commander of Fort Dearborn, Major William Whistler, to raise a Potawatomi screening force to patrol the area between Milwaukee and Green Bay. Accordingly, Whistler and Agent Thomas J. V. Owen sent Subagent Gholson Kercheval and a M. La Frambois to Milwaukee, still a predominantly Indian settlement, to recruit this force. Once again, the Potawatomis exhibited eagerness to serve the government, and once again their contributions were of negligible significance. Unaware that Black Hawk had never left the banks of the Mississippi, the Potawatomis searched in vain. By 4 September, Kercheval was back in Chicago to report that the operation had yielded no trace of the Winnebago Prophet or his disillusioned disciple. Other than later rounding up and delivering some belligerent Kickapoos who had broken ranks with the British Band, the Potawatomis had at this point concluded their service to the United States during the Black Hawk War.[96] Despite their meager contributions, the Potawatomis had grasped every opportunity to demonstrate their allegiance. Returning to their homes, they could only hope that it would be enough to distance themselves from the British Band and the actions of some of their disaffected brethren.

The Ho Chunks, too, had ample motive to make symbolic gestures, but the actions of their various bands put them in a perilous position. From the overt support of the Rock River Ho Chunks to the simmering enmity of the Decorah family, Black Hawk had elicited the broadest range of Ho Chunk sentiments. Now desperate fugitives, Black Hawk and Wabokieshiek, accompanied by approximately twenty women and children, fled toward Prairie la Crosse, a microcosm of Ho Chunk disunity. Two prominent men of the village, Winneshiek and One-Eyed Decorah, were, respectively, the brother-in-law of Black Hawk's advisor and the brother of his sworn enemy, Waukon Decorah. Warriors from the village had both actively supported Black Hawk and borne arms against him.

Whether Black Hawk had planned to continue his flight or, as he later claimed, to turn himself over to the Ho Chunks, it soon became evident that surrender was his only option. Stumbling upon the fugitives' camp about fifteen miles east of Prairie la Crosse, members of a Ho Chunk hunting party weighed their options before asking Black Hawk to submit to the Americans. With even sympathetic members of the Prairie la Crosse community now urging his surrender, Black Hawk resigned himself and his party to fate; on 27 August, the Ho Chunks of Prairie la Crosse delivered the fugitives to Joseph Street.[97] Capitalizing on the moment, the Ho Chunks hoped that "there would never more a black cloud hang over your Winnebeagoes" and that the gesture would quiet the "bad birds" who circulated rumors that the Great Father intended to punish his Ho Chunk children.[98] Yet even in turning Black Hawk and Wabokieshiek over to the Americans, the Ho Chunks continued to exhibit signs of support for their captives. When presented to Street, the captives wore newly manufactured vestments of white deerskin, which Ho Chunk women had sewn to convey the innocence of the wearers.[99]

With this symbolic gesture, both the Black Hawk War and active cooperation between the United States and its Indian allies came to a close. Whatever their operational significance, the final maneuvers of the Menominees, Dakotas, Potawatomis, and Ho Chunks illustrate well the disparity of their motives in terms of both ends and intensity. Pursuing their own aims first and cooperating with the Americans second, the Menominees and Dakotas took exceptional and sometime exceptionable measures to realize their war objectives. In contrast, the Potawatomis and Ho Chunks desired only to demonstrate allegiance to their Great Father and exhibited little eagerness to shed the blood of fellow Indians. Consequently, their contributions remained limited and their loyalty suspect. It remained to be seen whether their service was sufficient to offset the manifest evidence that other members of their tribe had shed white blood without reservation.

# 8

## LOSING THE PEACE

As stability returned to the Upper Mississippi following the capture of Black Hawk, it remained unclear whether Potawatomi and Ho Chunk participation in the war had achieved its desired effects. The Indians' objectives were meager: they wished only to retain the land they yet possessed and to avoid the undercompensated removal that awaited the Sauks and Mesquakies. Still, the Potawatomi and Ho Chunk campaigns were hardly the stuff of legend, and some Americans persisted in the belief that their Indian allies were "either ignorant or treacherous."[1] Both tribes had to contend with allegations of complicity—both warranted and unwarranted—with the British Band. Some charges, such as Potawatomi involvement in the "Indian Creek Massacre," were irrefutable, while others were fictions designed to expedite removal. Ultimately, Potawatomi and Ho Chunk cooperation with the United States succeeded in securing the loyalty of the Indian agents and army officers with whom the Indians worked most closely, but it failed to sway the popular opinion of frontier whites, who continued to regard all Indians as a threat. Although Indian agents and some army officers steadfastly defended the Potawatomis and Ho Chunks, the Indians discovered that they had allied not with the Great Father but with lower-level government functionaries who were powerless to keep their promises.

Following the conflict, the Dakotas and Menominees generally avoided such concerns. Although Billy Hamilton's mismanagement of the Prairie du Chien contingent had strained Dakota-U.S. relations, neither the Dakotas nor the Menominees had to contend with anti-American sentiments among their people, let alone violence against whites. Unthreatened by imminent removal, the Menominees and Dakotas pursued objectives conducive to U.S. policy and thereby earned the unqualified approbation of their Great Father and his agents. Not surprisingly, Samuel Stambaugh was effusive: "The Menomonie Chiefs and Warriors cannot be too highly extolled for their good conduct," he wrote George Boyd. "I have no doubt of the bravery & fidelity of these people, and I most respectfully and earnestly recommend them to the attention of our Government as faithful & useful allies of the U States."[2] Concurring, Winfield Scott exclaimed, "I wish to say to the Menominees that I am highly pleased with the zeal and promptitude with which they marched against the common enemy, & that I shall report their good conduct to the government."[3] Neither did citizens of Green Bay fail to appreciate the conduct of the Menominees, and they petitioned the U.S. Congress to show the tribe justice in its ongoing dispute with the New York Indians. One citizen later recalled that "in the Black Hawk war, they assembled *en masse,* and showed themselves efficient allies of the whites."[4] At the Red Cedar River, the Dakotas demonstrated their own "efficiency" as white allies, compelling Joseph Street to retract his earlier critique of Dakota resolve. "You have proved that you are warriors," he declared, "and I am pleased with the activity and bravery you have displayed against our common enemies the Sacs & Foxes."[5]

Because of their spotty wartime record, the Potawatomis were not assured of similar judgments, but they had reason for hope. Under Billy Caldwell's adroit guidance and with Thomas J. V. Owen's assistance, they had waged an effective public relations campaign to mollify white fears and publicize Potawatomi military contributions. Perhaps more important, Caldwell and the Potawatomi chiefs had been able to promulgate a relatively cohesive, multiband policy of modest but visible support for the Americans. Although much of the tribe sympathized with Black Hawk, Potawatomi elders distanced their people from the conflict and convinced the vast majority of their young men to stay out of the fight. Consequently, interrogation of Sauk and Mesquakie prisoners after the war largely exonerated the Potawatomis of charges of cooperating with the British Band.[6] Through his adjutant, a gratified Winfield Scott informed Thomas J. V. Owen "that all investigation results in a perfect acquittal of the Pottowatamies, of any participation in the recent hostilities against us, and he directs this to be communicated to those Indians through the Agent at Chicago, with the assurance that he has so advised the War Department."[7]

This testimony, combined with the Potawatomis' campaign service, distanced the tribe from the "well established fact that the Pottawattimes were concerned in the murders on Indian Creek."[8] Because the Potawatomis had demonstrated themselves to be faithful allies to their Great Father, the government tried the perpetrators of this attack as individuals and made no claim against Potawatomi possessions as war reparations. The Potawatomis' policy, it seemed, had succeeded.

The Ho Chunks had less reason for optimism. Decentralized and geographically dispersed, the bulk of the tribe congregated at the Portage and attempted to enforce a tribal policy of neutrality, but with limited success. On opposite ends of the Fox-Wisconsin water-

way, elements of the Lake Winnebago and Prairie du Chien bands
chose alliance with the Americans or, at least, the Americans' Menominee allies. Wabokieshiek and the people of his village, meanwhile, had openly assisted the British Band and bore some responsibility in Black Hawk's decision to reenter Illinois in 1832. Finally,
White Crow's upper Rock River Ho Chunks adhered to a policy of
studied duplicity, keeping all options open until the outcome of
the war was clear. Despite all this, for a moment it seemed as
though the Ho Chunks might replicate the diplomatic success of
the Potawatomis. Intermittent military contributions by various
parties and White Crow's "rescue" of the Hall sisters, they hoped,
would suffice to overcome the Ho Chunks' active and passive support of the British Band. As the Americans began to interrogate
Sauk and Mesquakie prisoners, however, it became evident that the
militia's suspicions about Ho Chunk loyalty had been more than
warranted.

Early evidence of Ho Chunk collaboration with the enemy came
from an elderly Sauk woman captured by the Green Bay Menominees. In addition to identifying the Ho Chunks involved in the
attacks at Blue Mounds, this woman confirmed that Ho Chunks
had provided both guides and sanctuary to the British Band, part
of which continued to hide among the Ho Chunks in the vicinity of the Four Lakes.[9] Although the Green Bay contingent's subsequent search of this area turned up nothing, the resident Ho
Chunks appeared anxious to learn whether the government intended to offer a reward for the capture of Black Hawk. Certain of
Ho Chunk perfidy, Samuel Stambaugh opined that the Ho Chunks
would bring the fugitive Sauk chief in for a bounty of thirty horses
and $100, but for no other reason: "Their *good feeling* toward our
Govrt would never prompt them to do so."[10] These and similar
reports reached Winfield Scott, who concluded "with great regret,

that many Winnebagos have been engaged in this lawless war against the Americans," and he enjoined the Ho Chunks to convene in council with him on 10 September 1832.[11]

In the meantime, the government interrogated survivors of the British Band, who uniformly testified that the Ho Chunks had not only assisted Black Hawk but also borne arms against the Americans. A Mesquakie named Ma-kauk identified Wabokieshiek and White Crow as their principal accomplices, and many prisoners depicted White Crow as an agitator who counseled against a peaceful return to Iowa.[12] According to Neapope, the principal civil chief of the British Band, ten lodges of Ho Chunks had provided active support to the Sauks and Mesquakies, furnishing corn and potatoes in exchange for durable goods and—more ominously—bringing in American scalps on eight different occasions.[13] Scott considered this evidence "conclusive as to certain acts of hostility committed by the Winnebagoes."[14] No longer desiring merely to speak with the Ho Chunk leaders in September, Scott now demanded that they also surrender all individuals guilty of acts of violence against whites.[15]

Meanwhile, Joseph Street's self-interests converged with those of the Ho Chunks of his agency, whom he defended vociferously. A prideful man, Street was especially sensitive to any allegation that Indians assigned to his agency had allied with the British Band, which he interpreted as an indictment of his performance. Thus, Street continued to proclaim the innocence of "his" Ho Chunks, pointing out that they had turned over dozens of prisoners and killed fifty or sixty Sauks and Mesquakies.[16] Indeed, following the Battle of Bad Axe, the Ho Chunks had abandoned their imperfect neutrality policy altogether by offering General Henry Atkinson the service of ranging parties, which scoured western Wisconsin in search of Sauk and Mesquakie stragglers.[17] In this final demonstration of loyalty to their Great Father, the Ho Chunks encountered considerable success, and they daily delivered prisoners and scalps to their agent in Prairie du Chien.[18] Street now pointed to these actions as proof that the Prairie du Chien Ho Chunks had behaved loyally during the war. Although Street suspected that Winneshiek and his family had supported Black Hawk, the agent attributed all other instances of Ho Chunk disloyalty to bands from south of the Wisconsin River—and hence beyond the range of his administrative responsibility.[19] Denied any defense by Street, the implicated Ho Chunks turned inward for deliverance. The task of extricating the upper Rock River Ho Chunks from their precarious position now fell to the man who was ultimately responsible for their predicament.

Although every Ho Chunk band from south of the Portage was present when Scott finally convened his council on 12 September at Rock Island, White Crow dominated the discourse. Drawing on his considerable rhetorical skills, White Crow admitted the irrefutable but otherwise manipulated the facts to his advantage. He protested his own innocence and good conduct, but he admitted "many of our foolish boys have raised the hatchet against the United States; and as I said before I am ashamed, on this account, to look the whites in the face."[20] Despite the overwhelming evidence against him, he was able to cite an equal amount of evidence in his favor: his deliverance of Henry Gratiot, his rescue of the Hall girls, and his military service beside the Americans. In an impressive display of oratorical legerdemain, White Crow eventually won over Scott, and the general even bestowed a medal upon the chief's son, "who served gallantly with General Dodge in the late campaign."[21] Indeed, Scott thanked many of the Ho Chunks for their service. According to Waukon Decorah, "he drew his sword and put it back into its scabberd, saying he had no use for it; his red brethren had made it of no use."[22]

Scott had hardly convened the council merely to congratulate his "red brethren," however. "This unfortunate war seems to say that no peace can last between the Winnebagoes and the whites," he argued, and he proposed to compensate the Indians for all of their lands south of the Wisconsin and Fox Rivers—minus a "small portion" the Americans would extract as reparations for the conduct of Wabokieshiek and his band.[23] Incredibly, Scott did not demand similar concessions from White Crow's band. As with the Potawatomis involved at Indian Creek, individuals would bear responsibility for their actions without any disadvantage to their communities. The Ho Chunks agreed to sell off their southern lands to distance themselves from the whites, but they requested that Henry Dodge, Joseph Street, and John Kinzie advise them whether or not they were being offered fair terms.[24]

Whether the terms were in fact fair is subject to debate. In exchange for a smaller and inferior tract of land west of the Mississippi, the Ho Chunks ceded their remaining lands south of the Wisconsin River—approximately 2.5 million acres—to the United States. Scott recognized that "the country hereby ceded by the Winnebago nation is more extensive and valuable than that given by the United States in exchange," and the final treaty also granted the Ho Chunks an annuity of $10,000 for a term of twenty-seven years.[25] Not having entirely abandoned hope of acculturating the Indians, the government further agreed to construct a school for Ho Chunk children near Prairie du Chien and provide their parents with the services of agriculturalists and blacksmiths.[26] These terms were generally agreeable to the Ho Chunks, but they expressed concern regarding the home the Americans intended for them on the western shore of the Mississippi—a forty-mile wide strip of land that would place the Ho Chunks between the still-warring Dakotas and the Sauks and Mesquakies. Anticipating Ho Chunk concerns, Scott averred that "we will keep over you a watchful eye, and extend a strong arm for your protection."[27] Too familiar with the Americans' mediocrity as peacekeepers, Carymaunee submitted, "We wish very much that you would remove the Sacs further off. The Mississippi is a good line [to separate the Ho Chunks and the whites], but that between the Sacs and us not so good."[28]

Good or not, the Americans' offer was better than the Ho Chunks had reason to expect. Although their cooperation with the British Band had been more widespread and systematic than that of the Potawatomis, the Ho Chunks were similarly able to parlay limited military cooperation into political capital. For an alternative fate, they had to look only to the Sauks and Mesquakies. Although the majority of these tribes had disavowed the actions of the British Band and maintained regular diplomatic relations with the United States, they were presented terms "on the blended grounds of conquest & contract." Consequently, the Sauks and Mesquakies relinquished six million acres valued at $7 million, receiving only $660,000 in compensation. By comparison, at least, the Ho Chunk treaty appeared reasonable. Indeed, Winfield Scott anticipated that his superiors would consider the treaty unduly advantageous to the Ho Chunks. If the treaty commissioners had "agreed to just & equitable provisions in favor of the Winnebagos," he explained, "it was because conscience required that they should be treated with justice & liberality."[29]

This outcome was hardly expected or desired by the region's settlers and politicians. For many, the Black Hawk War represented an opportunity to terminate immediately all Indian claims east of the Mississippi. While the campaign was still underway, the citizens of Shelbyville, Illinois, addressed a letter directly to Secretary of War Lewis Cass, calling on the government to extinguish all Indian claims around Lake Michigan. Citing the Indian Creek attack, they railed against the "two handed game played on us by the puta-wotomies & Wininbagoes" and assured Cass, "we should be very much pleased to see the Putawatomies and winnebagoes removed to the Arkansas river." In a sentence that speaks volumes, the authors added, "there is no time so suitable to remove those Indians as when you are secretary of war, and General Jackson President."[30] The frontiersmen's hopes were not misplaced.

Cass, Andrew Jackson, and Illinois governor John Reynolds were among the foremost advocates of Indian removal before Black Hawk's intransigence, and the war only strengthened their convictions. Cass dedicated a lengthy essay to the subject in 1828, while Jackson's historical legacy is substantially marred by his Indian removal policy.[31] Reynolds was perhaps the most ardent champion of removal from Illinois. He was never fond of Indians, but he began to push strongly for their removal on 15 August 1831. He warned Jackson of impending violence if measures were not taken to remove Indians offensive to the white population: "It is to be feared; if this is delayed much longer; that the people who feel the annoyance can not be restrained from adopting some very harsh measures of redress."[32] To Cass and kindred spirits, the Black Hawk War provided an opportunity to divest the Old Northwest of Indians once and for all. So much was evident when Cass ordered Winfield Scott to assume overall command of the war in June 1832. "It is very desirable," he informed the general, "that the whole country between Lake Michigan & the Mississippi, & south of the

Ouisconsin, should be freed from the Indians; & with this view, you will endeavor to prevail upon the friendly or neutral Chiefs of those tribes . . . to cede their claims, & to remove west of the Missis sippi."[33] No mention of tribes that were neither friendly nor neutral was warranted; their removal was a forgone conclusion. Yet the friendly and neutral Indians refused to accept the same fate, much to the chagrin of the chief executives of the United States and Illinois. Frustrated that the Potawatomis could not be compelled to cede their land as war reparations, Governor Reynolds informed Cass that "removal of . . . the Pottawatomie Indians is very interesting to the people of this State"—so much so that he was willing to "do all in my power to effect so desirable an object."[34]

As Reynolds wrote Cass, the federal government was doing its part to realize the Illinois governor's vision. In October 1832, treaty commissioners Jonathan Jennings, John W. Davis, and Marks Crume began negotiations with select bands of Potawatomis at Camp Tippecanoe, Indiana. Although present, Thomas J. V. Owen protested the timing, location, and organization of the proceedings. The purpose of the treaty was to purchase from the Potawatomis their remaining lands in Indiana, Illinois, and southern Michigan. These were lands held in common by the entire tribe, but the commissioners invited only Potawatomis from south of the Grand River in Michigan and east of the Illinois and Des Plaines rivers in Illinois. Moreover, the commissioners scheduled the treaty away from Chicago and at a time conflicting with the issuance of annuities, complicating attendance for those most interested in the outcome of the negotiations.[35] Between 20 and 27 October, delegates for the bands represented signed away nearly 800,000 acres of eastern Illinois, most of their remaining lands in Indiana, and Michigan lands south of the Grand River. Although the government agreed to pay the Potawatomis annuities totaling $50,000 over terms of twelve or twenty years and promised delivery of nearly a quarter million dollars in trade goods, irregularities marred the negotiations.[36] The commissioners—all from Indiana—ensured that the interests of their state and supposed Potawatomi creditors were well attended to, but they paid little heed to the Potawatomis' concerns.[37] Ignoring Owen's advice, the commissioners neither invited all elements of the Potawatomi tribe nor ensured that every band would receive the annuities to which they were entitled. At this point a champion of justice toward the Indians, Michigan Territory governor George Porter had been intentionally excluded from the proceedings.[38] Believing that the government was "much indebted to them for their good conduct, immediately previous to and during the late Indian disturbances," Porter was now disgusted by that same government's treatment of the Potawatomis.[39] "I am convinced," a surly Porter wrote Indian commissioner Elbert Herring, "that as a Nation great injustice has been done them."[40]

The citizens of Illinois, however, were not satisfied with the extent of the injustice. By the terms of Scott's treaty with the Ho Chunks, these Indians were not required to relocate until 1 June 1833. The Potawatomis, meanwhile, were free to use their ceded lands until the government released them for private sale. Impatient to realize their supposed dividends from the Black Hawk War, Illinoisans considered these delays intolerable.[41] Many of them sought redress by manufacturing fictional Indian "outrages" in order to press for the Indians' immediate removal. In November 1832, a veteran of Dodge's battalion passed to Governor Porter "a report in circulation" that the Ho Chunks were dissatisfied with their treaty of September and were sending war wampum as far as Missouri.[42] In the same month, complaints against the Potawatomis began to emanate from Peoria. Reynolds forwarded the complaints to William Clark and Lewis Cass, demanding action. Atkinson learned of the complaints and, although incredulous, sent a minion to admonish the Potawatomis for their own sake and requested Owen to initiate his own investigation of the disturbances, which included hunting on ceded lands (which they were allowed to do), stealing horses, firing the prairie, destroying fences, and burning a bridge.[43]

Although Owen dismissed the allegations as "vague and uncertain rumors," allegations against the Potawatomis continued to roll in, and Reynolds continued to advocate total removal on account of their "outrages" and their "forming combinations to resist the Government."[44] Most of the complaints ranged from exaggeration to total fabrication. An inquiry by Billy Caldwell and Alexander Robinson convinced Owen of the Potawatomis' innocence and led him to denounce "the reports of certain Commissioners of the Executive of this State" as apocryphal.[45] In his report, Caldwell demonstrated his adroit ability to manipulate the Potawatomis' image—and the white perception of that image—to further the ends of the tribe. Perhaps recognizing that a simple rebuttal of the allegations would be dismissed because of Caldwell's inherent bias, he attempted to exploit the paternal obligation of the Great Father to care for his indigent and loyal children. Caldwell pleaded that his people "would immediately retire, as they would rather encounter the fear of starvation, and forego the benefits of commerce" than to cause the slightest apprehension to their white brethren. Simultaneously catering to his audience and revealing a good deal of his own mind, Caldwell added that the Potawatomis "know in a contest with the whites, they have every thing to lose, and nothing to gain."[46] Regardless, Caldwell and Robinson's findings were those of "half breed" Indians and, hence, immediately suspect. They proved wholly insufficient to allay the paranoia of the white inhabitants of Illinois the following spring, when Native communities returned from their winter hunting grounds to resume residency in their summer villages along the Rock River.

During the winter of 1832–1833, rumors of Indian conniving blossomed into articles of faith among the white settlements of northern Illinois. Consequently, the large-scale return of entire Indian communities to their villages in the spring of 1833 incited a panic as settlers interpreted a routine, annual migration as another Indian "invasion."[47] A ludicrous report that Keokuk, leader of the Sauk peace party, had sent war wampum to the Potawatomis surfaced in Cook County, and another maintained that the Potawatomis were circulating war wampum among the Rock River Ho Chunks.[48] Tall tales grew taller yet when, in April 1833, Reynolds received reports from "respectable and unsuspected channels" and "sources greatly respected" that the Potawatomis, Ho Chunks, Sauks, Mesquakies, and possibly Ojibwas were marshaling for war. "The most moderate accounts" placed the number of warriors at four thousand.[49] Another rumor maintained that two thousand Indians were advancing on Galena.[50] Such stories gained wide circulation in the pages of the *Galenian* and other regional newspapers, which ran spectacular (albeit specious) stories about the impending Indian war.[51]

True to form, junior officials responsible for the administration of federal Indian policy were quick to defend the Indians. Often conflating the reputations of their assigned tribes with their own professional reputations, agents did not brook unsubstantiated allegations regarding the behavior of "their" Indians. During the war, Joseph Street served his own interests at least as much as the Ho Chunks' when he assured William Clark "that the Winnebagoes of my Agency will remain quiet" due "to my untiring zeal in the duties of my office."[52] Because the agents invested considerable pride in the extent to which their charges remained loyal to the government, they sometimes denigrated the behavior of bands or tribes assigned to other agencies—and even their fellow agents. Street in particular lost few opportunities to impugn his colleagues, and Samuel Stambaugh filed an official complaint against Kinzie, claiming that the Fort Winnebago subagent had deliberately obstructed Menominee participation in the war.[53] Other times, however, agents developed loyalties for their assigned tribes that transcended any regard for career; Thomas Forsyth and John Marsh lost their posts at least in part because of their advocacy for the Sauks and Dakotas, respectively. Regardless of their motivations, the agents steadfastly defended the conduct of "their" Indians and attempted—albeit unsuccessfully—to turn the tide of public opinion in favor of the Indians.

Henry Gratiot began lobbying on behalf of the Rock River Ho Chunks before the war had ended; he rode through the lead country offering assurances of their fidelity in the hopes of alleviating paranoia.[54] He continued to do so after the conflict, investigating rumors of Indian belligerence in the company of the Ho Chunk chief Whirling Thunder. Finding the reports to be either baseless or greatly exaggerated, Gratiot informed Porter that the Indians "were as much alarmed as the white people."[55] Visiting Turtle Village, the supposed staging area for thousands of hostile warriors, Gratiot found only a "thinly attended" "'Medicine Feast,' the object of which was to 'Smoke to the Great Spirit,' and consult with one another on their future prospects, such as planting corn, exploring their new country, the removal permanent location etc." White Crow dispelled the rumor that the Potawatomis had circulated war wampum when he showed Gratiot the actual belt, which was tied with green ribbon—a sign of peace. The Potawatomis, it turned out, were privy to white rumors of Ho Chunk war plans and had sent the wampum to dissuade their neighbors from going to war with the whites.[56] The Potawatomis had nothing to fear, however; Gratiot found "All of the Rock River Indians . . . destitute of ammunition and provisions" and incapable of waging war, had they so desired.[57]

To the north, John Kinzie, whose wife referred to the Ho Chunks of their agency as "our own people," told a similar story.[58] He lambasted the authors of newspaper articles "calculated to prejudice the minds of the Whites against those Indians, if not, to create new disturbances."[59] Having just himself traveled from Chicago to Fort Winnebago, Kinzie testified "that there is not the least ground for suspicion or alarm—that the Indians have never manifested a greater desire to remain at peace, and to cultivate good feelings, than at the present time."[60] Commenting on rampant rumors about a supposedly imminent Indian war, Kinzie assured Governor Porter that he had "never seen less to fear on that score than at present. All the principal men of the Winnebago nation, with whom I have conversed, are very anxious and desirous of remaining at peace."[61] From Chicago, Potawatomi agent Thomas J. V. Owen submitted a similar report: "The Indians are so perfectly acquainted with the Power and facilities of the Government & are so well aware of their own weakness and imbecility, that no further difficulties need be apprehended from them, for the present."[62] If Owen's appraisal was less then complimentary, it helped complete a clear picture of Indian relations in the Old Northwest—one devoid of hostilities initiated by the Indians.

Hostilities initiated by the whites, however, were an entirely dif-

ferent matter. Worried that John Reynolds's imprudent characterization of the Potawatomis would incite the Illinoisans to violence,
George Porter warned Elbert Herring of the probable consequences. Empathetically, he forwarded to the commissioner the admonishment of a Potawatomi chief in Chicago: "If we are to be
treated as enemies, behave as we may, who can blame us for joining
in with our brethren of the forest. But remember we are suspected
unjustly, and if any thing is done by our young men, it is not
our fault—we are driven into it, and the whites must blame themselves."[63]

The chief's concern was not unwarranted; in February 1833
Henry Gratiot warned the secretary of war, "I have great difficulty
in pacifying the white people, and preventing them from com-
mencing hostilities on the Indians."[64] The U.S. Army, which had
shown itself only modestly successful in preventing hostilities between Indian peoples, remained Gratiot's only option for preventing such a calamity; he asked Cass to furnish a military force to
preserve the peace in the coming spring.[65] From Prairie du Chien,
Joseph Street concurred. In the absence of a robust, permanent
force of peacekeepers, he opined, "there will in my opinion *be little
prospect of peace*" and "the first favourable moment will be seized
to do mischief."[66] Unfortunately for the Indians, the empathetic
Henry Atkinson had returned to Jefferson Barracks, Missouri, and
the Indian agents' pleas for help fell on deaf ears in Washington.
The citizens of Illinois, however, were listening to what the agents
had to say, and they did not like what they were hearing.

Although the Indians enjoyed the support of the agents, it was
becoming increasingly evident that they operated in isolation from
the Jackson administration and in opposition to white interests on
the frontier. Even before the Black Hawk War, relationships be-

tween federal officials and the ever-growing white population of the Old Northwest were often tense or even antagonistic, but a quasi state of martial law had helped subordinate the unruly frontiersmen to federal regulation. Involved in the defense of the frontier by Reynolds's call-up of the militia, the residents of Illinois now questioned the priorities of Indian agents who seemed to regard the "savages" above their own countrymen. During the war, a Galena resident complained directly to President Jackson about the supposed malfeasance of Henry Gratiot, who "will get angry when the people say his Indians are not friendly" and who jealously upheld Indian claims to the lead-mining region. Also complaining that the "Indian Agents act in cog. with the Indian traders"—principally Franco-Indian métis—the complainant charged, "There ought to be a change in the Indian Department . . . there is something radically wrong in it."[67]

Disinclined to heed the concerns of pro-Indian bureaucrats, frontier whites were far more receptive to the recommendations of Henry Dodge—a rowdy frontiersman and true "man of the people" who emerged from the Black Hawk War as one of its few heroes.[68] Although he shared the agents' sentiment that trouble was imminent, Dodge offered a solution more in line with local (and hence his own) interests: "I think it is important to the peace of the country that the Winnebagoes should be forced to leave the country ceded to the U States, & that there should be an entire separation between the Potawatomies & Winnebagoes." Dodge went on to accurately gauge "the dislike of the people of this frontier to these two nations of Indians" as well as the common (albeit exaggerated) impression "that they participated in the late war with the Sacs & Foxes."[69]

Dodge's conclusion, however, that "their present location will produce war between them & the U.S. troops, unless they are all re-moved" represented a potentially self-fulfilling prophesy.[70] Unlike Gratiot and others who saw the U.S. Army as a buffer between Indi-ans and the frontier white population, Dodge maintained the Jack-sonian view that the U.S. Army and the tribes of northern Illi-nois were intrinsically antagonistic. Interestingly, the U.S. Congress made Dodge's provisional "Battalion of Mounted Rangers" a regu-lar unit in the U.S. Army, renaming it the First Regiment of U.S. Dragoons and appointing Dodge commander on 5 March 1833. Al-though the appointment of regular army officers such as Stephen Watts Kearny, Jefferson Davis, and Philip St. George Cooke to sub-ordinate posts infused the unit with some of the discipline and reg-imentation of the U.S. Army, the First Dragoons retained the char-acter of the earlier Mounted Rangers, which is to say that it was a unit manned by frontier miners who wished to expel Indians from the region.[71] Dodge's prediction of imminent hostilities between the Indians and the U.S. Army is therefore not surprising—nor is the fact that the Ho Chunks of Kinzie's subagency grew convinced that Dodge's new regiment had "been organized purposely for their extermination."[72] In reality, Congress established the dragoons to free the War Department from the vagaries of relying on volunteer cavalrymen during times of war.[73] Still, the Ho Chunks breathed easier when Dodge's troopers rode off to their winter quarters in Arkansas in October 1833, thereby eliminating the supposedly im-minent clash of arms between Indians and federal troops.

In spite of Dodge's biased perspective, he correctly informed his superiors that "Whether the white inhabitants are in danger or not, they appear confident of the hostile dispositions of the Indians."[74] Having endured two Indian wars in the span of five years, the white inhabitants of the region eyed their Native neighbors with fear and loathing. Every movement proved cause for alarm, and every affront provided a pretext for retribution. Unfortunately, the Indians who returned to their summer villages along the Rock River in the spring of 1833 were desperate and starving, a circumstance that could not help but produce friction between the two peoples.

Economic hardship for the Indians of the region began with the Black Hawk War itself, which shattered the fragile subsistence economies of communities along the campaign trail. Seeking refuge at their respective agency houses to avoid being confused with the "hostiles" of the British Band, the Ho Chunks and Potawatomis of northern Illinois and southern Wisconsin relied on the beneficence of the Great Father to fill their stomachs in the summer of 1832. Recognizing the dimensions of the crisis, Indian agents spent beyond their authorization and requested additional funds.[75] Once the crisis had seemingly abated, these Indians returned to their villages, only to find that their untended crops had failed.[76] To make matters worse, cholera appeared among some communities around Chicago. Thomas J. V. Owen sent medical assistance but acknowledged its minimal help in the absence of "the necessary diet and attention."[77] Autumn brought no improvement. The growing season already past and their larders empty, Indian leaders again appealed to their agents for aid. Although agents were uniformly empathetic, they had to request additional funds to cover the unforecasted expenditures, which produced intolerable delays.[78] By the time supplies arrived, most Indian communities had dispersed to their winter hunting camps. Ironically, a mild winter actually compounded the problem; minimal snowfall hampered the winter hunts, making deer more difficult to track and their movements more unpredictable.[79] By March 1833 John Kinzie reported, "All of the Indians in this section of the country are actually in a state of starvation."[80] Deprived of venison, the Indians resorted to the staple of the deer and rooted acorns from the forest floor.

Hence, the Indians who reoccupied their summer villages in the spring of 1833 were in a pitiful state. In locations close to white settlements, their return seemed an ominous harbinger of another Indian "uprising." Recognizing their precarious standing in public opinion, Indian headmen implored their young men to be on their best behavior. Inevitably, however, in spite of their elders' pleas some Ho Chunks and Potawatomis pilfered crops, livestock, and even lead ore to fill their stomachs or provide the means to do so.[81] When they did, the whites made the perpetrators pay. Governor Reynolds's loyal subordinate Isaiah Stillman informed the governor "that the Whites had caught several of them & whipped them in a most inhuman manner."[82] Grasping the opportunity to use these "depredations" to further his case for immediate removal, Reynolds dispatched his own investigator to the scene. He was no doubt embarrassed, however, by S. C. Christy's 28 April report, which found stories of Indian transgressions greatly exaggerated. Indeed, all of the Indians he encountered professed friendship and convinced Christy that they had committed no depredations.[83] Although perhaps inclined to bury Christy's report, Reynolds had little reason to despair. His own views on the subject of Indian removal aligned neatly with those in Washington, and the destitute condition of the Illinois Indians provided the Jackson administration with all the leverage needed to see them gone.

Eager to improve their condition, Indians across the region planted their summer crops at the first opportunity. For the various Ho Chunk bands, this undertaking posed a problem. By the treaty of 15 September 1832, they had agreed to migrate either to the north side of the Wisconsin River or west of the Mississippi by

1 June 1833, and none of their crops would be ready for harvesting at that time. Consequently, Ho Chunk leaders appealed to their agents for permission to cultivate crops over the summer to prepare for the move and the ensuing winter.[84] They pointed out that they had already sown their fields and—assuming too much charity on the part of their white neighbors—that these lands could not possibly be of any use to the settlers until the following year. Acknowledging their good behavior and dire need, Kinzie forwarded the request to Governor Porter, who endorsed it before sending it on to the Indian Office. Conditioned to consider these men faithful representatives of the Great Father, who promised to look after and protect his "red children," the Ho Chunks were no doubt pleased with the initial response to their entreaty. They did not understand, however, the proscribed authority of their agents and territorial superintendents. Commissioner of Indian Affairs Elbert Herring's response to the Ho Chunk request dispelled at once any hope that these Indians would retain their lands through the summer. More important, it suggested that the agents of the Indian Office—who exhibited too much empathy for their Indian charges—were not true representatives of the Great Father, after all.

Despite the miserable state of the Ho Chunks, the reasonableness of their request, and the endorsement of government officials most familiar with the tribe, Herring informed Governor Porter that an extension of Ho Chunk occupancy was out of the question. Moreover, Herring directed Porter to make every exertion to urge the Ho Chunks westward beyond the Mississippi rather than north of the Wisconsin, as permitted by the treaty.[85] Just two weeks earlier, however, Herring had informed Porter that "It is not in the contemplation of the Government to press the removal of the Winnebagos West of the Mississippi. . . . The choice of their future abode in either region is left entirely to their own free will."[86] Not surprisingly, Porter was astonished by Herring's precipitous change in tune, especially since it contrasted with his own judgments on the subject. Porter submitted a scathing critique of this policy, which he deemed of no advantage to the United States and detrimental to the Indians. "I cannot," he protested to Herring, "while holding the responsible office of Superintendent of Indian Affairs [for Michigan Territory], suffer any arrangement to be made with regard to the Indians under my care, which I disapprove, without remonstrating against it." The Ho Chunks had never accepted Street's plan, whereby they would provide a buffer between the warring Dakotas, Sauks, and Mesquakies. Consequently, they informed Porter that they had no intention of migrating westward of the Mississippi, preferring instead to migrate to their own lands north of the Wisconsin. Although Porter pledged not to "interfere with what is adopted as the policy of the Government," this same policy left him befuddled and angry.[87]

Having forged diplomatic bonds and even military alliances with the tribes of the region, Porter and the agents under him (as well as those under William Clark) maintained relationships with the Indians that were now threatened by the policies of Washington. In response to Porter's tirade, Herring made it very clear that "this object is in conformity with what I am authorized to say, is the view of the President." And, while the Indian Office could not direct agents to violate the conditions of ratified treaties with Indian nations, Herring reminded Porter that it was the duty of officers of the Indian Office to take into account the views of the president.[88] Put simply, Herring put Porter and his agents on notice that, should they place loyalty to the Indians above loyalty to their president, they should be prepared for the consequences.

Although they were not yet entirely aware of it, the Indians of the Old Northwest had formed alliances with individuals rather than with the United States. While the agents of the Indian Office and officers of the U.S. Army pretended to wield plenipotentiary powers when dealing with Native people, their authority as ambassadors was actually quite limited. The practice of falsely claiming absolute power was a product of the militarization of Indian relations in the formative years of U.S. Indian policy. Aimed primarily at preventing Indian hostilities on the frontier, this policy operated on the principle of deterrence: the projection of might (whether real or imagined) to cow the Indians into passivity. Conducting council meetings in the presence of military force and addressing the Indians in grandiloquent fashion, agents and officers made it very clear that they spoke not for themselves but for the Great Father in Washington. Among the Indians addressed, there was little reason to question the veracity of this claim. The proceedings adhered to a familiar form, and many Indian societies similarly delegated responsibility for diplomacy to gifted orators while hereditary headmen either sat passively or remained at home. It was entirely understandable, then, that the Indians would believe that they engaged in formal diplomatic talks between sovereigns.

In reality, however, the Indians of Jacksonian America dealt with a congeries of midlevel bureaucrats from the Indian Office and tactical commanders from the U.S. Army, each interested in securing the allegiance of the various tribes of the Old Northwest, but none of them capable of influencing U.S. Indian policy to guarantee reciprocity. Now that the war was over, Indians who had offered military assistance or taken pains to ensure neutrality expected the Great Father to treat them like the loyal "children" they were. Having labored to foster good relations with the tribes they represented and consistently averring that the Great Father always looked after their interests, their agents expected the same. Both parties now found their expectations disappointed. Accustomed to gaining the loyalty of Indians with the carrot-and-stick approach, the agents of the Indian Office discovered that the Jackson administration was keen to wield the stick but parsimonious otherwise.

In the case of the Ho Chunks, Elbert Herring's Indian Office found a way to use the supposed benevolence of the Great Father to its advantage. In exchange for their lands south of the Wisconsin and east of the Mississippi River, the Ho Chunks received—in addition to their annuity and typical compensation package of "civilizing" influences—sixty thousand rations to offset any hardship endured by the migration.[89] Already starving when they signed the treaty, the Ho Chunks earned the empathy of Winfield Scott, who issued a third of these rations on the spot to ease their suffering. In the remaining rations and other treaty incentives, Herring saw an opportunity to adhere to the letter of the treaty—which promised the Ho Chunks the choice of their abode—while violating its spirit. Although only one sixth of the Ho Chunks reported to the Prairie du Chien Agency at this time, Herring directed that Joseph Street receive half of their annuity payment for disbursement there.[90] As a consequence of this decision, Ho Chunks deciding to remain in Wisconsin would receive only a paltry fraction of their share of the annuity. Worse yet, Herring sent all remaining treaty incentives—including the remaining rations—to Prairie du Chien as well.[91] Despite Herring's earlier insistence that "the choice of their future abode in either region is left entirely to their own free will," the Ho Chunks essentially had to choose between westward migration and starvation.[92]

Porter was disgusted with Herring's adopted course of action and openly challenged the fairness of a policy that left the choice of residence to free will but says "that if you go to one place you shall have rations—but if to the other you shall have none."[93] Predicting that this policy would produce starvation, Porter intoned that the ensuing loss of life would weigh on Herring's conscience, not his own. Still, Porter realized what he was up against, and he knew that a terrible alternative existed. Resigning himself to the injustice and inevitability of Ho Chunk removal, Porter sought a single concession from the Indian Office: a prohibition against the use of force. Although his advice had carried little weight to date, Porter submitted that the use of force for removal was unnecessary, that it should not be contemplated, and that any such consideration ought to be kept from the Indians.[94]

Officials in Washington did not share Porter's reservations. On 9 May 1833, Commanding General of the U.S. Army Alexander Macomb ordered Henry Atkinson to enforce the 1 June deadline. Although Atkinson displayed little enthusiasm for the edict, Colonel Henry Dodge compensated for his commander's lack of zeal. Less than a month earlier, Dodge had written directly to the War Department to protest the possibility of the Ho Chunks remaining on their lands through the summer: "This arrangement will not suit the people of the frontier. Nothing but the removal of the Rock River Indians will restore peace to the people of the mineral country."[95] From the mineral country himself, Dodge wasted no time in implementing Macomb's instructions. By mid-July, he had driven the Ho Chunks from their former lands south of the Wisconsin River.[96] In Prairie du Chien, one Ho Chunk chief explained to Joseph Street, "Genl. Dodge has hunted us from Lake to Lake like Deer—we could not hide from him—we wanted to remain where we were."[97]

So too did the Potawatomis, but Billy Caldwell was realistic about their prospects. When John Kinzie inquired about the Potawatomis' willingness to cede their remaining lands on the western shore of Lake Michigan, Caldwell resignedly requested that they be permitted to send a delegation to Iowa to inspect their new home and to make peace with the Sauks and Mesquakies. Aware that the Sauks and Mesquakies might not reciprocate his willingness to make amends, Caldwell also requested an army escort to ensure his party's safety.[98] Not all Potawatomis accepted this fate, however, and several surly chiefs demanded to know why the government summoned them to Chicago in September 1833. Although often critical of his president's Indian policy, treaty commissioner George Porter loyally responded to the Indians with "a forcible Jacksonian discourse" regarding the necessity of separating the Natives from the whites.[99] Conducting diplomacy as part of the Three Fires, the Potawatomis selected Ap-te-ke-zhick, an Ojibwa, as their spokesperson. When the council began in earnest on 16 September, the Indians made explicit their unwillingness to sell any additional land. "If we have to sell *all* our lands and go where you advise us, some great evil might happen to us," Ap-te-ke-zhick explained. Having enjoyed mutually beneficial relations with the French and métis of the region, the Indians did not accept Porter's assertion that they could no longer remain: "Here the Great Spirit allows us to live in peace amongst ourselves, with the white man and all. We are happy here."[100] Porter did not abandon his mission so easily. After browbeating the Potawatomis for over two weeks, Porter finally compelled the Indians to sign a treaty.[101] According to one resident of Chicago, "It should have been conducted upon the principals of truth and justice; but the whole thing was a farce, acted by those in office in our Government."[102] Harangued by Elbert Herring to mind his president more than his conscience, George Porter obeyed. Even as an individual, he was no longer an ally of the Potawatomis.

Despite their treaties, the Potawatomis and Ho Chunks remained reluctant to migrate westward. They had allied with their Great Father to influence their own fate and found their future almost entirely beyond their control. Both tribes, moreover, harbored considerable anxiety regarding their new home. Aware that the Sauks and Mesquakies considered them treacherous for their role in the recent conflict, the Ho Chunks were unenthusiastic about sidling in as neighbors. Worse yet, Black Hawk's defeat had done nothing to stem the Dakotas' war with the Sauks and Mesquakies, and the Ho Chunks' new home lay between the warring tribes. Unimpressed by Joseph Street's buffer plan in 1827, the Ho Chunks had not changed their minds since.[103]

Their reservations were well founded. In late November 1833, a Mesquakie war party attacked three Dakota lodges on the Root River. The initial raid turned into a day-long running engagement in which the Dakotas suffered nine killed.[104] Two of L'Arc's sons—including Enchankeeanazie (Red Pine), who was to have succeeded his father as chief—were among those killed.[105] Both sides protested their innocence to the Americans while simultaneously mobilizing for war in the spring.[106] Adhering to protocol, the Indians promised to stay their hands while they awaited their Great Father's justice, but everyone involved knew better. The Indians continued to trade blows in January and February 1834, and Fort Snelling's commander informed General Macomb, "Among the Indians I regret I perceive a distrust of the promptness and energy of the Americans."[107]

The Ho Chunks shared this lack of faith, and those who had migrated westward fled their new home for the familiar safety of Wisconsin.[108] A Sauk and Mesquakie war party added urgency to the exodus by attacking a party of Ho Chunks and their Menominee companions in late January.[109] Soon afterward, a disgusted Whirling Thunder protested to Lewis Cass, "We are tired of having no home—We are scattered all over the country like wild beasts, and whish to unite in the spring, and build a village and plant corn."[110] Refugee Ho Chunks overpopulated the area between the Mississippi and Wisconsin Rivers, overtaxing the region's resources and compounding the Indians' hardship. Lacking options, many of them returned to their ancient homeland around Lake Winnebago.[111]

Disturbed by the direction of Ho Chunk migration—eastward rather than westward—the government had more pressing problems with which to contend. Intertribal warfare again threatened to consume the frontier, and the government struggled to uphold its obligations to the warring tribes while simultaneously keeping the peace. Under the leadership of their respective "peace parties," the Sauks and Mesquakies appealed to the Americans for unfettered permission to wage war against the Dakotas. Throughout the Black Hawk War, these tribes' leaders had adhered to the government's every direction and, to their minds, demonstrated unflinching loyalty to their Great Father. "All we ask," a Sauk-Mesquakie shaman explained, "is to let us gow to war with our Ennemies." Anticipating the usual response, the religious leader asked his agent to forward this request to "the red Head" in St. Louis, William Clark.[112] The Sauks and Mesquakies misplaced their faith in Clark, their territorial superintendent, who was committed to assimilation and had been appalled by the disorderly conduct of the British Band.[113] Elbert Herring rejected the request as "totally inadmissible," which closed the issue for Clark.[114]

Lacking allies in the Indian Office since Thomas Forsyth's dismissal four years earlier, the Sauks and Mesquakies turned to Henry Atkinson for succor. On 27 March, leaders from both tribes met with the general at his command post in Missouri and told him, "It is your fault you hold us so fast, and the Sioux's know that you will hold us." Keokuk added, "And we hope that the President will release us from the treaty—and let the Sioux's and our nation settle our difficulties in our own way—as we used to do."[115] Formerly an advocate of using the army to maintain peace among the Indians, Atkinson now recognized that the practice created more problems than it solved.[116] Despite his empathy, Atkinson was powerless to grant the Indians' wish.

Sauk and Mesquakie disappointment, however, paled in comparison to the Dakotas' frustration. Speaking to Indian agent Lawrence Taliaferro in June, L'Arc was incredulous that the Americans remained incapable of enforcing the 1830 treaty line that established a boundary between his people and their enemies—and yet more astonished that the United States would treat its Dakota allies no better than these enemies. "I know not what to say my heart is getting *so full* now that I feel as a man that is getting drunk—for I see no signs of redress." Averring that the recent Mesquakie attacks were a direct consequence of Dakota participation in the Black Hawk War, L'Arc implied that the Americans were not upholding their obligations as allies. Unless they began to do so, another speaker warned Taliaferro, the Dakotas would build new alliances that did not include the Long Knives. "Messages have been sent to the *Seven fires*" of every Sioux tribe, Wah-koo-ta advised his agent. If the Americans did not act quickly, "there will be cutting of each other up worse than ever."[117]

Perhaps predictably, the Americans did not act fast enough, and the cutting continued. On 5 November 1834, a Mesquakie war party crossed the Mississippi five or six miles above Prairie du Chien and attacked a Ho Chunk band at daybreak. The band belonged to Waukon Decorah, who had fought with the Americans to avenge the death of his daughter in 1829. The Mesquakies responsible claimed that this assault was a mistake—that they had intended to strike Dakotas or Menominees—but Waukon regarded the attack as revenge for his helping the Americans during the Black Hawk War. In allying with them, Waukon had indeed avenged his daughter's death, but now ten women and children from his family—among them his wife—lay dead.[118] The cost of alliance with the Great Father was considerable and manifest; the dividends, however, were hard to discern.

Always perceptible in some degree, the differences between the American Great Father and his French and British forerunners became stark in the months and years following the Black Hawk War. Under these earlier regimes, military and economic alliance between the Natives and their European patrons had helped to create a world conducive to their mutual benefit. The fur trade, while it altered Indian economies and regional ecology, depended on the preservation of the Indians' way of life and continued ownership of their land. French and British military dependence on the Indians and the presence of other European suitors, moreover, compelled these regimes to treat the Indians fairly and even generously. For sixteen years following the War of 1812, American officials had labored to replicate this milieu. The Indians' dependence on a European trading partner helped offset the awkwardness of the Americans, who deliberately (if imperfectly) imitated the diplomatic forms of their predecessors and achieved a modicum of success in the first decade of their suzerainty over the Old Northwest. This success proved short-lived, however, as white miners flooded the region in the mid-1820s and lay bare the limits of America's loyalty to its Indian allies. Unlike earlier European interlopers, American miners and settlers were not subject to interdependency with the Indians. The only thing they required of the Natives was for them to be gone.

For the most part, the stewards of alliance—Indian agents and some army officers—faithfully defended Indian rights against white encroachment and abuse. Following the Winnebago War of 1827 and Andrew Jackson's ascendancy to the presidency in 1829, however, these men engaged in a quixotic campaign destined only to earn the enmity of frontier political leaders and thereby marginalize their own importance. By the eve of the Black Hawk War, it was evident to most Americans and men like Billy Caldwell that the Natives could not possibly preserve both their lands and their lifestyle any longer. Some Indians clung to the forlorn hope that, if Black Hawk could not restore Indian tribal sovereignty in the region, the Great Father would at least protect them from further assault by frontier whites. It was this hope that compelled most Ho Chunks and Potawatomis to suppress their sympathies and to offer military aid to the Americans, and it was this hope that was dashed by the treaties of 1832 and 1833. Disgusted and sometimes outraged by their government's abandonment of the Indians, the Natives' remaining white friends were powerless to intercede. Some, like Michigan Territory governor George Porter, resigned themselves to complicity. In the end, the United States' allies reached an inescapable conclusion, echoed years later by a member of the Decorah family: "We think the Big Father does not care for us any longer, now that he has all our best land."[119]

# 9

## An Indian War

When Dakota messengers notified Joseph Street of the final destruction of the British Band, the Indian agent asserted that "Your G. F. [Great Father] had no war of *his own* with the Sacs & Foxes—This [was] a war commenced for the sake of the Sioux & Menomines."[1] Although Street took considerable liberty with the truth, the Dakotas did not object. From the very beginning, the Dakotas, together with the Menominees, had considered this *their* war—an Indian war in which the Americans opted to interfere. In fact, every Native group that participated in the conflict did so with the design of realizing their own objectives and serving the interests of their people. In several instances, these designs compelled cooperation with the United States—but always with the goal of accomplishing their own objectives. Broadly defined, these objectives fell into four categories: the opportunity to reap material gain, to exert political leverage, to settle intertribal scores, and to fulfill male gender roles. Paradoxically, fulfillment of the last two objectives convinced many frontier whites of the Indians' savagery even as it restored peace to the region. Taking advantage of the new stability, white settlers surged into the region and demanded the final removal of the "red demons" who had, ironically, helped restore order.

Americans regarded the contributions of the Dakotas, Menominees, Potawatomis, and Ho Chunks as negligible to the outcome of the war. Following Stillman's Run and the disbandment of the first Illinois militia army, Henry Atkinson requested Indian assistance in a moment of desperation, but his tardy invitation to war and decision to place Billy Hamilton in command doomed the Prairie du Chien contingent of Menominees, Dakotas, and Ho Chunks to irrelevance. Receiving their summons a month later yet, the Menominees and Ho Chunks of Green Bay met a similar fate. Although Atkinson was grateful to accept the services of Caldwell's Potawatomis, the general rarely mentioned them in his orders or reports and later admitted, "I found it necessary to urge the Potawatomies to take sides not that I wanted their strength, but, to Know where to find them."[2] Similar considerations led Atkinson to employ Ho Chunk scouts, but he later concluded that "they told me lies—they deceived me when they told me where to find the Sacs."[3] Although Atkinson and Winfield Scott subsequently heaped praise on all of their Indian allies, their campaign conduct warranted only passing mention in the generals' official reports. Some officers remained open-minded or optimistic about the military potential of Indian allies or auxiliaries, but senior officials were circumspect. Alexander Macomb appears to have left no commentary on the topic, while Secretary of War Lewis Cass offered only that, rather than turning to the Indians, Atkinson should have relied on "a considerable force of regulars" from the Eastern Department, regional militia, and "mounted men authorized to be raised by a late act of Congress."[4]

If the War Department damned the military utility of Indians through faint praise, others within the Indian Office were more vocal in their disapproval of Native participation in the war. Indeed, only Samuel Stambaugh seems to have advocated the policy.[5] Most agents disagreed with Atkinson's decision because it ran against the government's long-standing efforts to quell intertribal violence. Writing Stambaugh's replacement in Green Bay, George Porter admitted, "I cannot well see how *you* could have prevented the Menominies from marching, after all that had been done to bring it about:—although my decided opinion would have been against the measure."[6] A champion of "civilization," Prairie du Chien agent Joseph Street similarly disapproved on the grounds that endorsing Indian warfare retarded their transformation into yeoman farmers. From St. Louis, a jaded Thomas Forsyth saw hypocrisy in the government's admonishment to the Indians not to make war on one another—except when such practice was condoned by the army. Forsyth found Atkinson's use of the Dakotas to pursue the "Battle of Bad Axe" survivors particularly loathsome: "was there not a sufficiency of Militia in the State of Illinois to fight and defeat the Black Hawk and party, without employing Indians to butcher the women and Children of the Sauk & Fox Indians[?]"[7] Forsyth was almost certainly the author of an anonymous editorial in the 21 May 1833 *St. Louis Times,* in which "F" railed against Atkinson's role in the massacre and demanded a government inquiry.[8]

Other agents objected to Atkinson's employment of Indians on more pragmatic grounds. Devoid of experience if not opinions, neophyte subagent Thomas Burnett protested that Indian alliances were not worth the trouble: "I have always considered Indians to be the most troublesome and expensive of all allies, at the same time that their services can be least relied upon. The result of this expedition is an additional evidence to support the opinion."[9] John Kinzie's opinion on the matter, conversely, was the product of decades of experience among the Indians as a fur trader. Officially, Kinzie deemed "the measure impolitic and contrary to treaty stipulations and to the views and wishes of Government," but Kinzie rarely held these views and wishes in high regard.[10] More likely, Kinzie objected because warfare disrupted the fur trade and brought economic hardship to both the Indians and his family. Personal motives aside, Kinzie sincerely believed that the Indians were best served by a policy of neutrality—a conviction many Ho Chunks shared after the war.[11]

Unique among American frontiersman, Henry Dodge sought to subvert this neutrality. While Dodge shared the common conviction that Indian societies would have to give way before the press of "civilization," he exhibited none of his contemporaries' paranoia of armed Indians or intertribal warfare. Rather, he distinguished himself by his willingness to harness Indian talents to expedite their removal. Recognizing that Indian warriors possessed skills not found in American troops, Dodge employed Ho Chunk guides for most of the war and approved of Atkinson's decision to encourage Indian participation. Learning that the Green Bay Menominees were to join the fight, Dodge was sure that they "would have good effect should they even reach the country after the battle." Anticipating that the British Band might "retire to the *swamps* & scatter," he opined that the Menominees "would be the best kind of Troops to hunt them up." But if Dodge appreciated Indian military capabilities, his grasp of Indian politics was less sure. Transposing his own sense of racial solidarity to the Indians of the Old Northwest, Dodge mistakenly assumed that allying with the Menominees would "shew the rest of the Indians that their own people could be braught to bear on them."[12] While one historian has suggested the emergence of a pan-Indian identity among the tribes of the Old Northwest at the time of the Black Hawk War, the Sauks and Mesquakies felt no more fraternity toward the Menominees than

Americans reserved for their European rivals.[13] Indeed, to the extent that a pan-Indian identity existed among these tribes, it appears to have achieved its greatest realization in the undiscerning imaginations of men like Dodge.

Outside of Dodge and the fur traders, most frontier civilians were suspicious or even fearful of the "friendly" Indians. William Campbell, a mining official and Jackson crony who observed the Prairie du Chien contingent on its way through Galena, feared that an appeal to Indian aid simply convinced the Indians "that we were not able to fight our own battles with the Sacs & Foxes." "We will have these same Indians in arms against us before the fall of the leaf," he predicted to President Jackson.[14] Although incorrect, Campbell's prognostication was not baseless. Unimpressed by their army allies during the Arikara War, the Sioux had little reason to reappraise the Americans' martial ability after the Black Hawk War. Still, Campbell's prophesy was thirty years premature. During the Sioux War of 1862, Dakota warriors interpreted the army's recruitment of métis militiamen as evidence of military weakness and went to war with their former allies.[15] Campbell's opposition to Indian alliances was not based entirely on the fear that it publicized American military weakness, however. Although singularly unsympathetic toward the Indians, Campbell shared with them a conception of alliance that involved reciprocal loyalty. The Indians, no mere auxiliaries, fought as independent people, and if they made concessions to their Great Father they expected something in return. "I do not believe in laying ourselves under any obligations to Indians," Campbell informed the president, who—to the collective fortune of Campbell's fellow Galenians—held similar convictions.[16]

Although disappointed by their Great Father, America's Indian allies were not the mercenaries, fools, or pawns depicted by some scholars.[17] Conditioned by over a century of alliances with powerful European partners, the Indians of the Old Northwest had learned the necessity of accommodation with the whites. Such unions had delivered the Menominees and Ho Chunks from the brink of extinction and had enabled the western Algonquians to roll back the tide of Iroquois expansion. As the Fox Wars of the eighteenth century and the Winnebago War of the nineteenth attested, Indian groups who rejected a patron-client relationship with a European or American power did so at their peril. Following the War of 1812, the Indians lost the luxury of choosing between a pair of competing suitors for their allegiance. Hence, although the Indians discerned and protested American deviations from the French and British precedent—especially the refusal to provide an acceptable outlet for martial ambition—they generally lacked recourse. Thanks to Henry Atkinson's willingness to field Indian allies, the Black Hawk War offered the Indians an opportunity to at once resurrect an older, more favorable conception of alliance and to realize their ambitions.

Certainly the least important of these ambitions was the acquisition of material wealth. The Potawatomis, for instance, derived almost no material benefit from the war whatsoever. Aside from taking ownership of the army's stockade at Lake Koshkonong and receiving remuneration for horses stolen during the war, they received only "a small pittance of flour & pork to prevent them from suffering"—and that was sometimes drawn from the "damaged" portion of the army's stocks.[18] Certainly some tribes—notably the Menominees and Ho Chunks—parlayed their service into material advantage, but no evidence suggests that their participation was predicated on a quest for profit. Instead, these Indians merely expected the Americans to uphold the obligations of a wealthy partner in alliance according to the practices of the French and British. Clearly, the Menominees and Dakotas did not join the Americans *because* Atkinson promised them provisions and arms, but the withholding of such presents would have communicated to the Indians a miserliness unbecoming a Great Father.[19] If rifles and ammunition were inducement enough to draw individual warriors into the government's service, they did little to win the endorsement of the broader communities whence these warriors came. Accordingly, many of the provisions issued to the Indians were of a distinctly nonmilitary character. In addition to six hundred pounds of lead and two hundred fifty pounds of powder, George Boyd issued the Green Bay Menominees three hundred needles, fifty yards of colored muslin, twenty yards of blue ribbon, two teakettles, and sundry other goods.[20] The domestic nature of these items indicated that the agent was not simply buying warriors but cementing a pact with the Menominee people collectively. In so doing, George Boyd acknowledged the voice of Menominee women in the decision for war and adhered to the Indians' expectations of alliance. Perhaps more so than his contemporaries, Samuel Stambaugh understood these expectations and urged the government to uphold them. According to Stambaugh, "Justice as well as sound policy will recommend that the Inds who marched at the call of the Govt, should be paid and *well paid* for every day they were in service. In future times the salutary effects of such a course will be experienced."[21] George Porter endorsed Stambaugh's recommendation, and the Menominees received land bounty warrants (which they subsequently sold) for their service.[22]

Stambaugh was less convinced of the propriety of rewarding the

Ho Chunks. Their motivation to capture Black Hawk and Wabo-kieshiek, he was sure, was sheerly financial; "Their *good feeling* to-wards our Govrt would never prompt them to do so."[23] Indeed, the Ho Chunks were perhaps the most opportunistic of the Americans' Indian allies, and they unashamedly—but not always successfully—attempted to parlay their service into material gain. Although White Crow's band earned the handsome sum of $2,000 for "rescu-ing" the Hall sisters, the Prairie la Crosse Ho Chunks were disap-pointed in their reward for capturing the fugitive leaders of the British Band.[24] Promised forty good horses and $100, Black Hawk's and Wabokieshiek's captors complained that they received only twenty mounts "so poor that we can't get them along."[25] After the war, the Ho Chunks attempted to obtain bounty land on account of their service (like the Menominees), but here, too, they were dis-appointed because no muster rolls existed to verify their claims.[26] Fundamentally, however, the Ho Chunks had not participated in the war for profit. Indeed, the conflict was ruinous to their fragile economy, and the meager rewards the Ho Chunks milked from the Americans only began to offset the damage. Opportunists rather than mercenaries, the Ho Chunks simply attempted to make the best of a bad situation.

The principal motivation of the Ho Chunks and Potawatomis alike was not to accrue wealth but to retain that which they already had: their remaining lands and continued existence as independent peoples. Since the early 1820s, members of both tribes had seen their sovereignty erode under a steady tide of white immigration. The Winnebago War of 1827 convinced most Indians in the region that the Americans were too numerous and powerful to contest by force of arms, but some retained the hope that a pantribal alliance could punish white transgressions and establish a more favorable balance of power. To these Indians, Black Hawk seemed to offer the promise of a better future. Those more familiar with the extent of American power, however, sensed that their situation was already tenuous and that Black Hawk's banner, while alluring, could only lead to ruin.

Ultimately, most Potawatomis and Ho Chunks followed an uneasy policy of neutrality, which disaffected elements of both tribes violated—usually discreetly but sometimes with spectacular violence. At Indian Creek, Kellogg's Grove, Blue Mounds, and elsewhere, Potawatomis and Ho Chunks exacted their revenge for a catalog of abuses that stretched back over a decade. More calculating than their passionate warriors, leaders from both tribes realized that such sanguinary outbursts, although conducted by individuals, implicated their entire tribes. Already the Ho Chunks' and Potawatomis' hold on northern Illinois was shaky, and these incidents provided the Americans ample justification to promptly and permanently pry the Indians from their lands.

The Potawatomis responded first and most decisively to this challenge. By virtue of history, geography, and kinship, the Potawatomis were better postured to understand the magnitude of the problem confronting them—and to respond to it. Under the better days of the French regime, the Potawatomis had parlayed their occupancy of Green Bay into a privileged position within the French-Algonquian alliance. Perhaps more readily than other tribes, the Potawatomis adapted their conceptions of leadership to meet French expectations, thereby giving rise to the "alliance chief." Although authority in Potawatomi society remained decentralized and noncoercive, the emergence of alliance, or "principal," chiefs permitted the formulation and (to a lesser extent) enforcement of multiband or even tribal policies that were previously infeasible.[27]

Selected jointly by the Indians and their European allies, the alliance chiefs were men capable of fulfilling the expectations of both groups. By the early nineteenth century, such men were most commonly found among clever or educated métis who opportunistically embraced the role of middle-man between the tribes and the government.[28]

In 1832 Chicago, Billy Caldwell was this man. A métis related to the Potawatomis only by marriage, Caldwell wielded unusual influence among both his adopted people and the government. Prevalent interpretations of such middlemen variously consider them "imposters" or "masters at accommodation."[29] The most ardent critic of intercultural brokers in general, and Billy Caldwell in particular, has been James Clifton, who has described them as "men who pursued their own ambitions by accepting the role of an alien-sponsored manager of tribal society."[30] Particularly offensive to Clifton was the attachment of the title "chief" to men who considered themselves white-skinned entrepreneurs. Clifton acknowledged that Caldwell eventually came to identify with the Potawatomis and sought to further their best interests, but Clifton saw this shift beginning with the Chicago Treaty of 1833. Caldwell's conduct during the Black Hawk War, however, suggests that his "conversion" predated this conflict.[31]

Indeed, Caldwell seems to have been a driving force behind the Potawatomi policy of neutrality and, later, alliance. Recognizing that the Potawatomis' days in Illinois were numbered, Caldwell aimed not to avert removal altogether, but rather to ensure that the government compensated the Indians for their lands. He knew that the Potawatomis' collaboration with Black Hawk would furnish the government with a pretext for seizing Potawatomi lands as war reparations, and he moved to preempt the possibility. In council at

Chicago and in his rides among remote villages, Caldwell—often assisted by Alexander Robinson and Shaubena—cobbled together a multiband policy of neutrality. Through the influence of village chiefs, such as Wabaunsee and Big Foot, the Potawatomis were able to subdue the martial aspirations of most of their young men, many of whom desired to join Black Hawk. With the help of their assigned agents, the Potawatomis publicly proclaimed their innocence and evacuated their villages from the campaign trail to avoid the wrath of the militia and to distance the tribe, physically and figuratively, from the hostile Indians.

These measures proved modestly successful through 19 May, but the "Indian Creek Massacre" represented a massive failure in Potawatomi policy. Realizing that the entire tribe would be held accountable for the actions of a single, disaffected band, the Potawatomis had to make a more convincing demonstration of their distance from the British Band. They consequently offered a traditional pledge of allegiance, military service, to an unlikely ally, the United States. Whereas in the past, however, the Potawatomis embraced a French or British Great Father for profit and security, they now affiliated themselves with the army of Andrew Jackson simply to hold on to what they had left.

Facing a nearly identical problem, the Ho Chunks ultimately arrived at the same solution, albeit by a more convoluted path. Like the Potawatomis', the formulation of Ho Chunk policy during the war was, at least in part, the product of history, geography, and kinship. Yet while these factors facilitated a relatively unified response among the Potawatomis, they virtually assured that the Ho Chunks would pursue divided and sometimes contradictory courses. Occupying the interior of Wisconsin throughout their known history, the Ho Chunks never enjoyed the privileged status of other Great Lakes tribes in the Western fur trade. Considered "warlike" by the Europeans, with whom the Ho Chunks were reluctant to intermarry, these Indians were never fully incorporated by the French, British, or American regimes. In a region of peoples to whom centralized, coercive leadership was anathema, the Ho Chunks were once notable for their recognition of a paramount, tribal chief. But as Ho Chunk bands dispersed along the Fox, Wisconsin, and Rock River Valleys during the relative security of the eighteenth century, political authority went with them. Despite nominal recognition of a principal, tribal chief, by the time of the Black Hawk War decisions for war or peace were the prerogative of village leaders. The geographic dispersion of bands also ensured that the Ho Chunks entertained no single opinion of the Americans. In the relative isolation of Wisconsin, the Ho Chunks encountered few Americans outside of Prairie du Chien and the Portage. But those who settled in northwestern Illinois did not know such bliss. Abused and dispossessed by white miners, these Ho Chunks withdrew from their Great Father, whose inability to control his white children or uphold his promises called into question his presumption of greatness.

Estranged from their agents and lacking the counsel of men like Billy Caldwell, the northern Illinois Ho Chunks brooded until Black Hawk's crossing of the Mississippi seemed to offer an opportunity for revenge in the spring of 1832. Like the Sauks and Mesquakies, however, the Ho Chunks may have been startled by the alacrity and intensity of the Illinoisans' response. Although his young men yearned to join Black Hawk, White Crow foreswore open alliance until he could tell whether Black Hawk was another Tecumseh or merely another Red Bird, who died in prison following the failure of his 1827 Winnebago War. By the time White Crow concluded the latter, overwhelming evidence indicted the chief and his followers of aiding the enemy and even slaying Americans. While the Potawatomis offered military services to distance themselves from renegade bands, White Crow's Ho Chunks now rendered military aid in the hopes of expunging their own conduct. Incredibly, White Crow's gambit succeeded, and his visible but modest contributions to the American effort proved sufficient to overshadow his earlier duplicity.

In truth, the contributions of both tribes were almost entirely symbolic. Unlike the Menominees and Dakotas, no evidence suggests that the Potawatomis and Rock River Ho Chunks engaged in the songs, dances, or other preparations indicative of traditional warfare. Rather than painting themselves for war, moreover, the Potawatomis and Ho Chunks merely donned white headbands to avoid falling prey to indiscriminant militiamen. Perhaps the most telling indicator of the proscribed nature of these tribes' involvement was their palpable reluctance to engage the Sauks and Mesquakies in combat. Although many young men in both tribes desired the opportunity to make names for themselves in war, they wished to do so beside, rather than against, Black Hawk. From both forces, only White Crow's son actually exchanged blows with the British Band. Willing to go to war with the Americans to realize their political objectives, the Rock River Ho Chunks and Potawatomis were less inclined to make war on fellow Indians with whom they sympathized.[32]

Ultimately, the alliance policies of the Rock River Ho Chunks and Potawatomis served each tribe admirably. As Billy Caldwell recognized and Winfield Scott's deployment orders reveal, removal of all Indians from Illinois was inevitable by 1832, but the Indians retained the ability to influence the terms of their migration. Black

Hawk's crossing of the Mississippi and ensuing rumors of Ho Chunk and Potawatomi collaboration with the enemy threatened to deprive the Indians of this prerogative, however. As evidence mounted that elements of both tribes were in league with Black Hawk, it appeared that all Ho Chunks and Potawatomis were destined to forfeit their land without compensation—the pitiful fate of "hostile" Indians. Timely and visible gestures of faithfulness permitted both tribes to avoid this fate without requiring a betrayal of their loyalties. Their postwar treaties may have left much to be desired, but they represented the best conceivable denouement to an impossible situation.

The Green Bay Menominees also parlayed their wartime contributions into political leverage, but their situation differed markedly from those of the Potawatomis and Ho Chunks. A small and vulnerable people, the Menominees grasped the benefits of close alliance with European powers during the Great Dispersal of the mid-seventeenth century. Because their survival and prosperity depended on it, the Menominees became masters of alliance politics, achieving their own ends while ostensibly accommodating the expectations of the prevailing regime. Accordingly, the French and British regarded the Menominees as the most steadfast and loyal of all Native peoples—a perception shared by the Americans following their occupation of Green Bay in 1816. Ensconced in Wisconsin's north woods, the Menominees were perhaps less disrupted by the arrival of the Americans than any other tribe in the Old Northwest. Climate and latitude helped isolate the Menominees from the doleful influences of white miners and settlers, and Indians and métis continued to dominate Green Bay's fur trade economy into the 1830s. Here, perhaps more than anywhere else in the years after the War of 1812, the Menominees and the United States successfully created an alliance based on trade, security, and reciprocity.

Menominee leaders thus believed that the United States was in no position to make demands after the Black Hawk War. The Green Bay Menominees had wanted to participate in the war from the very beginning, it was true, but they had also gone out of their way to accommodate the wishes of their Great Father—staying their hand until it was too late to play a meaningful role. Hence, the Menominees were not in a compromising mood when George Porter submitted for their approval a treaty to resolve a dispute with the New York Indians who occupied Menominee lands. For nearly a decade, the Menominees had labored to escape from the fraudulent land sales of 1821 and 1822, believing that they had reached favorable resolution in the so-called Stambaugh Treaty of 1831. The U.S. Senate modified this treaty before ratification, however, and Porter assumed that the government's liberal handling of the Menominees during the recent conflict with Black Hawk would ensure their acquiescence. Grizzly Bear promptly disabused the governor of this notion. The chief confirmed his people's commitment to their American allies but proclaimed that they would do nothing for the New York Indians, whom the Menominees regarded as trespassers.[33] To ward off any remonstrance from the governor, Grizzly Bear reminded Porter of the Menominees' service and sacrifices in the recent conflict: "We have done so much to please you under the hope that it will be satisfactory to our Great Father and the Senate."[34] The chief's statement was largely disingenuous, as Porter may well have recognized. Fundamentally, self-interest motivated the Menominees, but they were wise enough to the ways of alliance politics to grasp diplomatic leverage afforded by their participation. Ultimately, the Menominees forced a favorable compromise that the New York Indians accepted only grudgingly.[35]

Yet Menominee participation in the Black Hawk War had far less to do with the New York Indians than with the Sauks and Mesquakies. If there is a single, overriding explanation for Menominee campaign participation, it is that *this was their war.* Long before the United States existed, the Menominees harbored deep animosity for the Sauks and Mesquakies as separate tribes. In accordance with a code of justice common among North American Indians, the Sauks, Mesquakies, and Menominees had visited violence upon one another for over a hundred years, each trying to avenge the most recent wrong, none agreeing as to when the balance sheet of blood was correctly adjusted.[36]

Historian David Beck has recently acknowledged that "Menominee involvement in the war was not so much related to the Americans as to a long-standing dispute with the Mesquakies, whom they identified with the Sac and Fox"; but he understates the extent of Menominee animosity, specifically toward the Sauks.[37] According to Alanson Skinner, "the word 'enemy' at once connotes 'Sauk' to the mind of the Wild Rice People."[38] Oral traditions that postdate the Black Hawk War seem to support this contention. One fable relates the finding of a Sauk girl by the Menominee warriors during the Black Hawk War.

"Who are you?" they asked.

The girl responded, "I am Black Hawk's daughter."

"Where is he?"

"He fled because he was hungry."

At this the Menominee warriors broke into laughter and sang this derisive song: "Oh Black Hawk, why did you not await us? We would have fed you! With our bows and arrows, we would have fed you."[39]

The Menominees also believed they had recovered Black Hawk's breechcloth and composed a sarcastic song to commemorate the event, calling the Sauk war captain a cowardly dog for failing to come back for it.[40] By their ceremonial conduct during the campaign and their subsequent recording of the war's events in oral legend, the Menominees clearly demonstrated that this was no mere mercenary endeavor. From its outset through its conclusion— and in Menominee collective memory—the Black Hawk War was a Menominee affair.

The primary motivations for the Dakotas and Wisconsin River Ho Chunks were much the same. Sauk and Mesquakie migration during the seventeenth century placed them in economic competition with these Indians at a time when the European fur trade was already taxing the Upper Mississippi beyond its sustainable limits. During the 1820s, by which time the Indians had exhausted much of the region's peltry, this competition reached a sanguinary head in the Des Moines River Valley. The contest for furs resurrected a latent, historical animosity between the Mesquakies and the Dakotas, which expanded to involve the Sauks as well as western bands of Ho Chunks and Menominees. American efforts to broker a peace were unsuccessful, and the Black Hawk War was in large measure the most spectacular failure of many. Atkinson left Jefferson Barracks in April 1832 not to chastise Black Hawk but to prevent another episode in this western war. The debacle at Stillman's Run changed the general's mission and thereby presented an opportunity to the Dakotas and western Ho Chunks. Accepting Atkinson's permission to join the war while rejecting the man he sent to lead them, both Indian groups realized the objectives that, ironically, Atkinson had meant to deprive them.

Although not always the most culturally sensitive observer, Samuel Stambaugh understood better than most the consequences of denying the Indians the right to wage their own wars. "An Indian knows of no other way to acquire *fame* but by his feats in War," he explained. Further, if the government persisted in denying an Indian warrior this opportunity, "he would be unable to acquire any, except by *fighting on the side of the enemy against the U States.*"[41] A generation of warriors had availed themselves of such an opportunity during the War of 1812, but opportunities for martial glory diminished significantly as the Great Father extended his control over the Old Northwest and forbade intertribal warfare altogether (albeit unsuccessfully). Hence, an anxious generation of Indian warriors saw in the Black Hawk War a chance to realize their ambitions—a powerful motive in itself. Traditional foes of the Sauks and Mesquakies, the Dakotas, Menominees, and western Ho Chunks had no qualms about striking Black Hawk's followers, whom the warriors regarded as hated enemies rather than fellow Indians.

In the end, the Black Hawk War provided few opportunities for Indians to distinguish themselves in battle, but they contented themselves with those available. Although the aptly named Big Soldier, a venerated Menominee war leader, boasted that the Black Hawk War was "child's play," he acknowledged its importance in giving his young warriors vital experience.[42] He might not have realized it at the time, but opportunities for martial glory were fleeting, and his "child's play" represented a defining moment for a generation of Indian warriors in the *pays d'en haut*. While Dakotas and removed Potawatomis continued to hone their skills and reputations against their trans-Mississippi enemies, the Native populations of Wisconsin and Illinois had helped to expunge their domain of foes and, by extension, occasions for war. Years later, Menominee and Ho Chunk warriors journeyed far in search of enemies, again donning their red and black paint, this time to fight renegade Long Knives wearing gray.[43] The Civil War notwithstanding, opportunities for martial glory were rare following the Black Hawk War, which signaled the end of an era in the Old Northwest. Once mighty warriors and vital components of a powerful Franco-Indian alliance, many Ho Chunks and Potawatomis now submitted to removal to Iowa and economic dependence on annuity payments. While their loyalty garnered respect and gratitude from Indian agents and some army officers, it did little to placate the fears of white settlers and politicians. Citing "the many outrages these hell-hounds committed on our frontier settlements" during the conflict, Black Hawk War veteran John Wakefield saw no room for Indians in postwar Illinois.[44] By bearing arms against the British Band, the Indians had confirmed their "savagery" in the eyes of some whites, demonstrating that they were a potential threat, uncomfortably close to white settlements and possessing valuable land. Hence, although they were able to reap some small advantage from their contributions, the Ho Chunks and Potawatomis had also helped men like John Reynolds and Henry Dodge realize their visions of the future.

Just as the termination of the Winnebago War in 1827 had opened the lead country to a deluge of miners, Black Hawk's defeat signaled that the Americans had finally subdued the Old Northwest in its entirety. During that earlier conflict, the territorial governor had traversed the region's waterways in bark canoes that were flying the stars and stripes but were manned by French *engagés*, who wore the red sashes of *Canadiens* and sang in their native tongue.[45] Now, steamboats bearing Yankee émigrés in almost inconceivable numbers drowned out the lusty Frenchmen's voices. In 1830, the non-Indian populations of Illinois and the Wisconsin part of Michigan Territory were 157,445 and 3,635, respectively. Ten years later, Illinois had almost half a million citizens, while the population of

Wisconsin increased nearly tenfold—a demographic feat replicated in the ensuing decade. Made a state in 1848, Wisconsin boasted 305,391 citizens two years later.[46] Like a glacier, the onrush of white settlers dramatically altered the landscape over which it passed— pushing communities out of its way in places and overwhelming them in others. Formerly cosmopolitan outposts in the wilderness, Green Bay, Prairie du Chien, and Chicago lost their earlier character as English subsumed the French-Ojibwa lingua franca, and their métis residents migrated westward or "slipped into impoverished anonymity."[47] Until 1838, Indian villages still dotted the prairies around Milwaukee, but they soon moved north or westward, leaving little to remind the Americans of the people they had supplanted.[48] After two centuries of tumultuous but remarkable existence, the *pays d'en haut* had ceased to exist.

# EPILOGUE

Describing the advent of white miners in the lead country years earlier, the Indians likened the Americans to "a drop of Racoons Grease falling on a new Blanket," which "at first is scarcely perceptible, but in time covers almost the whole Blanket."[1] Yet this observation did not prepare the Indians for the surge of whites that enveloped their homes after the Black Hawk War. It began before the ink had dried on their cession treaties of 1832 and 1833. At Rock Island, anxious speculators gathered to await the outcome of General Winfield Scott's negotiations with the Ho Chunks in September 1832. According to one witness, "Thousands of adventurers lined the eastern shore of the Mississippi, ready to seize upon the possession and pre-emption rights in the new territory the moment they became perfect."[2] Similarly, settlers and speculators occupied the proposed Potawatomi cession of 1833 before the U.S. Senate ratified the treaty, eliciting complaints from the Indians but no response from the government—other than to amend the treaty to the benefit of Missouri and the disadvantage of the Potawatomis.[3] Unabated, the tide of white immigration convinced some—but not all—Indians that it was time to accept removal.

Led by Billy Caldwell, many Potawatomis of Illinois and southern Wisconsin prepared to leave their homeland in the autumn of

1835. Before departing, they conducted a powwow, which Judge John D. Caton observed: "They appreciated that it was the last on their native soil—that it was a sort of funeral ceremony of old associations and memories, and nothing was omitted to lend to it all the grandeur and solemnity possible. Truly, I thought it an impressive scene, of which it is quite impossible to give an adequate idea by words alone."[4]

Over the next year, nearly sixteen hundred Potawatomis settled in the Platte Country in what is today northwest Missouri. Hoping to annex this area in 1837, Missourians reacted adversely to the Potawatomi settlement. Removal brought no respite for the Indians, who contended with white squatters almost immediately upon arriving in their new homes. On 19 June 1836, the Potawatomis exchanged shots with a band of horse thieves known as the Heatherly Gang, killing two of the Missourians.[5]

This episode drew the U.S. Army into the business of removing its former allies from the Old Northwest. Like its earlier efforts to maintain peace between the Indians and the white settlers, the army's role in Indian removal was ambiguous, trying, and destined to frustrate the officers charged with its execution. Because the Platte Country was not yet part of Missouri, the army moved promptly to defend the Indians from what it deemed illegal encroachments—even after Missouri governor Daniel Durkin mobilized his state's militia to drive the Potawatomis from the Platte. Compelled to use other channels, Missouri politicians pressured the federal government to remove the Potawatomis again, this time to the Osage River in Iowa. Knowing that the Potawatomis would not go willingly, the government ordered Henry Atkinson to effect its wishes in June 1836. Atkinson, a stickler for just treatment of the Indians and a personal acquaintance of Billy Caldwell, did not make things easy for his government. Learning that the Potawatomis had yet to receive many of the provisions promised by the 1833 treaty, Atkinson effectively refused to move the Indians until the government upheld its obligations.[6] Atkinson's superior, Edmund Gaines, added to the government's inconvenience by issuing provisions to the relocating Potawatomis at government expense and without authorization—a measure that earned censure from the secretary of war. Unrepentant, Gaines spent additional government money on steamboats to transport the aged and infirm to their new homes.[7]

Near the end of their careers and politically isolated, Generals Gaines and Atkinson may have taken sanctimonious satisfaction in compelling the government to afford the Indians justice and humanity. Unfortunately, later tasks were less agreeable to these and other officers charged with removing by force Indians who refused to relinquish their former lands. Poor fortune continued to befall the Ho Chunks, who lost nearly one quarter of their number to smallpox in 1834. According to Pierre Paquette's son, Moses, "the Indians had never heard of its like before. The medicine men soon abandoned their futile efforts to stay the ravages of the pest, and the survivors simply fled before it like a herd of stricken deer, leaving their dead and dying behind them, unburied."[8] West of the Mississippi, Sauks and Mesquakies attacked those survivors who resettled in accordance with the Great Father's wishes, while east of the Mississippi timber interests conspired to deprive the Ho Chunks of their remaining Wisconsin lands.[9] In 1837, the Ho Chunks dispatched a twenty-man delegation to Washington to seek redress. Led by Carymaunee, the mission included Waukon Decorah, One-Eyed Decorah, Waukaunkaw, and others who had aided the Americans during the Black Hawk War. But their recent fidelity meant little to the Americans, who coerced the delegates into ceding their remaining lands east of the Mississippi.[10] According to Henry Merrell, an early Wisconsin state senator, "the poor Red Men were deceived and out-witted by those who ought to have been their wards and protectors."[11] Not surprisingly, many Ho Chunks proved unwilling to abide by the treaty, and in February 1840 the government once more called on Henry Atkinson to chastise Indians who had encamped on the wrong side of the Mississippi.

Henry Dodge, at that point governor of Wisconsin Territory and a driving force behind the removal of Indians from his domain, advised Atkinson that most of the Ho Chunks would relocate peaceably, but that those residing around the Portage would require encouragement.[12] Atkinson discovered this to be true when he convened a council with the Portage Ho Chunks on 1 May 1840.[13] Reluctantly, Atkinson threatened to withhold rations and annuity payments if they refused to relocate and finally arrested two of the most recalcitrant chiefs, Yellow Thunder and Little Soldier. Perhaps sensitized by his part in this distasteful duty, Atkinson reacted immediately when he learned that the War Department intended to renege on its promise to station troops between the Ho Chunks and their enemies in Iowa. He had personally pledged to "establish a garrison in the neutral ground," he advised Secretary of War Joel Poinsett, "a promise I feel bound in honor, as an officer of the army, to faithfully preserve."[14] Poinsett deferred to Atkinson, but it remained necessary to escort the reluctant Ho Chunks from their homes with military force.

From 26 May to 3 June 1840, elements of the Fifth and Eighth Regiments of U.S. Infantry ushered the Ho Chunks from the Portage to their new land on the Turkey River in Iowa.[15] While transporting the Indians to Prairie du Chien, one removal detail came across three wigwams at the head of the Kickapoo River. Captain Edwin V. Sumner, a veteran of the Black Hawk War who later commanded a corps in the Army of the Potomac, enjoined the occupants to break camp and join the procession. According to Sumner's interpreter, three elderly Ho Chunk women responded by "throwing themselves on their knees, crying and beseeching Captain Sumner to kill them; that they were old, and would rather die, and be buried with their fathers mothers and children, than be taken away; and that they were ready to receive their death blows."[16] Moved, Sumner not only permitted them to remain, but he also released three young Ho Chunk warriors to stay with the women to hunt for them.[17]

A little further on, the detail encountered another Ho Chunk camp. Captain Sumner again attempted to perform his duty and ordered them to break camp and accompany the removal detail. They loaded "their little property" into a wagon but then began to walk south. When Sumner enquired where they were going, the Ho Chunks replied that "they were going to bid good bye to their fathers, mothers, and children." Uncertain that the Indians would return, Sumner and his interpreter followed at a distance. "We found them on their knees, kissing the ground, and crying very loud, where they relations were buried," the interpreter recalled. "This touched the Captain's feelings, and he exclaimed 'Good God! What harm could these poor Indians do among the rocks!'"[18]

As it turned out, they did precious little harm among the rocks, in the swamps, or along other backwaters of the Old Northwest, where many Ho Chunks and Potawatomis remained in spite of government efforts to remove them. Although perhaps fewer than four hundred Ho Chunks remained in Wisconsin by 1848, their numbers recovered thereafter as kinsmen quit the reservation to return home, and the Homestead Act allowed them to reclaim a meager portion of their former land base.[19] Sharing the Ho Chunk assessment of reservation life, fewer than half of the Potawatomis ever moved west of the Mississippi, and many of these likewise returned.[20] Some Potawatomis avoided removal by adopting the trappings of Anglo-American society and entrusting their political leadership to métis brokers, making them less conspicuous to their white neighbors, while others moved north to live with their Three Fires allies in northern Michigan and Canada.[21] Until 1862, vagabond bands of "strolling Potawatomis" remained in southern Wisconsin, but the Dakota uprising of that fall excited a regional panic and exhausted white tolerance of their perambulations. The strolling Potawatomis migrated northward and found refuge with the Menominees, who, owing to their remote station and relatively friendly relations with the white residents of northern Wisconsin, had narrowly averted removal in the 1850s.[22] In nearby Minnesota, the Dakotas enjoyed no such circumstances. Abused by settlers, cheated by traders, and manipulated by the federal government, the Dakotas lashed out in a paroxysm of violence in August 1862. To their collective misfortune, they finally received convincing evidence of American martial prowess only a month later at the decisive Battle of Wood Lake. Together with the bulk of the Dakota people, the United States' war against the Sioux migrated to the Great Plains in the years to come, but the American conquest of the Upper Mississippi was complete.[23]

Following the Dakota War, relative tranquility returned to the Native communities of the Old Northwest. Despite modern, misguided efforts to assimilate them into mainstream society, the Indians of the former *pays d'en haut* have retained their identities and rebuilt their communities. As of 2000, nearly half a million people of Indian descent reside in the states surrounding the western Great Lakes.[24] Borne by traditional values through decades of wrenching change, many continue to venerate the warrior as a paragon of virtue. In the twentieth century, the American Indian's proclivity for military service is well documented and celebrated; in the twenty-first century, Indian men continue to join the U.S. armed forces at twice the rate of the general population.[25] Yet while historical precedent encouraged Grizzly Bear, Wabasha, White Crow, and Wabaunsee to ally with their Great Father, their descendants join his ranks *in spite* of their own historical memory. And although many American Indians proclaim a profound sense of patriotism, it remains a peculiar brand of the sentiment that combines love of country with abiding resentment of its government and admiration of the soldier with uneasiness toward the army in which he serves. Unlike the Indian allies of the Black Hawk War, today's Indian warriors must selectively draw upon a problematic past, but—like their forbears—they continue to serve the United States foremost as a means of serving their own people.[26]

# NOTES

### INTRODUCTION

1. John Dean, "Wisconsin—Early History," George A. Hyer News-clippings, 1820–1824, 1830–1860, Wis Mss AX, Wisconsin Historical Society, Madison, no. 5, 12; Perry A. Armstrong, *The Sauks and the Black Hawk War, with Biographical Sketches, etc.* (Springfield, Ill.: H. W. Rokker, Printer, 1887), 473; Cecil Eby, *"That Disgraceful Affair," the Black Hawk War* (New York: W. W. Norton & Co., 1973), 253; E. Duis, *The Good Old Times in McLean County, Illinois, Containing Two Hundred and Sixty-one Sketches of Old Settlers: A Complete Historical Sketch of the Black Hawk War, and Descriptions of All Matters of Interest Relating to McLean County* (Bloomington, Ill.: Leader Publishing and Printing House, 1874), 117–118.

2. Philip St. George Cooke, *Scenes and Adventures in the Army: Or, Romance of Military Life* (Philadelphia: Lindsay & Blakiston, 1857), 188.

3. John A. Wakefield, *Wakefield's History of the Black Hawk War,* ed. Frank E. Stevens (1834; reprint, Chicago: Caxton Club, 1904), 133.

4. William H. Perrin, ed., *History of Crawford and Clark Counties, Illinois* (Chicago: O. L. Baskin & Co., 1883), 232.

5. Council between Henry Atkinson and the Winnebago and Menominee Indians, 6 August 1832, in *The Black Hawk War, 1831–1832,* ed. Ellen M. Whitney, vol. 37, Collections of the Illinois State

Historical Library (Springfield: Illinois State Historical Library, 1975), 950; Cooke, *Scenes and Adventures in the Army*, 188.

6. Kerry A. Trask, *Black Hawk: The Battle for the Heart of America* (New York: Henry Holt, 2006), 280; Felix Keesing, *The Menomini Indians of Wisconsin: A Study of Three Centuries of Cultural Contact and Change* (Philadelphia: American Philosophical Society, 1939), ix; Armstrong, *The Sauks and the Black Hawk War*, 475, 481. Richard White and Thomas Dunlay have refuted similar characterizations of Plains Indian tribes who did not resist or ostensibly aided American expansion into their domains. Richard White, "The Winning of the West: The Expansion of the Western Sioux in the Eighteenth and Nineteenth Centuries," *Journal of American History* 65, no. 2 (September 1978): 320, 342; Thomas W. Dunlay, *Wolves for the Blue Soldiers: Indian Scouts and Auxiliaries with the United States Army, 1860–90* (Lincoln: University of Nebraska Press, 1982).

7. Eby, *"That Disgraceful Affair,"* 201; Patrick J. Jung, *The Black Hawk War of 1832* (Norman: University of Oklahoma Press, 2007), 5.

8. W. J. Eccles, "The Fur Trade and Eighteenth-Century Imperialism," *William and Mary Quarterly* 40, no. 3 (July 1983): 356.

9. Robert E. Bieder, *Native American Communities in Wisconsin, 1600–1960: A Study of Tradition and Change* (Madison: University of Wisconsin Press, 1995), 80–81.

10. For a broad assessment of the implications of Manifest Destiny for native peoples in the United States, see Jeffrey Ostler, *The Plains Sioux and U.S. Colonialism from Lewis and Clark to Wounded Knee*, Studies in North American Indian History series (Cambridge: Cambridge University Press, 2004), 38–39.

11. With some reservations, I have elected to use "Ojibwa" instead of "Anishinaabe" to avoid usage problems. The use of "Sioux" is retained for reference to the broader linguistic and cultural group to which the Dakotas belonged.

12. Quoted in Joseph J. Ellis, "The Farewell: Washington's Wisdom at the End," in *George Washington Reconsidered*, ed. Don

Higginbotham (Charlottesville: University Press of Virginia, 2001), 237.

### 1. ROOTS OF CONFLICT

1. Alanson Skinner, *Folklore of the Menomini Indians,* vol. 13, part 3, Anthropological Papers of the American Museum of Natural History (New York: American Museum of Natural History, 1915), 434.

2. Charles J. Kappler, ed., *Indian Affairs: Laws and Treaties,* vol. 2 (Treaties) (Washington, D.C.: U.S. Government Printing Office, 1904), 74-77.

3. David R. M. Beck, *Siege and Survival: History of the Menominee Indians, 1634–1856* (Lincoln: University of Nebraska Press, 2002), 1; Patricia K. Ourada, *The Menominee Indians: A History* (Norman: University of Oklahoma Press, 1979), 4.

4. Beck, *Siege and Survival,* 1.

5. Reuben G. Thwaites, Winnebago Notes, US Mss 7E Folder 3, Wisconsin Historical Society, Madison, 1; Nancy O. Lurie, *Wisconsin Indians,* rev. and expanded ed. (Madison: Wisconsin Historical Society Press, 2002), xii; Nancy O. Lurie, "Winnebago," in *Northeast,* ed. Bruce G. Trigger, vol. 15, Handbook of North American Indians (Washington, D.C.: Smithsonian Institution, 1978), 690, 706.

6. Paul Radin, *The Winnebago Tribe* (Lincoln: University of Nebraska Press, 1970), 18.

7. Ibid., 73.

8. Bacqueville de la Potherie, "History of the Savage Peoples Who Are Allies of New France," in *The Indian Tribes of the Upper Mississippi Valley and Region of the Great Lakes,* ed. Emma Helen Blair, vol. 1 (Lincoln: University of Nebraska Press, 1996), 293.

9. Ibid., 293-295.

10. The usual practice was for a village to disperse into several smaller bands for the winter hunt to avoid overburdening a particular hunting ground with too many hunters.

11. Thwaites, Correspondence . . . on Wisconsin Indians, Folder 3, 1.

Even by the end of the seventeenth century, one French official placed the number of Ho Chunk men at a scant 150. Potherie, "History of the Savage Peoples," 295-300.

12. Earlier interpretations maintain that the Mesquakies originated from the south shore of Lake Superior; William T. Hagan, *The Sac and Fox Indians* (Norman: University of Oklahoma Press, 1958), 5. Others suggest that they relocated from Michigan during the more general Great Dispersal of the 1640s and 1650s. David Edmunds and Joseph Peyser provide a convincing argument for an earlier migration from Michigan. R. David Edmunds and Joseph L. Peyser, *The Fox Wars: The Mesquakie Challenge to New France*, Civilization of the American Indian Series (Norman: University of Oklahoma Press, 1993), 9-10, 224-226n13.

13. Beck, *Siege and Survival*, 26.

14. Ibid., 17.

15. Ibid., 28.

16. Radin, *The Winnebago Tribe*, 11.

17. Daniel K. Richter, *The Ordeal of the Longhouse: The Peoples of the Iroquois League in the Era of European Colonization* (Chapel Hill: University of North Carolina Press, 1992), 57-65.

18. Skinner, *Folklore of the Menomini Indians*, 435.

19. Felix Keesing, *The Menomini Indians of Wisconsin: A Study of Three Centuries of Cultural Contact and Change* (Philadelphia: American Philosophical Society, 1939), 15.

20. Beck, *Siege and Survival*, 28, 32, 44, 46.

21. James Axtell, *The Invasion Within: The Contest of Cultures in Colonial North America* (New York: Oxford University Press, 1985), 285.

22. Susan Sleeper-Smith, *Indian Women and French Men: Rethinking Cultural Encounter in the Western Great Lakes* (Amherst: University of Massachusetts Press, 2001), 42.

23. W. J. Eccles, "The Fur Trade and Eighteenth-Century Imperialism," *William and Mary Quarterly* 40, no. 3 (July 1983): 341-342.

24. R. David Edmunds, *The Potawatomis: Keepers of the Fire* (Norman:

University of Oklahoma Press, 1978), 7-9; James A. Clifton, *The Prairie People: Continuity and Change in Potawatomi Indian Culture, 1665-1965* (Iowa City: University of Iowa Press, 1998), 40-41; Keesing, *The Menomini Indians of Wisconsin*, 57; Richard White, *The Middle Ground: Indians, Empires, and Republics in the Great Lakes Region, 1650-1815* (Cambridge: Cambridge University Press, 1991), 35.

25. Clifton, *The Prairie People*, 19-20; White, *The Middle Ground*, 38-39, 177, 313-314.

26. Richter, *The Ordeal of the Longhouse*, 210-211; White, *The Middle Ground*, 49; Francis Jennings, *The Ambiguous Iroquois Empire: The Covenant Chain Confederation of Indian Tribes with English Colonies from Its Beginnings to the Lancaster Treaty of 1744* (1984; reprint, New York: W. W. Norton & Co., 1990), 210-211.

27. Edmunds and Peyser, *The Fox Wars*, 19.

28. Ibid.

29. Ibid., 9.

30. Ibid., 11.

31. Harold Hickerson, "The Virginia Deer and Intertribal Buffer Zones in the Upper Mississippi Valley," in *Man, Culture, and Animals: The Role of Animals in Human Ecological Adjustments*, ed. Anthony Leeds and Andrew P. Vayda (Washington, D.C.: American Association for the Advancement of Science, 1965), 47; Edmunds and Peyser, *The Fox Wars*, 19-20.

32. Beck, *Siege and Survival*, 28.

33. Edmunds and Peyser, *The Fox Wars*, 60-129.

34. Ibid., 129-33; Paul Radin and Jasper Blowsnake, "A Semi-Historical Account of the War of the Winnebago and the Foxes," in *Proceedings of the State Historical Society of Wisconsin, Oct. 22, 1914* (Madison: State Historical Society of Wisconsin, 1915), 192-207; Joseph Marin to Governor de Beauharnois, 11 May 1730, in Reuben G. Thwaites, ed., *Collections of the State Historical Society of Wisconsin*, vol. 17 (Madison: State Historical Society of Wisconsin, 1906), 88-100.

35. Edmunds and Peyser, *The Fox Wars*, 134-179.

36. Lucy Eldersveld Murphy, *A Gathering of Rivers: Indians, Métis, and Mining in the Western Great Lakes, 1737–1832* (Lincoln: University of Nebraska Press, 2000), 40; Nicolas Perrot, "Memoir on the Manners, Customs, and Religion of the Savages of North America," in *The Indian Tribes of the Upper Mississippi Valley and Region of the Great Lakes,* ed. Emma Helen Blair, vol. 1 (Lincoln: University of Nebraska Press, 1996), 77–78.

37. Alanson Skinner, *Social Life and Ceremonial Bundles of the Menomini Indians,* vol. 13, part 1, Anthropological Papers of the American Museum of Natural History (New York: American Museum of Natural History, 1913), 79.

38. Clifton, *The Prairie People,* 173–178; Skinner, *Social Life and Ceremonial Bundles,* 96–128; Keesing, *The Menomini Indians of Wisconsin,* 40–41; Beck, *Siege and Survival,* 15–20; Radin, *The Winnebago Tribe,* 107–111; Lurie, "Winnebago," 695; Gary Clayton Anderson, *Kinsmen of Another Kind: Dakota-White Relations in the Upper Mississippi Valley, 1650–1862* (Lincoln: University of Nebraska Press, 1984; reprint, with a new introduction, St. Paul: Minnesota Historical Society Press, 1997), 1–2; Anthony F. C. Wallace, *Prelude to Disaster: The Course of Indian-White Relations Which Led to the Black Hawk War of 1832* (Springfield: Illinois State Historical Library, 1970), 7–9.

39. Wallace, *Prelude to Disaster,* 8–9.

40. Several scholars have noted the militarizing effects of the Beaver Wars on the Iroquois Confederacy and their enemies. Anthony F. C. Wallace, *The Death and Rebirth of the Seneca* (New York: Alfred A. Knopf, 1970), 39–48; Richter, *The Ordeal of the Longhouse,* 50–65; Edmunds and Peyser, *The Fox Wars,* 51–52; Murphy, *A Gathering of Rivers,* 38; Colin G. Calloway, *The American Revolution in Indian Country: Crisis and Diversity in Native American Communities,* Cambridge Studies in North American Indian History (Cambridge: Cambridge University Press, 1995), 6.

41. Edmunds and Peyser, *The Fox Wars,* 51–52.

42. Ibid., 51; Murphy, *A Gathering of Rivers,* 38.

43. Donald Jackson, ed., *Black Hawk: An Autobiography* (Chicago: Illini Books, 1964; reprint, Chicago: University of Illinois Press, 1990), 91.

44. Thomas Forsyth, "Manners and Customs of the Sauk and Fox Nations of Indians etc. with Anecdotes, etc.," Draper Mss T, vol. 9, Wisconsin Historical Society, Madison, 6-7.

45. Anderson, *Kinsmen of Another Kind*, 1. Indeed, suicide rates for Dakota women were high by comparative standards, suggesting a gender-based discontentment unusual among Eastern Woodland Indians, who generally achieved a higher degree of gender equality than did European societies at the time.

46. Ibid., 2.

47. Lamothe Cadillac, "Description of Michillimackinac; Indian Tribes of that Region," in *Collections of the State Historical Society of Wisconsin*, ed. Reuben G. Thwaites, vol. 16 (Madison: State Historical Society of Wisconsin, 1902), 362.

48. Anderson, *Kinsmen of Another Kind*, 21-22.

49. Ibid., 3.

50. Ibid., 41-42.

51. Edmunds and Peyser, *The Fox Wars*, 173, 189-190.

52. Anderson, *Kinsmen of Another Kind*, 2.

53. Edmunds and Peyser, *The Fox Wars*, 193.

54. Eccles, "The Fur Trade and Eighteenth-Century Imperialism," 353-356.

55. Murphy, *A Gathering of Rivers*, 42.

56. Eccles, "The Fur Trade and Eighteenth-Century Imperialism," 356-362; White, *The Middle Ground*, 199-246.

57. Ian K. Steele, *Betrayals: Fort William Henry and the "Massacre"* (New York: Oxford University Press, 1990); Fred Anderson, *Crucible of War: The Seven Years' War and the Fate of Empire in British North America, 1754-1766* (New York: Alfred A. Knopf, 2000), 199.

58. Gregory Evans Dowd, *War under Heaven: Pontiac, the Indian Nations, and the British Empire* (Baltimore: Johns Hopkins University Press, 2002), 177-185; Fintan O'Toole, *White Savage: William Johnson and the*

*Invention of America* (New York: Farrar, Straus and Giroux, 2005), 248–249.

59. Colin G. Calloway, *Crown and Calumet: British-Indian Relations, 1783–1815* (Norman: University of Oklahoma Press, 1987), 58–59.

60. Anderson, *Kinsmen of Another Kind*, 62.

61. Wayne E. Lee, "From Gentility to Atrocity: The Continental Army's Ways of War," *Army History* 62 (Winter 2006): 10–15; Calloway, *The American Revolution in Indian Country*, 46–56.

62. Anderson, *Kinsmen of Another Kind*, 78.

63. Francis Paul Prucha, *The Sword of the Republic: The United States Army on the Frontier, 1783–1846* (New York: Macmillan, 1968), 40.

64. Such decisions sundered many Indian communities in close proximity to the Americans. Ultimately, none of the Indians realized their objective of protecting their people from further American encroachment. Gregory Evans Dowd, *A Spirited Resistance: The North American Indian Struggle for Unity, 1745–1815* (Baltimore: Johns Hopkins University Press, 1992), 194–195. For an interesting examination of divergent courses pursued by various Potawatomi bands during both wars, see Sleeper-Smith, *Indian Women and French Men*, 69–70, 87–89.

65. Anderson, *Kinsmen of Another Kind*, 65, 88–90.

66. Colin G. Calloway, "The End of an Era: British-Indian Relations in the Great Lakes Region after the War of 1812," *Michigan Historical Review* 12, no. 2 (Fall 1986): 3–4.

2. A NEW ONONTIO

1. Richard White, *The Middle Ground: Indians, Empires, and Republics in the Great Lakes Region, 1650–1815* (Cambridge: Cambridge University Press, 1991), 371.

2. Donald Jackson, ed., *The Journals of Zebulon Montgomery Pike, with Letters and Related Documents*, vol. 1 (Norman: University of Oklahoma Press, 1966), 216.

3. James Monroe to William Clark, 25 March 1833, *American State Pa-*

*pers: Indian Affairs,* ed. Walter Lowrie and Walter S. Franklin, vol. 2 (Washington: Gales and Seaton, 1834), 6.

4. Gary Clayton Anderson, *Kinsmen of Another Kind: Dakota-White Relations in the Upper Mississippi Valley, 1650–1862* (Lincoln: University of Nebraska Press, 1984; reprint, with a new introduction, St. Paul: Minnesota Historical Society Press, 1997), 85–86.

5. W. Sheridan Warrick, "The American Indian Policy in the Upper Old Northwest Following the War of 1812," *Ethnohistory* 3 (Spring 1956): 109–120.

6. Samuel S. Storrow, "The North-West in 1817," in *Report and Collections of the State Historical Society of Wisconsin, for the Years 1869, 1870, 1871, and 1872,* ed. Lyman C. Draper, vol. 6, Collections of the State Historical Society of Wisconsin (Madison: Atwood & Culver, State Printers, Journal Block, 1872) (hereafter WHC 6), 155.

7. Thomas Forsyth, "Journal of a Voyage from St. Louis to the Falls of St. Andrews in 1819," in ibid., 190.

8. Anderson, *Kinsmen of Another Kind,* 95–96.

9. Colin G. Calloway, "The End of an Era: British-Indian Relations in the Great Lakes Region after the War of 1812," *Michigan Historical Review* 12, no. 2 (Fall 1986): 9–20; Robert S. Allen, "His Majesty's Indian Allies: Native Peoples, the British Crown, and the War of 1812," *Michigan Historical Review* 14, no. 2 (Fall 1988): 23–24.

10. For evidence of early intransigence among these tribes, see *American State Papers: Indian Affairs,* vol. 2, 7–10, 12, 94.

11. Thomas Forsyth, "Maj. Thomas Forsyth to Gov. Wm. Clark, 23 September 1819," in WHC 6, 219.

12. Forsyth, "Journal of a Voyage from St. Louis to the Falls of St. Andrews in 1819," 202.

13. William Crawford to John Gallard, 13 March 1816, *American State Papers: Indian Affairs,* vol. 2, 26.

14. Anderson, *Kinsmen of Another Kind,* 100.

15. Forsyth, "Maj. Thomas Forsyth to Gov. Wm. Clark, 23 September 1819," 217.

16. Augustin Grignon, "Seventy-Two Years' Recollections of Wisconsin," in *Third Annual Report and Collections of the State Historical Society of Wisconsin for the Year 1856*, ed. Lyman C. Draper, Collections of the State Historical Society of Wisconsin (Madison: Calkins & Webb, Printers, 1857), 282.

17. Proceedings of a Court-Martial for the Trial of Colonel Talbot Chambers, 16 May 1826, *American State Papers: Military Affairs*, ed. Asbury Dickins and John W. Forney, vol. 3 (Washington, D.C.: Gales and Seaton, 1860), 307–326; John Shaw, "Personal Narrative of Col. John Shaw, of Marquette County, Wisconsin," in *Second Annual Report and Collections of the State Historical Society of Wisconsin for the Year 1855*, ed. Lyman C. Draper, vol. 2, Collections of the State Historical Society of Wisconsin (Madison: Calkins & Proudfit, Printers, 1856) (hereafter WHC 2), 229.

18. Forsyth, "Journal of a Voyage from St. Louis to the Falls of St. Andrews in 1819," 202.

19. Samuel Storrow considered Fort Howard at Green Bay pivotal: "At no part of the Indian frontier could a fortress be more useful or indispensable. It is in the chain of connection with the Indian settlements between the Mississippi and the Lakes. It opens a way to their retreats in the West, and commands their thoroughfare towards the East. The Fals Avoines [Menominees], Ottawas, Pottowotomies and dangerous Winnebagoes consider this place as their accustomed and privileged haunt." Storrow, "The North-West in 1817," 167.

20. Tomah quoted in Grignon, "Seventy-Two Years' Recollections of Wisconsin," 282.

21. Reuben G. Thwaites, Winnebago Notes, US Mss 7E Folder 3, Wisconsin Historical Society, Madison, 3–4; Nancy O. Lurie, "Winnebago," in *Northeast*, ed. Bruce G. Trigger, vol. 15, Handbook of North American Indians series (Washington, D.C.: Smithsonian Institution, 1978), 692–693.

22. Reuben G. Thwaites, Correspondence . . . on Wisconsin Indians, US Mss 7E Folder 3, Wisconsin Historical Society, Madison, 4.

23. James W. Biddle, "Recollections of Green Bay in 1816-17," in *Collections of the State Historical Society of Wisconsin*, ed. Lyman C. Draper, vol. 1 (Madison: Wisconsin State Historical Society, 1855; reprint, with the addition of a memoir of Dr. Draper and the early records of the Society, Madison: Wisconsin State Historical Society, 1903) (hereafter WHC 1), 52.

24. Ibid.

25. Ibid.

26. Albert G. Ellis, "Fifty-Four Years' Recollections of Men and Events in Wisconsin," in *Report and Collections of the State Historical Society of Wisconsin, for the Years 1873, 1874, 1875 and 1876*, ed. Lyman C. Draper, vol. 7, Collections of the State Historical Society of Wisconsin (Madison: E. B. Bolens, State Printer, 1876) (hereafter WHC 7), 225.

27. William J. Snelling, "Early Days at Prairie du Chien, and Winnebago Outbreak of 1827," in *Report and Collections of the State Historical Society of Wisconsin, for the Years 1867, 1868, and 1869*, ed. Lyman C. Draper, vol. 5, Collections of the State Historical Society of Wisconsin (Madison: Atwood & Rublee, State Printers, 1868; reprint, Madison: State Historical Society of Wisconsin, 1907), 142.

28. Records of Ho Chunk participation in various campaigns are available in Thwaites, Correspondence . . . on Wisconsin Indians, Folder 3, 1-2.

29. Charles Whittlesey, "Recollections of a Tour through Wisconsin in 1832," in WHC 1, 74.

30. Forsyth, "Maj. Thomas Forsyth to Gov. Wm. Clark, 23 September 1819," 219; John Dean, "Wisconsin—Early History," George A. Hyer Newsclippings, 1820-1824, 1830-1860, Wis Mss AX, Wisconsin Historical Society, Madison, no. 1, 6.

31. Jacqueline Peterson, "Prelude to Red River: A Social Portrait of the Great Lakes Métis," *Ethnohistory* 25, no. 1 (Winter 1978): 52-54; Lucy Eldersveld Murphy, *A Gathering of Rivers: Indians, Métis, and Mining*

*in the Western Great Lakes, 1737–1832* (Lincoln: University of Nebraska Press, 2000), 47.

32. William Crawford to John Gallard, 13 March 1816, *American State Papers: Indian Affairs,* vol. 2, 28.

33. A. J. Dallas to William Harrison, Duncan McArthur, and John Graham, 9 June 1815, ibid., 13.

34. Forsyth, "Journal of a Voyage from St. Louis to the Falls of St. Andrews in 1819," 214; James H. Lockwood, "Early Times and Events in Wisconsin," in WHC 2, 130–131.

35. Ellis, "Fifty-Four Years' Recollections," 222.

36. *American State Papers: Indian Affairs,* vol. 2, 326–364. For a thorough examination of the causes of the factory system's failure, see Ora Brooks Peake, *A History of the United States Indian Factory System* (Denver: Sage Books, 1954), 218–256. A concise overview of the system is available in Francis Paul Prucha, *The Great Father: The United States Government and the American Indians,* abridged ed. (Lincoln: University of Nebraska Press, 1995), 35–40.

37. Forsyth, "Journal of a Voyage from St. Louis to the Falls of St. Andrews in 1819," 214.

38. Francis Paul Prucha, *American Indian Policy in the Formative Years: The Indian Trade and Intercourse Acts, 1790–1834* (Cambridge, Mass.: Harvard University Press, 1962), 56–57.

39. McKenney to John Eaton, 17 November 1829, Indian Office Letter Books, vols. 1–15, US Mss BN Box 47, Wisconsin Historical Society, Madison, vol. 6, 166.

40. McKenney to William Clark, 10 April 1828, ibid., vol. 4, 396.

41. Prucha, *American Indian Policy in the Formative Years,* 57–60.

42. "Report of a tour of inspection commenced on the 11th December, 1826, and completed in April, 1827, by Edmund P. Gaines, major general by brevet in the army of the United States," *American State Papers: Military Affairs,* ed. Asbury Dickins and John W. Forney, vol. 4 (Washington, D.C.: Gales and Seaton, 1860), 129;

James W. Silver, *Edmund Pendleton Gaines: Frontier General* (Baton Rouge: Louisiana State University Press, 1949), 106.

43. *American State Papers: Military Affairs,* vol. 4, 130.

44. Ibid.

45. Ibid., 131.

46. Ibid., 132-133.

47. McKenney to Lewis Cass, 14 December 1827, Indian Office Letter Books, vol. 4, 180-181.

48. Herman J. Viola, *Thomas L. McKenney: Architect of America's Early Indian Policy, 1816-1830* (Chicago: Sage Books, 1974), 144.

49. John Eaton to Treaty Commissioners, 30 March 1829, Letter Book of Gen. John McNeil concerning the 1829 treaty of Prairie du Chien, US Mss 4E, Wisconsin Historical Society, Madison, 6.

50. Report of a tour of inspection . . . by Edmund P. Gaines, *American State Papers: Military Affairs,* vol. 4, 132.

51. George D. Lyman, *John Marsh, Pioneer: The Life Story of a Trail-Blazer on Six Frontiers* (Chautauqua, N.Y.: Chautauqua Press, 1931), 59-60.

52. *Oshkosh City Times,* 1 December 1869, in George A. Hyer, Newsclippings, 1820-1824, 1830-1860, Wis Mss AX, Wisconsin Historical Society, Madison, 1-2.

53. Anderson, *Kinsmen of Another Kind,* 115.

54. Accounts of Jefferson Davis's relations with Indian women range from unwarranted familiarity at a dance to the fathering of an illegitimate child who fought for the Union during the Civil War. Most appear to be post–Civil War fabrications, although it seems probable that they have a basis in fact. Zachary Taylor's biographer has asserted that Taylor objected to Davis on the simple and sole grounds that he was an army officer. William J. Cooper, Jr., *Jefferson Davis, American* (New York: Alfred A. Knopf, 2000), 52; Dean, "Wisconsin—Early History," no. 1, 7; K. Jack Bauer, *Zachary Taylor: Soldier, Planter, Statesman of the Old Southwest* (Baton Rouge: Louisiana State University Press, 1985), 69.

55. Lyman, *John Marsh, Pioneer,* 59–60.

56. Ibid., 147–148, 150–151.

57. Dean, "Wisconsin—Early History," no. 1, 7.

58. Murphy, *A Gathering of Rivers,* 31.

59. Samuel W. Pond, *The Dakota or Sioux in Minnesota as They Were in 1834* (1908; reprint, St. Paul: Minnesota Historical Society Press, 1986), 137.

60. R. David Edmunds, *The Potawatomis: Keepers of the Fire* (Norman: University of Oklahoma Press, 1978), 215–216.

61. McKenney to Eaton, 21 December 1829, Indian Office Letter Books, vol. 6, 199; Viola, *Thomas L. McKenney,* 162; *American State Papers: Indian Affairs,* vol. 2, 6.

62. McKenney to Eaton, 17 November 1829, Indian Office Letter Books, vol. 6, 166.

63. Anderson, *Kinsmen of Another Kind,* 119.

64. McKenney to Eaton, 17 November 1829, Indian Office Letter Books, vol. 6, 166.

65. Forsyth, "Journal of a Voyage from St. Louis to the Falls of St. Andrews in 1819," 213.

66. Ibid., 198.

67. Snelling, "Early Days at Prairie du Chien," 143.

68. Ibid., 134.

69. Eager to avert retaliation by the Ojibwas, a Dakota delivered two more of the perpetrators to Colonel Snelling; the latter likewise turned these over to the Ojibwas for execution. Ibid., 134–135, 138–141.

70. Samuel S. Hamilton to Samuel C. Stambaugh, 8 September 1831, Indian Office Letter Books, vol. 7, 383.

71. Anderson, *Kinsmen of Another Kind,* 119–121.

72. Lyman, *John Marsh, Pioneer,* 58.

73. Edward M. Coffman, *The Old Army: A Portrait of the American Army in Peacetime, 1784–1898* (New York: Oxford University Press, 1986), 73–78.

74. Storrow, "The North-West in 1817," 177.

75. Juliette Kinzie, *Wau-bun: The Early Day in the North West* (1873; reprint, Philadelphia: Bibliobazaar, 2006), 233.

76. Henry Smith, "Indian Campaign of 1832," in *Collections of the State Historical Society of Wisconsin for the Years of 1883, 1884, and 1885*, ed. Lyman C. Draper, vol. 10, Collections of the State Historical Society of Wisconsin (Madison: Democrat Printing Co., State Printer, 1888), 154.

77. Dean, "Wisconsin—Early History," no. 1, 8.

78. William Powell, "William Powell's Recollections, in an Interview with Lyman C. Draper," in *Proceedings of the Annual Meeting of the State Historical Society of Wisconsin* (Madison: The Society, 1912), 160.

79. Draper, WHC 2, 89n.

80. Dean, "Wisconsin—Early History," no. 1, 8.

81. Ibid., 4.

82. Robert E. Bieder, *Native American Communities in Wisconsin, 1600–1960: A Study of Tradition and Change* (Madison: University of Wisconsin Press, 1995), 85–86.

83. Lockwood specifically addresses the importance of British-made firearms to the Indians. Lockwood, "Early Times and Events in Wisconsin," 130–131.

84. Prucha, *American Indian Policy in the Formative Years*, 102–130.

85. Anonymous to Thomas Burnett, 3 May, 1831, Alfred Brunson, "Memoir of Hon. Thomas Pendleton Burnett," in WHC 2, 243.

86. Francis Paul Prucha, *The Sword of the Republic: The United States Army on the Frontier, 1783–1846* (New York: Macmillan, 1968), 45.

87. Knox quoted in Reginald Horsman, *Expansion and American Indian Policy, 1783–1812* (Norman: University of Oklahoma Press, 1992), 64.

88. William Crawford to William Clark, Ninian Edwards, and Auguste Chouteau, 7 May 1816, *American State Papers: Indian Affairs*, vol. 2, 97.

89. "Exchange of Lands with Indians," 9 January 1817, ibid., 124.

90. George Graham to William Clark, 10 November 1815, ibid., 10–11.

91. Henry S. Baird, "Recollections of the Early History of Northern Wisconsin," in *Report and Collections of the State Historical Society of Wisconsin for the Years 1857 and 1858,* ed. Lyman C. Draper, vol. 4, Collections of the State Historical Society of Wisconsin (Madison: James Ross, State Printer, 1859) (hereafter WHC 4), 212–213.

92. Ibid., 213.

93. Lockwood, "Early Times and Events in Wisconsin," 128–129.

94. Henry S. Baird, "Early History and Condition of Wisconsin," in WHC 2, 84.

95. Ibid.

96. Ibid., 90.

97. Ellen M. Whitney, ed., *The Black Hawk War, 1831–1832,* vol. 36, Collections of the Illinois State Historical Library (Springfield: Illinois State Historical Library, 1973), 82n5.

98. Henry Merrell, "Pioneer Life in Wisconsin," in WHC 7, 375.

99. Dean, "Wisconsin—Early History," no. 1, 9.

100. Merrell, "Pioneer Life in Wisconsin," 375; Dean, "Wisconsin—Early History," no. 1, 9.

101. Spoon Decorah, "Narrative of Spoon Decorah," in *Collections of the State Historical Society of Wisconsin,* ed. Reuben G. Thwaites, vol. 13 (Madison: Democrat Printing Co., State Printers, 1895), 461.

102. Lyman, *John Marsh, Pioneer,* 108.

103. Twiggs to John McNeil and Col. Menard, 18 June 1829, Letter Book of Gen. John McNeil concerning the 1829 treaty of Prairie du Chien, 43.

104. Ebenezer Childs, "Recollections of Wisconsin since 1820," in WHC 4, 175–180.

105. Beverly Hayward Johnson, *Queen Marinette: Spirit of Survival on the Great Lakes Frontier* (Amasa, Mich.: White Water Associates, 1995), 26–27; Baird, "Early History and Condition of Wisconsin," 84–86.

106. Charles B. Hempstead to Col. Willoughby Morgan, 31 December 1831, National Archives, Letters Received by the Office of the Adju-

tant General (Main Series), 1822–1860, Microcopy No. 567, Roll 66: 1832 (Washington, D.C.: National Archives and Records Service, General Services Administration, 1964), F30-33.

107. "On the Claims of Officers of the Army for Expenses Incurred in Defending Suits for Acts Done in Performance of their Official Duties," 9 April 1832, *American State Papers: Military Affairs,* ed. Asbury Dickins and John W. Forney, vol. 5 (Washington, D.C.: Gales and Seaton, 1860), 10.

### 3. A MOUNTING STORM

1. Lucy Eldersveld Murphy, *A Gathering of Rivers: Indians, Métis, and Mining in the Western Great Lakes, 1737–1832* (Lincoln: University of Nebraska Press, 2000), 80. By 1811, Nicholas Boilvin, agent to the Ho Chunks, reported that lead had become the cornerstone of the Sauk and Mesquakie economy and that in 1810 they had manufactured 400,000 pounds of the metal, which they traded with French Canadians. Reuben G. Thwaites, "Notes on Early Mining in the Fever (or Galena) River Region," in *Collections of the State Historical Society of Wisconsin,* ed. Reuben G. Thwaites, vol. 13 (Madison: Democrat Printing Co., State Printers, 1895) (hereafter WHC 13), 285.

2. John Shaw, "Personal Narrative of Col. John Shaw, of Marquette County, Wisconsin," in *Second Annual Report and Collections of the State Historical Society of Wisconsin for the Year 1855,* ed. Lyman C. Draper, vol. 2, Collections of the State Historical Society of Wisconsin (Madison: Calkins & Proudfit, Printers, 1856) (hereafter WHC 2), 228–229.

3. Thwaites, "Notes on Early Mining," 277–278.

4. Treaty with the Sauks and Foxes, 3 November 1804, *Indian Affairs: Laws and Treaties,* ed. Charles J. Kappler, vol. 2 (Treaties) (Washington, D.C.: U.S. Government Printing Office, 1904), 74–77.

5. Thwaites, "Notes on Early Mining," 289–290.

6. Ibid., 284.

7. Treaty with the Ottawa, etc., 24 August 1816, *Indian Affairs*, vol. 2, 132–133.

8. Americans operated small-scale, illegal mines in the region as early as 1810. Duane K. Everhart, "The Leasing of Mineral Lands in Illinois and Wisconsin," *Journal of the Illinois State Historical Society* 60, no. 2 (Summer 1967): 120.

9. Thwaites, "Notes on Early Mining," 288–290.

10. Moses Meeker, "Early History of the Lead Region of Wisconsin," in *Report and Collections of the State Historical Society of Wisconsin, for the Years 1869, 1870, 1871 and 1872*, ed. Lyman Draper, vol. 6, Collections of the State Historical Society of Wisconsin (Madison: Atwood & Culver, State Printers, 1872) (hereafter WHC 6), 272.

11. Spoon Decorah, "Narrative of Spoon Decorah," in WHC 13, 458.

12. James E. Wright, *The Galena Lead District: Federal Policy and Practice, 1824–1847* (Madison: State Historical Society of Wisconsin, 1966), 11, 14–15.

13. Street to Edwards, 27 November 1827, Joseph M. Street, "Prairie du Chien in 1827: Letters of Joseph M. Street to Gov. Ninian Edwards, Illinois," in *Collections of the State Historical Society of Wisconsin*, ed. Reuben G. Thwaites, vol. 11 (Madison: Democrat Printing Co., State Printers, 1888) (hereafter WHC 11), 358, 360; *Indian Affairs*, vol. 2, 250–255.

14. Adèle Maria Antoinette de Perdreauville Gratiot, "An Interesting Narrative: The Reminiscences of Mrs. Adele B. Gratiot," *Galena Weekly Gazette*, 2 May 1879, 3.

15. Thomas Forsyth to William Clark, 20 July 1827, Thomas Forsyth Papers, 1804–1833, Draper Mss T, vol. 6 (Letter Books), Wisconsin Historical Society, Madison, 66.

16. Meeker, "Early History of the Lead Region," 273.

17. Ibid., 272.

18. Thwaites, "Notes on Early Mining," 290.

19. Meeker, "Early History of the Lead Region of Wisconsin," 282.

20. Thwaites, "Notes on Early Mining," 291.

21. George D. Lyman, *John Marsh, Pioneer: The Life Story of a Trail-Blazer on Six Frontiers* (Chautauqua, N.Y.: Chautauqua Press, 1931), 106.

22. Forsyth to William Clark, 6 August 1826, Forsyth Papers, vol. 6, 54.

23. Lyman, *John Marsh, Pioneer,* 106.

24. Draper, WHC 6, 275n.

25. Meeker, "Early History of the Lead Region," 283.

26. Meeker "covered" the offense with a gift of flour, pork, tobacco, a new gun, and a keg of whiskey. Ibid.

27. Ebenezer Childs, "Recollections of Wisconsin since 1820," in *Report and Collections of the State Historical Society of Wisconsin for the Years 1857 and 1858,* ed. Lyman C. Draper, vol. 4, Collections of the State Historical Society of Wisconsin (Madison: James Ross, State Printer, 1859) (hereafter WHC 4), 181-182; Meeker, "Early History of the Lead Region," 271n; Murphy, *A Gathering of Rivers,* 130.

28. Decorah, "Narrative of Spoon Decorah," 459.

29. Charles Whittlesey, "Recollections of a Tour through Wisconsin in 1832," in *Collections of the State Historical Society of Wisconsin,* ed. Lyman C. Draper, vol. 1 (Madison: Wisconsin State Historical Society, 1855; reprint, with the addition of a memoir of Dr. Draper and the early records of the Society, Madison: Wisconsin State Historical Society, 1903), 81.

30. Thomas Forsyth to William Clark, 15 October 1826, Forsyth Papers, vol. 6, 57.

31. Gary Clayton Anderson, *Kinsmen of Another Kind: Dakota-White Relations in the Upper Mississippi Valley, 1650-1862* (Lincoln: University of Nebraska Press, 1984; reprint, with a new introduction, St. Paul: Minnesota Historical Society Press, 1997), 106-107; Harold Hickerson, "The Virginia Deer and Intertribal Buffer Zones in the Upper Mississippi Valley," in *Man, Culture, and Animals: The Role of Animals in Human Ecological Adjustments,* ed. Anthony Leeds and Andrew P. Vayda (Washington, D.C.: American Association for the Advancement of Science, 1965), 43-62.

32. Anthony F. C. Wallace, *Prelude to Disaster: The Course of Indian-White Relations Which Led to the Black Hawk War of 1832* (Springfield: Illinois State Historical Library, 1970), 24-25.

33. Anderson, *Kinsmen of Another Kind*, 106-107.

34. John Shaw, "Sketches of Indian Chiefs and Pioneers of the North-West," in *Report and Collections of the State Historical Society of Wisconsin For the Years 1883, 1884, and 1885*, ed. Lyman C. Draper, vol. 10, Collections of the State Historical Society of Wisconsin (Madison: Democrat Printing Co., State Printer, 1888), 213.

35. Treaty with the Sioux, etc., 19 August 1825, *Indian Affairs*, vol. 2, 250-255; Anderson, *Kinsmen of Another Kind*, 122-123.

36. McKenney to Clark, 21 October 1829, Indian Office Letter Books, vols. 1-15, US Mss BN Box 47, Wisconsin Historical Society, Madison, vol. 6, 129.

37. Anderson, *Kinsmen of Another Kind*, 123.

38. Lyman, *John Marsh, Pioneer*, 98-99, 115, 354; William J. Snelling, "Early Days at Prairie du Chien, and Winnebago Outbreak of 1827," in *Report and Collections of the State Historical Society of Wisconsin, for the Years 1867, 1868, and 1869*, ed. Lyman C. Draper, vol. 5, Collections of the State Historical Society of Wisconsin (Madison: Atwood & Rublee, State Printers, 1868; reprint, Madison: State Historical Society of Wisconsin, 1907), 126-129; James H. Lockwood, "Early Times and Events in Wisconsin," in WHC 2, 155-156.

39. Lyman, *John Marsh, Pioneer*, 107.

40. Martin Zanger, "Red Bird," in *American Indian Leaders: Studies in Diversity*, ed. R. David Edmunds (Lincoln: University of Nebraska Press, 1980), 69.

41. Lyman, *John Marsh, Pioneer*, 107.

42. Anderson, *Kinsmen of Another Kind*, 124-125.

43. Lockwood, "Early Times and Events in Wisconsin," 156; Snelling, "Early Days at Prairie du Chien," 134-141.

44. Snelling's son flatly refuted the allegation that riverine soldiers sexually assaulted any Ho Chunk women. Instead, he maintained

that the riverboat crews traded peaceably with the Indians before passing north. The studious historian-archivist Lyman Copeland Draper endorsed Snelling's account after reviewing all available facts. Snelling, "Early Days at Prairie du Chien," 144.

45. John Connolly to William Clark, 12 February 1828, National Archives, Letters Received by the Office of Indian Affairs, 1824-81: Prairie du Chien Agency, 1824-1847, Microcopy No. 234, Roll 696: 1824-1842 (Washington, D.C.: National Archives and Records Service General Services Administration, 1957), 73v.

46. Reuben G. Thwaites, Winnebago Notes, US Mss 7E Folder 3, Wisconsin Historical Society, Madison, 7.

47. Snelling, "Early Days at Prairie du Chien," 146; Thomas Loraine McKenney, *Memoirs, Official and Personal* (Lincoln: University of Nebraska Press, 1973), 127-129; Zanger, "Red Bird," 70-71.

48. "Certificate of the inhabitants of Prairie du Chien, Dec. 3, 1827, relating to the occupancy of Fort Crawford by private citizens," US Mss BM Folder 11, Wisconsin Historical Society, Madison, 1.

49. John A. Wakefield, *Wakefield's History of the Black Hawk War*, ed. Frank E. Stevens (1834; reprint, Chicago: Caxton Club, 1904), 26-27; Zanger, "Red Bird," 71-72.

50. Snelling, "Early Days at Prairie du Chien," 152.

51. Alexander Wolcott to James Barbour, 25 July 1827, Letters Received by the Office of Indian Affairs, 1824-81: Chicago Agency, 1824-1847, National Archives Microcopy No. 234, Roll 132: 1824-1834 (Washington, D.C.: National Archives and Records Service General Services Administration, 1959), F32.

52. Thomas Forsyth to William Clark, 15 October 1827, Forsyth Papers, vol. 6, 78; Letters Received by the Office of Indian Affairs, 1824-81: Chicago Agency, 1824-1847, F32; Childs, "Recollections," 171.

53. Decorah, "Narrative of Spoon Decorah," 450.

54. Nancy O. Lurie, "Winnebago," in *Northeast*, ed. Bruce G. Trigger, vol. 15, Handbook of North American Indians (Washington, D.C.:

Smithsonian Institution, 1978), 693; Nancy O. Lurie, "In Search of Chaetar: New Findings on Black Hawk's Surrender," *Wisconsin Magazine of History* 71, no. 3 (Spring 1988): 166.

55. Kinzie to E. A. Brush, 4 September 1827, John H. Kinzie, Letters, 1827-1832, Wisconsin Historical Society, Madison, 1.

56. McKenney, *Memoirs, Official and Personal,* 105.

57. Ibid., 105-113; John Kinzie to E. A. Brush, 4 September 1827, Kinzie, Letters, 1827-1832, 1-2; Lyman, *John Marsh, Pioneer,* 128-131.

58. Kinzie to E. A. Brush, 4 September 1827, Kinzie, Letters, 1827-1832, 2.

59. Roger L. Nichols, *General Henry Atkinson: A Western Military Career* (Norman: University of Oklahoma Press, 1965), 119-120.

60. Joseph Street to Ninian Edwards, 27 November 1827, Street, "Prairie du Chien in 1827: Letters of Joseph M. Street to Gov. Ninian Edwards, Illinois," 358.

61. Henry B. Brevoort to Thomas L. McKenney, 18 August 1827, National Archives, Letters Received by the Office of Indian Affairs, 1824-81: Green Bay Agency, 1824-1880, Microcopy No. 234, Roll 315: 1824-1832 (Washington, D.C.: National Archives and Records Service General Services Administration, 1959), F0031-0034; Nichols, *General Henry Atkinson,* 132; Childs, "Recollections," 172-173. The Stockbridges and Oneidas occupied lands supposedly ceded by the Menominees in 1822, although the Menominees continued to dispute the legitimacy of this exchange.

62. Patricia K. Ourada, *The Menominee Indians: A History* (Norman: University of Oklahoma Press, 1979), 35.

63. Lamothe Cadillac, "Description of Michillimackinac; Indian Tribes of that Region," in *Collections of the State Historical Society of Wisconsin,* ed. Reuben G. Thwaites, vol. 16 (Madison: State Historical Society of Wisconsin, 1902), 360.

64. Augustin Grignon, "Seventy-Two Years' Recollections of Wisconsin," in *Third Annual Report and Collections of the State Historical Society of Wisconsin for the Year 1856,* ed. Lyman C. Draper, Collections of

the State Historical Society of Wisconsin (Madison: Calkins & Webb, Printers, 1857), 266.

65. Ourada, *The Menominee Indians,* 59.

66. Henry S. Baird, "Recollections of the Early History of Northern Wisconsin," in WHC 4, 217.

67. Thomas McKenney to John Bell (Chairman of the Committee of Indian Affairs), 8 March 1830, Indian Office Letter Books, vol. 6, 314.

68. Annual Report from the Department of War, Showing the Operations of that Department in 1829, 8 December 1829, *American State Papers: Military Affairs,* ed. Asbury Dickins and John W. Forney, vol. 4 (Washington, D.C.: Gales and Seaton, 1860), 154.

69. John Kinzie reported that the Potawatomis killed hogs and poultry and might have committed graver "acts of general violence" were it not for the movements of Atkinson's force. Lewis Cass to Thomas L. McKenney, 23 November 1827, Letters Received by the Office of Indian Affairs, 1824-81: Chicago Agency, 1824-1847, F15-17.

70. Wolcott to James Barbour, 25 July 1827, ibid., F27-31.

71. Juliette Kinzie, *Wau-bun: The Early Day in the North West* (1873; reprint, Philadelphia: Bibliobazaar, 2006), 207.

72. Cass to John C. Calhoun, 23 July 1827, and Wolcott to James Barbour, 20 March 1828, Letters Received by the Office of Indian Affairs, 1824-81: Chicago Agency, 1824-1847, F12-13, F43-44.

73. McKenney to Clark, 10 April 1828, Indian Office Letter Books, vol. 4, 395.

74. Ibid.

75. Annual Report from the Department of War, with the President's Message, Showing the Operations of that Department in 1828, 2 December 1828, *American State Papers: Military Affairs,* vol. 4, 5; United States War Department, Adjutant General's Office, "Order" dated 19 AUG 1828, US Mss BM Folder 4, Wisconsin Historical Society, Madison, 1-2.

76. Street to Secretary of War, 15 November 1827, National Archives,

Letters Received by the Office of Indian Affairs, 1824-81: Prairie du Chien Agency, 1824-1847, 44v.

77. McKenney to Macomb, 2 June 1828, Indian Office Letter Books, vol. 4, 479.

78. McKenney to Clark, 10 April 1828, ibid., vol. 4, 396.

79. H. A. Tenney, "Early Times in Wisconsin," in *First Annual Report and Collections of the State Historical Society, of Wisconsin, for the Year 1854*, ed. Lyman C. Draper, vol. 1, Collections of the State Historical Society of Wisconsin (Madison: Beriah Brown, Printer, 1855; reprint, 1903), 97.

80. Lyman, *John Marsh, Pioneer*, 143.

81. Ibid., 140.

82. Joseph Street to Secretary of War, 17 February 1828, National Archives, Letters Received by the Office of Indian Affairs, 1824-81: Prairie du Chien Agency, 1824-1847, 91v; Lyman, *John Marsh, Pioneer*, 142; Morgan L. Martin, "Narrative of Morgan L. Martin," in WHC 11, 397; Ronald Rayman, "Confrontation at the Fever River Lead Mining District: Joseph Montfort Street vs. Henry Dodge, 1827-1828," *Annals of Iowa* 44 (Spring 1978): 283-292.

83. Rayman, "Confrontation at the Fever River Lead Mining District," 293.

84. Thomas to William Clark, 7 July 1828, National Archives, Letters Received by the Office of Indian Affairs, 1824-81: Prairie du Chien Agency, 1824-1847, 71r.

85. Treaty with the Winnebago, etc., 1828, *Indian Affairs*, vol. 2, 292-294; Lyman, *John Marsh, Pioneer*, 140-142.

86. John W. Spencer, *Reminiscences of Pioneer Life in the Mississippi Valley* (Davenport, Iowa: Watson, Day, 1872); Thomas Forsyth, "Original causes of the troubles with a party of Sauk and Fox Indians under the direction or Command of the Black Hawk who is no Chief," 1 October 1832, Draper Mss T, vol. 9, Wisconsin Historical Society, Madison, 56.

87. Wallace, *Prelude to Disaster*, 28.

88. Forsyth to William Clark, 24 May 1828, Forsyth Papers, vol. 6, 81.

89. Forsyth to William Clark, 17 May 1829, ibid., 97.

90. Wallace, *Prelude to Disaster,* 29–30.

91. Thomas Forsyth to William Clark, 12 May, 30 May, and 15 June 1827, Forsyth Papers, vol. 6, 57–61.

92. Forsyth to William Clark, 22 May 1829, *The Governors' Letter Books 1818–1834,* ed. Evarts Boutell Greene and Clarence Walworth Alvord, vol. 4, Collections of the Illinois State Historical Library (Springfield: Illinois State Historical Library, 1909), 144–145.

93. Ibid., 145.

94. Treaty with the Chippewa, etc., 1829, 29 July 1829, and Treaty with the Winnebago, 1829, 1 August 1829, *Indian Affairs,* vol. 2, 297–303.

95. John McNeil, Col. Pierre Menard, and Caleb Atwater to Sec. of War, 7 August 1829, Letter Book of Gen. John McNeil concerning the 1829 treaty of Prairie du Chien, US Mss 4E, Wisconsin Historical Society, Madison, 60–67.

96. Eaton to Treaty Commissioners, 30 March 1829, ibid., 4.

97. McKenney to Barbour, 24 January 1828, Indian Office Letter Books, vol. 4, 267.

98. *Washington Intelligencer,* 25 October 1828, Correspondence, Articles, Miscellany on Wisconsin Indians, US Mss 7E Folder 3, Wisconsin Historical Society, Madison, 1.

99. McKenney to Barbour, 24 January 1828, Indian Office Letter Books, vol. 4, 267.

100. *Washington Telegram* (undated) cited in *New York Evening Post,* 29 October 1828, Correspondence . . . on Wisconsin Indians, US Mss 7E Folder 3, 4.

101. John Quincy Adams, Pardon Granted Wa-nu-ga (the Sun) and Chick-hong-sic (Little Beuffe), 3 November 1828, MAD 4/14/SC 352, Wisconsin Historical Society, Madison.

102. Alexander Wolcott to Lewis Cass, 25 March 1828, National Archives, Letters Received by the Office of Indian Affairs, 1824–81: Chicago Agency, 1824–1847, Microcopy No. 234, Roll 132: 1824–1834

(Washington, D.C.: National Archives and Records Service, General Services Administration, 1959), F37; Draper, WHC 4, 174n.

103. Tenney, "Early Times in Wisconsin," 97.

104. Annual Report from the Department of War, with the President's Message, Showing the Operations of that Department in 1828, 2 December 1828, *American State Papers: Military Affairs*, vol. 4, 3.

105. *House Journal*, 20th Cong., 2nd sess., 2 December 1828, 16.

106. Herman J. Viola, *Thomas L. McKenney: Architect of America's Early Indian Policy: 1816–1830* (Chicago: Sage Books, 1974), 185, 192–193, 197.

107. For a critical assessment of the supposedly humanitarian motives for removing the Indians of the Old Northwest, see Ronald N. Satz, "Indian Policy in the Jacksonian Era: The Old Northwest as a Test Case," *Michigan History* 60 (Spring 1976): 71–93.

108. McKenney, "Circular To Superintendents & Agents of Indian Affairs," 17 February 1829, Indian Office Letter Books, vol. 5, 309.

109. Ibid., vol. 5, 310.

110. William Clark to Henry Atkinson, 7 July 1828, and Atkinson to Col. McNeil, 7 July 1828, National Archives, Letters Received by the Office of Indian Affairs, 1824-81: Prairie du Chien Agency, 1824–1847, 63v, 66r-67r; P. G. Randolph (Acting Sec. of War) to Clark, 23 March 1831, Indian Office Letter Books, vol. 7, 163-164; *American State Papers: Military Affairs*, vol. 4, 588.

111. Annual Report from the Department of War, Showing the Operations of that Department in 1830, 7 December 1830, *American State Papers: Military Affairs*, vol. 4, 586-587.

112. Annual Report from the Department of War, Showing the Operations of that Department in 1831, 7 December 1831, ibid., 713.

113. Anderson, *Kinsmen of Another Kind*, 131.

114. Extracts from Minutes of a Council held at Prairie du Chien, etc., 7 July 1830, US Mss BM Box 63, Wisconsin Historical Society, Madison, 12; Wallace, *Prelude to Disaster*, 33.

115. Lyman, *John Marsh, Pioneer*, 145; Anderson, *Kinsmen of Another Kind*, 133.

116. Extracts from Minutes of a Council held at Prairie du Chien, etc., 7 July 1830, 13-14.

117. Street to Ninian Edwards, 28 December 1827, Street, "Prairie du Chien in 1827: Letters of Joseph M. Street to Gov. Ninian Edwards, Illinois," 366.

118. Anderson, *Kinsmen of Another Kind*, 133-134.

119. Wallace, *Prelude to Disaster*, 33.

4. CRISIS ON THE UPPER MISSISSIPPI

1. The actual numbers of participants and casualties in this episode are difficult to determine from the primary sources. Joseph Street reported that the attacking Menominees and Dakotas numbered 118 and that the Mesquakies numbered 25, 10 of whom died. Writing on behalf of the Mesquakie chief Morgan two days after the attack, Joseph Hardy likewise placed the number of Mesquakies killed at ten, but he claimed that the Mesquakie party had consisted of only sixteen men and one woman and that the aggressors numbered about fifty. Most secondary accounts, however, endorse the figures of Sauk and Mesquakie agent Thomas Forsyth, who reported a single Mesquakie survivor (who was half Mesquakie, half Ho Chunk) from a party of sixteen men and one woman. Joseph Street to William Clark, 7 May 1830, Indian Office Files St. Louis, 1830-1833, US Mss BN Box 63, Wisconsin State Historical Society, Madison, 1-2; Joseph Hardy to Wynkoop Warner, 7 May 1830, Indian Office Files St. Louis, 1828-1830, US Mss BN Box 63, Wisconsin State Historical Society, Madison, 1-2; Thomas Forsyth to William Clark, 7 May 1830, ibid., 2-3; Mrs. Henry S. Baird, "Indian Customs and Early Recollections," in *Report and Collections of the State Historical Society of Wisconsin for the Years 1880, 1881, and 1882*, ed. Lyman C. Draper, vol. 9, Collections of the State Historical Society of Wisconsin (Madison: David Atwood, State Printer, 1882), 324-325; Anthony F. C. Wallace, *Prelude to Disaster: The Course of Indian-White Relations Which Led to the Black Hawk War*

*of 1832* (Springfield: Illinois State Historical Library, 1970), 33;
George D. Lyman, *John Marsh, Pioneer: The Life Story of a Trail-Blazer
on Six Frontiers* (Chautauqua, N.Y.: Chautauqua Press, 1931), 152.

2. John H. Fonda, "Early Reminiscences of Wisconsin," in *Report and
   Collections of the State Historical Society of Wisconsin, for the Years 1867,
   1868, and 1869,* ed. Lyman C. Draper, vol. 5, Collections of the State
   Historical Society of Wisconsin (Madison: Atwood & Rublee, State
   Printers, 1868) (hereafter WHC 5), 257.

3. Baird, "Indian Customs and Early Recollections," 325–326.

4. Fonda, "Early Reminiscences of Wisconsin," 257.

5. Address of Col. Willoughby Morgan to delegates of the Sauk, Fox,
   Ioway, Menomonee, Sioux, Omahas, Ottawa, and Winnebago assembled in council on 7 July 1830, National Archives, Letters Received by the Office of Indian Affairs, 1824–81: Prairie du Chien
   Agency, 1824–1847, Microcopy No. 234, Roll 696: 1824–1842 (Washington. D.C.: National Archives and Records Service General Services Administration, 1957), F188.

6. Extracts from Minutes of a Council held at Prairie du Chien, etc.,
   7 July 1830, US Mss BM Box 63, Wisconsin Historical Society,
   Madison, 7.

7. Ibid., 16, 7.

8. Ibid., 10.

9. Ibid., 11.

10. Ibid., 12.

11. Ibid.

12. Ibid., 19.

13. Ibid., 19–20.

14. Ibid., 15.

15. Thomas McKenney to William Clark, 7 June 1830, Indian Office
    Letter Books, vols. 1–15, US Mss BN Box 47, Wisconsin Historical
    Society, Madison, vol. 6, 455.

16. During the War of 1812, Forsyth enjoyed such warm relations with
    the Indians that a U.S. Army captain assumed he must have been

employed by the British and placed him under arrest. Lyman C. Draper, ed., *Report and Collections of the State Historical Society of Wisconsin, for the Years 1869, 1870, 1871 and 1872,* vol. 6, Collections of the State Historical Society of Wisconsin (Madison: Atwood & Culver, State Printers, 1872) (hereafter WHC 6), 188n; Ellen M. Whitney, ed., *The Black Hawk War, 1831–1832,* vol. 36, Collections of the Illinois State Historical Library (Springfield: Illinois State Historical Library, 1973), 108n.

17. Anonymous to Forsyth, 14 March 1832, Thomas Forsyth Papers, 1804–1833, Draper Mss T, vol. 2 (Letters Received), Wisconsin Historical Society, Madison, 2.

18. Lyman C. Draper, WHC 6, 188n.

19. Randolph quoted in Thomas Loraine McKenney, *Memoirs, Official and Personal* (Lincoln: University of Nebraska Press, 1973), 262.

20. Lyman, *John Marsh, Pioneer,* 150-151.

21. Alfred Brunson, "Memoir of Hon. Thomas Pendleton Burnett," in *Second Annual Report and Collections of the State Historical Society of Wisconsin for the Year 1855,* ed. Lyman C. Draper, vol. 2, Collections of the State Historical Society of Wisconsin (Madison: Calkins & Proudfit, Printers, 1856), 242.

22. Ibid., 235, 236.

23. Herman J. Viola, *Thomas L. McKenney: Architect of America's Early Indian Policy, 1816–1830* (Chicago: Sage Books, 1974), 223-224.

24. McKenney lambasted the Jackson administration for its patronage in his memoirs, originally published in 1846. McKenney, *Memoirs, Official and Personal,* 193-200.

25. Treaty with the Sauk and Foxes, Etc., 15 July 1830, Charles J. Kappler, ed., *Indian Affairs: Laws and Treaties,* vol. 2 (Treaties) (Washington, D.C.: U.S. Government Printing Office, 1904), 305.

26. Fort Armstrong Council, 13 April 1832, *The Black Hawk War, 1831–1832,* ed. Ellen M. Whitney, vol. 36, Collections of the Illinois State Historical Library (Springfield: Illinois State Historical Library, 1973), 252.

27. P. G. Randoloph (Acting Sec. of War) to Morgan, 30 August 1830, Indian Office Letter Books, vol. 7, 19.

28. Joseph M. Street to John Eaton, 2 March 1831, Transcripts from Indian Office Files, US Mss BN Box 64, Wisconsin Historical Society, Madison, 1.

29. Ibid.

30. Ibid.

31. Ibid.

32. Street issued such warnings on 11 November, 2 February, and 2 March. Street to Eaton, 2 March 1831, Transcripts from Indian Office Files, Box 64, 1.

33. Thomas Burnett to William Clark, 18 May 1831, Brunson, "Memoir of Hon. Thomas Pendleton Burnett," 246-247.

34. Reynolds to William Clark, 26 May 1831; Gaines to Reynolds, 29 May 1831, *Black Hawk War,* vol. 36, 13, 23.

35. Donald Jackson, ed., *Black Hawk: An Autobiography* (Chicago: Illini Books, 1964; reprint, Chicago: University of Illinois Press, 1990), 109-110.

36. Edmund Gaines to Roger Jones, 8 June 1831, *Black Hawk War,* vol. 36, 36.

37. George Archibald McCall, *Letters from the Frontier during Thirty Years Service in the U.S. Army* (Philadelphia: J. B. Lippincott & Co., 1868), 228.

38. Jackson, ed., *Black Hawk: An Autobiography,* 114.

39. Ibid., 113.

40. James W. Silver, *Edmund Pendleton Gaines: Frontier General* (Baton Rouge: Louisiana State University Press, 1949), 144-145.

41. Gaines to Reynolds, 5 June 1831, *The Governors' Letter Books 1818–1834,* ed. Evarts Boutell Greene and Clarence Walworth Alvord, vol. 4, Collections of the Illinois State Historical Library (Springfield: Illinois State Historical Library, 1909), 169.

42. William Clark to Secretary of War, 12 August 1831, *Black Hawk War,* vol. 36, 136-138.

43. Nehemiah Matson, *Memories of Shaubena* (Chicago: D. B. Cooke Co., 1878), 100–101.

44. Thomas Loraine McKenney, "The Winnebago War," in WHC 5, 193.

45. Extracts from Minutes of a Council held at Prairie du Chien, etc., 7 July 1830, 16.

46. Whitney, *Black Hawk War*, vol. 36, 469n7.

47. Joseph Street to Wynkoop Warner, 22 April 1830, National Archives, Letters Received by the Office of Indian Affairs, 1824–81: Prairie du Chien Agency, 1824–1847, 208.

48. Moses Meeker, "Early History of the Lead Region of Wisconsin," in WHC 6, 289.

49. Thomas Forsyth to William Clark, 10 June 1828, Forsyth Papers, vol. 6, 84–85.

50. Gregory Evans Dowd, *A Spirited Resistance: The North American Indian Struggle for Unity, 1745–1815* (Baltimore: Johns Hopkins University Press, 1992), 193.

51. Thomas Forsyth to William Clark, 25 June and 1 July 1828, Forsyth Papers, vol. 6, 90–91; Frank E. Stevens, ed., *Wakefield's History of the Black Hawk War* (Chicago: Caxton Club, 1903), 210.

52. Jackson, ed., *Black Hawk: An Autobiography*, 119.

53. Clark to Secretary of War, 12 August 1831, *Black Hawk War*, vol. 36, 137.

54. Street to Secretary of War, 1 August 1831, ibid., 117.

55. According to the Mesquakie chief Wapello (or Prince), roughly equal numbers of Sauks and Mesquakies were involved in the attack. Black Hawk maintained, however, that the party consisted primarily of Mesquakies. Fort Armstrong Council, 13 April 1832, *Black Hawk War*, vol. 36, 253; Jackson, ed., *Black Hawk: An Autobiography*, 115.

56. Journal of Council between Samuel C. Stambaugh and the Menominee Indians in Green Bay, 15 August 1831, National Archives, Letters Received by the Office of Indian Affairs, 1824–81:

Green Bay Agency, 1824–1880, Microcopy No. 234, Roll 315: 1824–1832 (Washington. D.C.: National Archives and Records Service General Services Administration, 1959), F534. John Fonda, who helped bury the victims, recalled that every one was "killed with the knife and tomahawk, except the Fox shot by a boy." Fonda, "Early Reminiscences of Wisconsin," 258.

57. Street to Secretary of War, 1 August 1831, *Black Hawk War,* vol. 36, 117.

58. Journal of Council between Samuel C. Stambaugh and the Menominee Indians in Green Bay, 15 August 1831, National Archives, Letters Received by the Office of Indian Affairs, 1824–81: Green Bay Agency, 1824–1880, F531, F537.

59. Ibid., F531. Street placed the dead at twenty-five (eight men, six women, and eleven children). Street to Secretary of War, 1 August 1831, *Black Hawk War,* vol. 36, 117. John Fonda reports burying twenty-seven dead Indians, one of whom he believed to be a Mesquakie. Fonda, "Early Reminiscences of Wisconsin," 258.

60. Street to Gustavus Loomis, 31 July 1831, *Black Hawk War,* vol. 36, 114–115. Joseph Street described the slain Dakotas as "a brother of the principal chief, and the other a brave—both men of considerable consequence in the Tribe." Street to Secretary of War, 31 August 1831, *The Territorial Papers of the United States: Michigan Territory, 1829–1837,* ed. Clarence Edwin Carter, vol. 12 (Washington, D.C.: U.S. Government Printing Office, 1945), 343.

61. Street to Secretary of War, 1 August 1831, *Black Hawk War,* vol. 36, 118.

62. Ibid.

63. Clark to Secretary of War, 26 August 1831, National Archives, Letters Received by the Office of Indian Affairs, 1824–81: Green Bay Agency, 1824–1880, F358.

64. Street to Secretary of War, 1 August 1831, *Black Hawk War,* vol. 36, 119.

65. Street to Clark, 9 August 1831, National Archives, Letters Received

by the Office of Indian Affairs, 1824-81: Green Bay Agency, 1824-1880, F362-363.

66. Ibid., F362-364.

67. Ibid., F363.

68. Journal of Council between Samuel C. Stambaugh and the Menominee Indians in Green Bay, 15 August 1831, ibid., F530-35.

69. Stambaugh to Cass, 16 August 1831, ibid., F527.

70. Indian Office Letter Books, vol. 7, 344.

71. National Archives, Letters Received by the Office of Indian Affairs, 1824-81: Green Bay Agency, 1824-1880, F528A-28B, F538.

72. Samuel S. Hamilton to Samuel C. Stambaugh, 8 September 1831, *Territorial Papers*, vol. 12, 351.

73. Morgan to Henry Atkinson, 4 January 1832, National Archives, Letters Received by the Office of the Adjutant General (Main Series), 1822-1860, Microcopy No. 567, Roll 66: 1832 (Washington, D.C.: National Archives and Records Service, General Services Administration, 1964), 34-35.

74. Joseph M. Street to William Clark, 11 January 1832, *Black Hawk War,* vol. 36, 206-207.

75. Patricia K. Ourada, *The Menominee Indians: A History* (Norman: University of Oklahoma Press, 1979), 91.

76. Elbert Herring to John H, Kinzie, 6 April 1832, *Black Hawk War,* vol. 36, 229.

77. Quoted in Street to Atkinson, 29 April 1832, ibid., 333.

78. Macomb to Henry Atkinson, 17 March 1832, ibid., 220.

79. Silver, *Edmund Pendleton Gaines,* 146. Regarding Indian removal, Gaines said, "For my own part I would just as soon seek for fame an attempt to remove the Shakers, or the Quakers, as to break up the Indians." Ibid., 137.

80. Atkinson to Macomb, 3 April 1832, *Black Hawk War,* vol. 36, 224.

81. Matson, *Memories of Shaubena,* 92.

82. Felix St. Vrain to William Clark, 6 April 1832, *Black Hawk War,* vol. 36, 230.

83. Jackson, ed., *Black Hawk: An Autobiography*, 116-117.

84. In April 1830, Waukon had pledged to Street that he would encourage his people to remain at peace despite the killing of his daughter. Street to Wynkoop Warner, 22 April 1830, National Archives, Letters Received by the Office of Indian Affairs, 1824-81: Prairie du Chien Agency, 1824-1847, 208.

85. Street to Loomis, 9 April 1832, ibid., 239; Gustavus Loomis: Special Order 2, 9 April 1832, ibid., 240. Later in the month, Marsh reported to Joseph Street, "I find that I am much blamed by the Indians for having gone below to stop the war party." Marsh to Street, 17 April 1832, Joseph Montfort Street Papers, Iowa Department of Archives and History, Des Moines.

86. John Bliss to Atkinson, 12 April 1832, and Atkinson to John Reynolds, 13 April 1832, *Black Hawk War*, vol. 36, 238, 245; Wallace, *Prelude to Disaster*, 40. Black Hawk considered the 1831 attack on the Menominees "lawful and right" and granted those involved asylum. Jackson, ed., *Black Hawk: An Autobiography*, 115.

87. Fort Armstrong Council, 13 April 1832; Henry Atkinson to Alexander Macomb, 19 April 1832, *Black Hawk War*, vol. 36, 252-253, 278-279.

88. Fort Armstrong Council, 19 April 1832, ibid., 281.

89. Henry Smith, "Indian Campaign of 1832," in *Report and Collections of the State Historical Society of Wisconsin for the Years of 1883, 1884, and 1885*, ed. Lyman C. Draper, vol. 10, Collections of the State Historical Society of Wisconsin (Madison: Democrat Printing Co., State Printer, 1888), 154.

90. John H. Kinzie to Atkinson, 21 April 1832, ibid., 292.

91. Marsh to Street, 17 April 1832, Street Papers.

92. Conference between Joseph M. Street and a Menominee Delegation, 21 April 1832, *Black Hawk War*, vol. 36, 292-294.

93. Street to Henry Atkinson, 13 May 1832, ibid., 369; Street to Atkinson, 16 May 1832, ibid., 376-77; Street to William Clark, 29 April 1832, Street Papers.

94. Stambaugh to George B. Porter, 7 June 1832, *Black Hawk War*, vol. 36, 545.

### 5. EVERYTHING TO LOSE

1. Margaret Connell Szasz, ed., *Between Indian and White Worlds: The Cultural Broker* (Norman: University of Oklahoma Press, 1994), 10–20.

2. Billy Caldwell to Thomas Forsyth, 8 April 1832, *The Black Hawk War, 1831–1832*, ed. Ellen M. Whitney, vol. 36, Collections of the Illinois State Historical Library (Springfield: Illinois State Historical Library, 1973), 234.

3. The 1830 census placed the white population of Illinois at 157,445. Illinois experienced relatively uniform growth during the ensuing two decades. The 1840 census reported 466,576 residents, and the 1850 census reported 787,043 residents, indicating an average annual increase of approximately 31,480 persons. Bureau of the Census, *1990 Census of Population and Housing: Population and Housing Unit Counts, United States*, Bureau of the Census (Washington, D.C.: U.S. Department of Commerce, Economics and Statistics Administration, Bureau of the Census, 1990), 44.

4. The absence of a substantial Ho Chunk–métis population also posed a problem for the U.S. government, which habitually struggled to secure the services of qualified Ho Chunk interpreters.

5. Spoon Decorah, "Narrative of Spoon Decorah," in *Collections of the State Historical Society of Wisconsin*, ed. Reuben G. Thwaites, vol. 13 (Madison: Democrat Printing Co., State Printers, 1895), 450.

6. Edward E. Hill, *The Office of Indian Affairs, 1824–1880: Historical Sketches* (New York: Clearwater Publishing Co., 1974), 143.

7. Street to Montfort Stokes, 26 August 1833, Joseph Montfort Street Papers, Iowa Department of Archives and History, Des Moines.

8. Forsyth to William Clark, 6 August 1826, Thomas Forsyth Papers, 1804-1833, Wisconsin Historical Society, Madison, 54; Lyman C. Draper, Draper's Notes, Draper Mss 22S, Microcopy 1034, Reel 50,

Wisconsin Historical Society, Madison, F213-214; Adèle Maria Antoinette de Perdreauville Gratiot, "An Interesting Narrative: The
Reminiscences of Mrs. Adele B. Gratiot," *Galena Weekly Gazette*,
2 May 1879.

9. Reuben G. Thwaites, ed., *Collections of the State Historical Society of
Wisconsin*, vol. 20 (Madison: State Historical Society of Wisconsin,
1911), 315-316n; Juliette Kinzie, *Wau-bun: The Early Day in the North
West* (1873; reprint, Philadelphia: Bibliobazaar, 2006), 130.

10. James Ryan Haydon, "John Kinzie's Place in History," in *Transac-
tions of the Illinois State Historical Society for the year 1932*, ed. Paul M.
Angle (Springfield: By the authority of the State of Illinois, 1932),
191.

11. Kinzie, *Wau-bun*, 84.

12. Former governor Ninian Edwards argued such a point to Senator
Elias Kent Kane on 19 April 1832. *The Black Hawk War, 1831–1832*, ed.
Ellen M. Whitney, vol. 36, Collections of the Illinois State Historical Library (Springfield: Illinois State Historical Library, 1973),
649n.

13. Bliss to Atkinson, 9-12 April 1832, ibid., 238; Davenport to
Atkinson, 13 April 1832, ibid., 247; Atkinson to Macomb, 13 April
1832, ibid., 245; Atkinson to Reynolds, 13 April 1832, ibid., 245.

14. Atkinson to Macomb, 10 April 1832, ibid., 243.

15. Henry Gratiot to Clark, 12 June 1832, ibid., 577.

16. Donald Jackson, ed., *Black Hawk: An Autobiography* (Chicago: Illini
Books, 1964; reprint, Chicago: University of Illinois Press, 1990),
120-121.

17. Henry Gratiot to Clark, 12 June 1832, *Black Hawk War*, vol. 36, 577-
578.

18. Lyman C. Draper, Draper's Historical Miscellanies, 2Q, Reel 43,
Wisconsin Historical Society, Madison, F139r.

19. James A. Clifton, "Merchant, Soldier, Broker, Chief: A Corrected
Obituary of Captain Billy Caldwell," *Journal of the Illinois State Historical Society* 71 (August 1978): 193.

20. Caldwell had fought for the British at the River Raisin, Fort Stephenson, Fort Meigs, Dudley's Defeat, and the Thames during the War of 1812. Draper, Draper's Notes, Draper Mss 17S, Microcopy 1034, Reel 49, F232.

21. Draper, Draper's Historical Miscellanies, F139r–139v; Kinzie, *Waubun*, 126.

22. Draper, Draper's Historical Miscellanies, F139.1. Sau-ga-nash literally translates as "peninsula," by which name the British were known for their earlier reluctance to stray from the Michigan Peninsula. Juliette Kinzie to Lyman C. Draper, 7 June 1865, Draper, Draper's Historical Miscellanies, F140.2.

23. Thomas J. V. Owen to Elbert Herring, 12 May 1832, National Archives, Letters Received by the Office of Indian Affairs, 1824–81: Chicago Agency, 1824–1847, Microcopy No. 234, Roll 132: 1824–1834 (Washington, D.C.: National Archives and Records Service, General Services Administration, 1959), F180–182; Nehemiah Matson, *Memories of Shaubena* (Chicago: D. B. Cooke Co., 1878), 97–98.

24. Atkinson to Edmund Gaines, 18 April 1832, *Black Hawk War*, vol. 36, 272; Felix St. Vrain to William Clark, 18 April 1832, ibid., 277; Benjamin M. Young, Benjamin Mills, and James M. Strode to Thomas M. Neal and James D. Henry, 20 April 1832, ibid., 287, 288; Benjamin M. Young, Benjamin Mills, and James M. Strode to John Reynolds, 20 April 1832, ibid., 289.

25. Fort Armstrong Council, 13 April 1832, ibid., 251.

26. Atkinson to Reynolds, 27 April 1832, ibid., 320.

27. Atkinson to Reynolds, 13 April 1832, ibid., 246.

28. Kerry A. Trask, *Black Hawk: The Battle for the Heart of America* (New York: Henry Holt, 2006), 158–159.

29. Reynolds to Atkinson, 16 April 1832, *Black Hawk War*, vol. 36, 263.

30. Atkinson to Henry Gratiot, 15 April 1832, ibid., 257; Atkinson to John H. Kinzie, 16 April 1832, ibid., 257–258; Atkinson to Gustavus Loomis, 16 April 1832, ibid., 258; Atkinson to the Commanding Officer Fort Winnebago, 16 April 1832, ibid., 259; Atkinson to Sam-

uel C. Stambaugh, 16 April 1832, ibid., 259–260; Atkinson to Joseph
M. Street, 16 April 1832, ibid., 260–261.

31. Atkinson to Hugh Brady, 8 May 1832, ibid., 354–355; Atkinson to
Owen, 18 May 1832, ibid., 379.

32. Minutes of a Talk between Henry Atkinson and Whirling Thunder
and White Crow, 28 April 1832, ibid., 322.

33. Matson, *Memories of Shaubena*, 185; Henry H. Hurlbut, ed., *Chicago
Antiquities: Comprising Original Items and Relations, Letters, Extracts,
and Notes, Pertaining to Early Chicago; Embellished with Views, Portraits,
Autographs, Etc.* (Chicago: Fergus Printing Co., 1881), 456–457.

34. Atkinson to Reynolds, 5 May 1832, *Black Hawk War*, vol. 36, 348; Isaiah Stillman to Reynolds, 4 May 1832, ibid., 346; William Clark to
Lewis Cass, 8 May 1832, ibid., 357; Henry Dodge to John Reynolds,
8 May 1832, ibid., 358.

35. Thomas J. V. Owen to John Reynolds, 12 May 1832, ibid., 365.

36. Dodge to Atkinson, 13 May 1832, ibid., 368.

37. Jackson, ed., *Black Hawk: An Autobiography*, 122; Matson, *Memories
of Shaubena*, 106, 109–111.

38. Philip St. George Cooke, *Scenes and Adventures in the Army: Or, Romance of Military Life* (Philadelphia: Lindsay & Blakiston, 1857), 156.

39. Whitney, *Black Hawk War*, vol. 36, 387n5; Jackson, ed., *Black Hawk:
An Autobiography*, 124–125.

40. John Reynolds: Proclamation, 15 May 1832, *Black Hawk War*, vol. 36,
373.

41. William Marshall to George B. Porter, 5 June 1832, ibid., 526;
Atkinson to Henry Dodge, 17 May 1832, ibid., 378; Thomas J. V.
Owen to George B. Porter, 18 May 1832, ibid., 383.

42. Jackson, ed., *Black Hawk: An Autobiography*, 127.

43. Minutes of an Examination of Prisoners, 19 August 1832, *The Black
Hawk War, 1831–1832*, ed. Ellen M. Whitney, vol. 37, Collections of
the Illinois State Historical Library (Springfield: Illinois State Historical Library, 1975), 1028–1033.

44. "War News from Galena," 30 May 1832, *Black Hawk War,* vol. 36, 489; Jackson, ed., *Black Hawk: An Autobiography,* 128.

45. Matson, *Memories of Shaubena,* 147-148; Whitney, *Black Hawk War,* vol. 37, 129n5.

46. Matson, *Memories of Shaubena,* 121-123.

47. Correspondence, Articles, Miscellany on Wisconsin Indians, US Mss 7E Folder 1, Wisconsin Historical Society, Madison, 1.

48. Ibid., 1-2.

49. Survivor John Hall estimated the attackers to number between sixty and eighty. Ibid., 3.

50. Matson, *Memories of Shaubena,* 153, 163.

51. Ibid., 174.

52. Matson, *Memories of Shaubena,* 118-119; Hurlbut, ed., *Chicago Antiquities,* 457.

53. Contrary to Big. Gen. Hugh Brady's report, Big Foot joined the Potawatomi company in the service of the United States. Hugh Brady to Winfield Scott, ca. 21 May 1832, *Black Hawk War,* vol. 36, 398. Brady's suspicion of Big Foot's allegiance, however, was at least partly warranted. Related to the Ho Chunks by marriage, the Potawatomi chief evinced considerable disaffection toward the Americans at the 1828 annuity payment in Chicago and subsequently (albeit unsuccessfully) circulated war wampum among other Potawatomi bands. Draper, Draper's Notes, Draper Mss 22S, Microcopy 1034, Reel 50, F89-91.

54. Reddick Horn to Reynolds, 22 May 1832, *Black Hawk War,* vol. 36, 407; Zachary Taylor to Atkinson, 26 May 1832, ibid., 453; Samuel Whiteside to Atkinson, 27 May 1832, ibid., 461-462; James M. Strode to Lewis Cass, 22 May 1832, ibid., 410; Clark to Cass, 29 May 1832, ibid., 471.

55. Thomas J. V. Owen to the Superintendent of Indian Affairs at Detroit, 24 May 1832, ibid., 433; Owen to Atkinson, 3 June 1832, ibid., 506; Chicago Residents to James Stewart, 29 May 1832, ibid., 475.

56. Richard R. Johnson, "The Search for a Usable Indian: An Aspect of the Defense of Colonial New England," *Journal of American History* 64, no. 3 (December 1977): 625–627, 634; James D. Drake, *King Philip's War: Civil War in New England, 1675–1676* (Amherst: University of Massachusetts Press, 1999), 4.

57. Jill Lepore, *King Philip's War and the Origins of American Identity* (New York: Alfred A. Knopf, 1998), 88–89.

58. Thomas W. Dunlay, *Wolves for the Blue Soldiers: Indian Scouts and Auxiliaries with the United States Army, 1860–90* (Lincoln: University of Nebraska Press, 1982), 14.

59. Colin G. Calloway, *The American Revolution in Indian Country: Crisis and Diversity in Native American Communities* (Cambridge: Cambridge University Press, 1995), 100.

60. Richard White, *The Middle Ground: Indians, Empires, and Republics in the Great Lakes Region, 1650–1815* (Cambridge: Cambridge University Press, 1991), 375.

61. St. Clair's Chickasaw scouts wore white handkerchiefs around their heads, each adorned with a single red feather, in order to distinguish them from the enemy. Wiley Sword, *President Washington's Indian War: The Struggle for the Old Northwest, 1790–1795* (Norman: University of Oklahoma Press, 1985), 168. Potawatomi and Ho Chunk scouts donned similar headwear during the Black Hawk War for the same purpose.

62. Gregory Evans Dowd, *A Spirited Resistance: The North American Indian Struggle for Unity, 1745–1815* (Baltimore: Johns Hopkins University Press, 1992), 186–190.

63. William Trimble to Poosh-a-mat-a-haw, 19 January 1818, Trimble to Thomas Wright, 15 January 1818, and Trimble to William King, 12 February 1818, William A. Trimble Papers, Ohio Historical Society, Columbus; Francis Paul Prucha, *The Sword of the Republic: The United States Army on the Frontier, 1783–1846* (New York: Macmillan, 1968), 132, 155.

64. Richard White, "The Winning of the West: The Expansion of the

Western Sioux in the Eighteenth and Nineteenth Centuries," *Journal of American History* 65, no. 2 (Sep. 1978): 333.

65. E. Duis, *The Good Old Times in McLean County, Illinois, Containing Two Hundred and Sixty-one Sketches of Old Settlers: A Complete Historical Sketch of the Black Hawk War, and Descriptions of All Matters of Interest Relating to McLean County* (Bloomington, Ill.: Leader Publishing and Printing House, 1874), 113.

66. Atkinson to Alexander Macomb, 30 May 1832, *Black Hawk War,* vol. 36, 478.

67. Henry Atkinson to William Davenport, 20 May 1832, ibid., 477; Cooke, *Scenes and Adventures in the Army,* 157.

68. Taylor to Atkinson, 2 June 1832, *Black Hawk War,* vol. 36, 503.

6. WARPATH

1. Atkinson to Joseph M. Street, 26 May 1832, *The Black Hawk War, 1831–1832,* ed. Ellen M. Whitney, vol. 36, Collections of the Illinois State Historical Library (Springfield: Illinois State Historical Library, 1973), 445.

2. Atkinson to Joshua B. Brant, 27 May 1832, ibid., 457.

3. Atkinson to Macomb, 30 May 1832, ibid., 478.

4. Street to Atkinson, 6–7 June 1832, ibid., 535.

5. George D. Lyman, *John Marsh, Pioneer: The Life Story of a Trail-Blazer on Six Frontiers* (Chautauqua, N.Y.: Chautauqua Press, 1931), 151, 171.

6. Street to Burnett, 30 May 1832, *Black Hawk War,* vol. 36, 488.

7. Lyman, *John Marsh, Pioneer,* 170.

8. Whitney, *Black Hawk War,* vol. 36, 525n.

9. Lyman, *John Marsh, Pioneer,* 170.

10. This village would furnish warriors and, Street observed, "Maney of the Winnebeagos who go, are related to & connected with the Menomines and Sioux." Street to Atkinson, 6 June 1832, *Black Hawk War,* vol. 36, 535.

11. One-Eyed Decorah was also known as Wadge-hut-ta-kaw or

Waugh-ha-ta-kau (Big Canoe or Big Boat). In 1829, anthropologist and treaty commissioner Caleb Atwater visited Prairie la Crosse and described Winneshiek and One-Eyed Decorah as coequal civil chiefs, but One-Eyed Decorah did not actually achieve formal status as a chief until the treaty of 15 September 1832. Caleb Atwater, *Remarks Made on a Tour of Prairie du Chien, Thence to Washington City, in 1829* (Columbus, Ohio: Isaac N. Whiting, 1831), 97; Mauchhewemahnigo, "Narrative of Walking Cloud," in *Collections of the State Historical Society of Wisconsin*, ed. Reuben G. Thwaites, vol. 13 (Madison: Democrat Printing Co., State Printers, 1895) (hereafter WHC 13), 465; Nancy O. Lurie, "In Search of Chaetar: New Findings on Black Hawk's Surrender," *Wisconsin Magazine of History* 71, no. 3 (Spring 1988): 164, 175.

12. Lyman, *John Marsh, Pioneer,* 170.

13. The *Galenian,* 13 June 1832, *The Black Hawk War, 1831–1832,* ed. Ellen M. Whitney, vol. 37, Collections of the Illinois State Historical Library (Springfield: Illinois State Historical Library, 1975), 790n4; Lurie, "In Search of Chaetar," 168. Winneshiek's elder son, Wawkonchawkoohaw, would help guide the British Band from Four Lakes (Madison, Wisconsin) to their intended crossing point of the Mississippi. Minutes of an Examination of Prisoners, 27 August 1832, *Black Hawk War,* vol. 37, 1056–1057. After the war, Winneshiek and both of his sons were detained, and Ellen Whitney suggests the possibility that both of them rendered assistance to Black Hawk. Atkinson to Zachary Taylor, 29 August 1832, Whitney, *Black Hawk War,* vol. 37, 1081n2.

14. *The Galenian,* 13 June 1832, Whitney, *Black Hawk War,* vol. 37, 790n4.

15. Lyman, *John Marsh, Pioneer,* 171. According to the recorder of a later talk between Street and the Dakotas, L'Arc was half Ho Chunk. Talk between Joseph M. Street and the Sioux, 22 June 1832, *Black Hawk War,* vol. 36, 652.

16. Atkinson to Street, 26 May 1832, *Black Hawk War,* vol. 36, 445.

17. Lyman, *John Marsh, Pioneer,* 171.

18. "The Winnebagoes and Black Hawk War," in *Report and Collections of the State Historical Society of Wisconsin, for the Years 1867, 1868, and 1869*, ed. Lyman C. Draper, vol. 5 (Madison: Atwood & Rublee, State Printers, 1868), 307.

19. Street to Atkinson, 6 June 1832, *Black Hawk War*, vol. 36, 536.

20. Marsh biographer George Lyman placed the number at twenty, while Street estimated that thirty to forty arrived with Marsh's party. Street to Atkinson, 6 June 1832, Lyman, *John Marsh, Pioneer*, 171; *Black Hawk War*, vol. 36, 535.

21. Street to Atkinson, 6-7 June 1832, *Black Hawk War*, vol. 36, 535.

22. Ibid.

23. Memorandum of purchase of firearms for the Black Hawk War, 7 June 1832, Joseph Montfort Street Papers, Iowa Department of Archives and History, Des Moines.

24. Albert S. Johnston to Hamilton, 26 May 1832, *Black Hawk War*, vol. 36, 444.

25. Robert Anderson, "Reminiscences of the Black Hawk War," in *Report and Collections of the State Historical Society of Wisconsin for the Years 1883, 1884, and 1885*, ed. Lyman C. Draper, vol. 10, Collections of the State Historical Society of Wisconsin (Madison: Democrat Printing Co., State Printer, 1888) (hereafter WHC 10), 171.

26. Memorandum of purchase of firearms for the Black Hawk War, 7 June 1832, Street Papers; Street to Atkinson, 6-7 June 1832, and Street to William Clark, 7 June 1832, *Black Hawk War*, vol. 36, 537, 547. Of the 225, Street identified eighty to ninety as Dakotas, forty as Menominees, and the remainder as Ho Chunks affiliated with Waukon Decorah. *Black Hawk War*, vol. 36, 547.

27. Kinzie to Porter, 31 May 1832, Whitney, *Black Hawk War*, vol. 36, 495n.

28. Juliette Kinzie, *Wau-bun: The Early Day in the North West* (1873; reprint, Philadelphia: Bibliobazaar, 2006), 257.

29. Ibid.

30. Four Lakes Council, 26 May 1832, *Black Hawk War*, vol. 36, 455.

31. Street to Atkinson, 7 June, 1832, ibid., 537.

32. Winnebago Indian Talk, 7 June 1832, ibid., 543.

33. Blue Mounds Council, 28 May 1832, ibid., 467.

34. Henry Gratiot's Journal, 28 May 1832, *Black Hawk War,* vol. 37, 1303.

35. Porter's Grove Council, 3 June 1832, *Black Hawk War,* vol. 36, 506–507; Nehemiah Matson, *Memories of Shaubena* (Chicago: D. B. Cooke Co., 1878), 172–173.

36. H. A. Tenney, "Early Times in Wisconsin," in *First Annual Report and Collections of the State Historical Society, of Wisconsin, for the Year 1854,* ed. Lyman C. Draper, vol. 1, Collections of the State Historical Society of Wisconsin (Madison: Beriah Brown, Printer, 1855; reprint, 1903), 98.

37. Daniel M. Parkinson, "Pioneer Life in Wisconsin," in *Second Annual Report and Collections of the State Historical Society of Wisconsin for the Year 1855,* ed. Lyman C. Draper, vol. 2, Collections of the State Historical Society of Wisconsin (Madison: Calkins & Proudfit, Printers, 1856), 339–340; Peter Parkinson, Jr., "Notes on the Black Hawk War," in WHC 10, 186–188.

38. Henry Gratiot to William Clark, 12 June 1832, *Black Hawk War,* vol. 36, 578.

39. Parkinson, "Notes on the Black Hawk War," 190.

40. Ibid., 185.

41. Porter's Grove Council, 3–4 June 1832, *Black Hawk War,* vol. 36, 512.

42. Parkinson, "Notes on the Black Hawk War," 185.

43. Henry Gratiot, Journal, 14 June 1832, *Black Hawk War,* vol. 37, 1304.

44. Atkinson to Taylor, 11 June 1832, *Black Hawk War,* vol. 36, 570.

45. Atkinson to Owen, 31 May 1832, ibid., 491–492.

46. Owen to Atkinson, 3 June 1832, ibid., 505–506.

47. Atkinson also specifically requested that Billy Caldwell join the force. Atkinson to Thomas J. V. Owen, 11 June 1832, ibid., 571.

48. Thomas J. V. Owen to the Public, 5 June 1832, ibid., 527–528; Matson, *Memories of Shaubena,* 112–114.

49. Atkinson to Commanding Officer at Hennepin, 7 June 1832, *Black Hawk War,* vol. 36, 540.

50. Owen to Stevens T. Mason, 17 June 1832, ibid., 615. Owen identified the attacking Indians as members of the British Band, but historian Patrick Jung has questioned the veracity of his report. Noting that the main body of Black Hawk's warriors was further west at this time—and that this attack occurred in the heart of Potawatomi country—Jung has contended that Potawatomis were responsible for this attack, as well as the deaths of Adam Payne on 24 May and three settlers on 24 June. Patrick J. Jung, *The Black Hawk War of 1832* (Norman: University of Oklahoma Press, 2007), 112–113.

51. Owen to Elbert Herring, 21 June 1832, Letters Received by the Office of Indian Affairs, 1824–81: Chicago Agency, 1824–1847, National Archives Microcopy No. 234, Roll 132: 1824–1834 (Washington, D.C.: National Archives and Records Service, General Services Administration, 1959), F188–F189.

52. Owen to Porter, 24 July 1832, ibid., F211–212.

53. William Campbell to Andrew Jackson, 13 July, 1832, *Black Hawk War,* vol. 37, 788.

54. *The Galenian,* 13 June 1832, ibid., 790n4.

55. Taylor to Atkinson, 13 June 1832, *Black Hawk War,* vol. 36, 585.

56. Hamilton to Atkinson, 13 June 1832, ibid., 582.

57. A volunteer at the Blue Mounds Fort placed the Wisconsin River Ho Chunk force at twenty-four warriors; Henry Gratiot counted thirty warriors, while Edward Beouchard (who accompanied the force from Blue Mounds) placed it at forty-nine warriors. It is likely that the volunteer tallied Waukaunkaw's band, that Gratiot tallied Waukon Decorah's band, and that Beouchard reported an aggregate number. Ebenezer Brigham to John H. Kinzie, 15 [16] June 1832, *Black Hawk War,* vol. 36, 605; Henry Gratiot Journal, 15 June 1832, *Black Hawk War,* vol. 37, 1304; Edward D. Beouchard,

"Beouchard's Narrative," in *The History of Wisconsin: In Three Parts, Historical, Documentary, and Descriptive.,* ed. William R. Smith, vol. 3 (Madison: Beriah Brown, Printer, 1854), 210; Edward D. Beouchard, "Edward D. Beouchard's Vindication," in *Report and Collections of the State Historical Society of Wisconsin, for the Years 1873, 1874, 1875 and 1876,* ed. Lyman C. Draper, vol. 7, Collections of the State Historical Society of Wisconsin (Madison: E. B. Bolens, State Printer, 1876) (hereafter WHC 7), 292.

58. Beouchard, "Beouchard's Narrative," 210; Charles Bracken and Peter Parkinson, Jr., "Pekatonica Battle Controversy," in WHC 2, 388–389.

59. Beouchard, "Edward D. Beouchard's Vindication," 293.

60. Paul Radin, *The Winnebago Tribe* (Lincoln: University of Nebraska Press, 1970), 110; Samuel W. Pond, *The Dakota or Sioux in Minnesota as They Were in 1834* (1908; reprint, St. Paul: Minnesota Historical Society Press, 1986), 128.

61. Dodge to Atkinson, 18 June 1832, *Black Hawk War,* vol. 36, 623.

62. Bracken and Parkinson, "Pekatonica Battle Controversy," 367; John A. Wakefield, *Wakefield's History of the Black Hawk War,* ed. Frank E. Stevens (1834; reprint, Chicago: Caxton Club, 1904), 70; Parkinson, "Pioneer Life in Wisconsin," 350–351.

63. Henry Atkinson to the Winnebago Indians, 11 June 1832, *Black Hawk War,* vol. 36, 572.

64. Dodge to Atkinson, 18 June 1832, ibid., 623–624.

65. Dodge to Captain John Sherman, Hamilton Fort, 16 June 1832, William Henry Papers, 1823–1849, SC 773, Wisconsin Historical Society, Madison, 2–3.

66. Gratiot to Atkinson, 19 June 1832, and Dodge to Atkinson, 18 June, 1833, *Black Hawk War,* vol. 36, 631, 623–624.

67. Hamilton to Atkinson, 24 June 1832, *Black Hawk War,* vol. 37, 663.

68. William Campbell to Andrew Jackson, 16 June 1832, and Talk between Joseph M. Street and the Sioux, 22 June 1832, *Black Hawk War,* vol. 36, 612, 653; Parkinson, "Pioneer Life in Wisconsin," 350.

69. Street to William Clark, 13 July 1832, Street Papers.

70. Talk between Joseph M. Street and the Sioux, 22 June 1832, *Black Hawk War,* vol. 36, 652-653.

71. Street to Atkinson, 17 July 1832, *Black Hawk War,* vol. 37, 818.

72. On 25 July, Sault Ste. Marie agent Henry Schoolcraft convened a council with the Dakotas at the Saint Peters Agency in Minnesota. On a diplomatic mission to broker a peace between the Dakotas and the Ojibwas, Schoolcraft inquired about the Dakota war party and the extent of its attachment to the United States. Refuting the insinuation that his warriors' loyalty was wanting, the Dakota chief assured Schoolcraft that the war party was prepared to sally forth once more: "The Sioux war club . . . was ready to be lifted again. They were ready to hear the Commanding officer, who was sitting present, say, Strike." National Archives, Letters Received by the Office of Indian Affairs, 1824-81: Michigan Superintendency, 1824-1851, Microcopy No. 234, Roll 421: 1832-1835 (Washington, D.C.: National Archives and Records Service, General Services Administration, 1959), F206.

73. Dodge to Atkinson, 18 June 1832, *Black Hawk War,* vol. 36, 624; Gratiot to Atkinson, 19 June 1832, ibid., 631; Report of Oliver Emmell and White Crow, 27 June 1832, *Black Hawk War,* vol. 37, 694; Gratiot, Journal, 15, 27 June 1832, *Black Hawk War,* vol. 37, 1304.

74. Report of Oliver Emmell and White Crow, 27 June 1832, *Black Hawk War,* vol. 37, 694-696.

75. Council with the Rock River Winnebago, 11 September 1832, ibid., 1133; Tenney, "Early Times in Wisconsin," 99.

76. Minutes of an Examination of Prisoners, 20 August 1832, *Black Hawk War,* vol. 37, 1036; Minutes of an Examination of Prisoners, 27 August 1832, ibid., 1055-1056.

77. Minutes of an Examination of Prisoners, 20 August 1832, ibid., 1035.

78. Henry Gratiot Journal, 5 July 1832, *Black Hawk War,* vol. 37, 1304; Thwaites, WHC 13, 452n; Charles Bracken, "Further Strictures on Gov. Ford's History of the Black Hawk War," in WHC 2, 404.

79. R. David Edmunds, *The Potawatomis: Keepers of the Fire* (Norman: University of Oklahoma Press, 1978), 239.
80. Roll of Potawatomi Indians in United States Service, *The Black Hawk War, 1831–1832*, ed. Ellen M. Whitney, vol. 35, Collections of the Illinois State Historical Library (Springfield: Illinois State Historical Library, 1970), 560–562.
81. Journal of Albert S. Johnston, *Black Hawk War*, vol. 37, 1315.
82. Wakefield, *Wakefield's History of the Black Hawk War*, 76.
83. Ibid.
84. Atkinson to Owen, 31 May, 1832, *Black Hawk War*, vol. 36, 491; Albert S. Johnston, Journal, *Black Hawk War*, vol. 37, 1315.
85. Philip St. George Cooke, *Scenes and Adventures in the Army: Or, Romance of Military Life* (Philadelphia: Lindsay & Blakiston, 1857), 163; Wakefield, *Wakefield's History of the Black Hawk War*, 77–78.
86. Albert S. Johnston Journal, 3 July 1832, *Black Hawk War*, vol. 37, 1316; Wakefield, *Wakefield's History of the Black Hawk War*, 78–79.
87. After receiving Emmell's first scouting report on 27 June, Henry Gratiot ordered this smaller Ho Chunk party back into the field on 29 June. Henry Gratiot Journal, 29 June and 8 July 1832, and Ninevah Shaw Journal, 3 July 1832, *Black Hawk War*, vol. 37, 1304, 1334.
88. Robb to Atkinson, 12 June 1832, *Black Hawk War*, vol. 36, 580.
89. Lewis Cass to Scott, 15 June 1832, ibid., 590–93; Cass to John Reynolds, 15 June 1832, ibid., 594; Adjutant General's Office Order No. 51, 16 June 1832, ibid., 599–601; Zachary Taylor to Thomas Lawson, 16 August 1832, ibid., 1016.
90. Allan Peskin, *Winfield Scott and the Profession of Arms* (Kent, Ohio: Kent State University Press, 2003), 83.
91. Contemporary correspondence almost invariably refers to the Bark as "White Water Creek," which was in fact a small tributary of the Bark River.
92. Ninevah Shaw Journal, 6 July 1832, *Black Hawk War*, vol. 37, 1334.
93. Donald Jackson, ed., *Black Hawk: An Autobiography* (Chicago: Illini

Books, 1964; reprint, Chicago: University of Illinois Press, 1990), 133.

94. Henry Smith, "Indian Campaign of 1832," in WHC 10, 160.

95. After the war, Ho Chunks identified six participants in this attack, although the United States ultimately held only a man named Waukeeaunskaw and his son (the latter as the actual shooter) accountable. Council with the Winnebago from the Fort Winnebago Agency, 10 September 1832, Council with the Rock River Winnebago, 11 September 1832, Treaty with the Winnebago, 15 September 1832, *Black Hawk War*, vol. 37, 1131–1132, 1133, 1155. A militiaman with the army later recorded that these Indians were among those guiding Atkinson's force—a claim echoed by several historians. Yet Ninevah Shaw and Henry Gratiot place the number of Ho Chunks with Emmell at ten and eleven, respectively, the first reporting on 3 July and the latter on 8 July. Extant records suggest that the only Ho Chunks with Atkinson's main body on the morning of 7 July were those under Emmell. Hence, if any of these guides participated in this attack, they must have recrossed the Bark River and rejoined Atkinson's command before Henry Gratiot entered Atkinson's camp. James Justice Reminiscences, 7 July 1832, Ninevah Shaw Journal, 4 [3] July 1832, and Henry Gratiot Journal, 8 July 1832, *Black Hawk War*, vol. 37, 1323, 1334, 1304; Jung, *The Black Hawk War of 1832*, 131; Crawford B. Thayer, ed., *Hunting a Shadow: The Search for Black Hawk* (Fort Atkinson, Wis.: Crawford B. Thayer, 1981), 93; Kerry A. Trask, *Black Hawk: The Battle for the Heart of America* (New York: Henry Holt, 2006), 250.

96. E. Buckner, "A Brief History of the War with the Sac and Fox Indians in Illinois and Michigan, in 1832, with Twenty-One Letters and Orders," in *Collections and Researches Made by the Pioneer and Historical Society of the State of Michigan*, vol. 12, Historical Collections (Lansing: Thorp & Godfrey, State Printers and Binders, 1888), 430.

97. Parkinson, "Pioneer Life in Wisconsin," 353–354.

98. Parkinson, "Notes on the Black Hawk War," 207.

99. Wakefield, *Wakefield's History of the Black Hawk War,* 83.

100. Ibid., 83–84; Albert S. Johnston Journal, 9 July 1832, *Black Hawk War,* vol. 37, 1317.

101. Parkinson, "Pioneer Life in Wisconsin," 354; Smith, "Indian Campaign of 1832," 160; Wakefield, *Wakefield's History of the Black Hawk War,* 84; Parkinson, "Notes on the Black Hawk War," 207; Charles Bracken, "Personal Narrative of Lieutenant Charles Bracken," in *The History of Wisconsin: In Three Parts, Historical, Documentary, and Descriptive.,* ed. William R. Smith, vol. 3 (Madison, Wis.: Beriah Brown, Printer, 1854), 219.

102. Atkinson to Roger Jones, 19 November 1832, *Black Hawk War,* vol. 37, 1209. On 9 July 1832, Atkinson informed Winfield Scott that "the surrounding tribes seem more disposed to be neutral than taking part with us." Atkinson to Scott, 9 July 1932, ibid., 753.

103. Roll of Menominee Indians, *Black Hawk War,* vol. 35, 562–563.

104. Gratiot, Journal, 10 June 1832, *Black Hawk War,* vol. 37, 1304.

105. Atkinson to Scott, 11 July 1832, ibid., 763.

106. Ibid.

107. Atkinson to Boyd, 12 July 1832, ibid., 770.

108. Ibid., 770–771; Atkinson to Hamilton, 12 July 1832, ibid., 771–772.

109. On 14 July, Hamilton arrived at Fort Winnebago, where he discussed his mission with John Kinzie. Hamilton believed that Black Hawk would attempt to use canoes to cross Lake Michigan and ultimately escape to Drummond Island. Hamilton's plan was to position himself at the head of canoe-mounted Menominee warriors and intercept the British Band while still on the lake. John H. Kinzie to George B. Porter, 14 July 1832, ibid., 796.

110. Dodge to Atkinson, 14 July 1832, ibid., 791.

111. Kinzie to George B. Porter, 12 July 1832, ibid., 774.

112. Dodge to Atkinson, 14 July 1832, ibid., 791.

113. Henry Merrell, "Pioneer Life in Wisconsin," in WHC 7, 383.

114. Ibid., 382–383.

115. Satterlee Clark, "Pierre Paquette: The Early History of Fort

Winnebago as Narrated by Hon. Sat. Clark at the Court House in Portage, on Friday Eve., Mar. 21, '79," *Portage Democrat,* 28 March 1879, 2.

116. Spoon Decorah, "Narrative of Spoon Decorah," in WHC 13, 452. After the war, one of Dodge's officers categorically dismissed allegations by two Illinois governors—Reynolds and Thomas Ford—that members of Paquette's party were spies: "No man who knew him, ever suspected the honesty or patriotism of Poquette"; he "possessed unbounded influence over the Indians." Bracken, "Further Strictures on Gov. Ford's History of the Black Hawk War," 407.

117. Decorah, "Narrative of Spoon Decorah," 453.

118. Spoon Decorah and John De la Ronde both recalled that White Crow himself accompanied this party, but they appear to have confused White Crow with his son. The issue is further confused by the fact that two Indians named Pania Blanc (White Pawnee)—one of them White Crow's son—were members of this party. Ibid; John T. De la Ronde, "Personal Narrative," in WHC 7, 350; Moses Paquette, "The Wisconsin Winnebagoes," in *Collections of the State Historical Society of Wisconsin,* ed. Reuben G. Thwaites, vol. 12 (Madison: Democrat Printing Co., 1892), 431; *Black Hawk War,* vol. 37, 1305-1306n21.

119. Present-day Hustisford, Wisconsin. Bracken, "Further Strictures on Gov. Ford's History of the Black Hawk War," 405.

120. Dodge to Atkinson, 18 July 1832, *Black Hawk War,* vol. 37, 820; Bracken, "Further Strictures on Gov. Ford's History of the Black Hawk War," 406-407; Parkinson, "Pioneer Life in Wisconsin," 355.

121. Journal of James J. Justice, *Black Hawk War,* vol. 37, 1324. Although the villagers at Hustis' Rapids may have intentionally misled Dodge's and Henry's brigades, Charles Bracken emphatically refuted allegations that the Ho Chunk guides from Fort Winnebago were in any way treacherous. Bracken, "Further Strictures on Gov. Ford's History of the Black Hawk War," 407.

122. Albert S. Johnston, Journal, 16 July 1832, *Black Hawk War,* vol. 37, 1318; Atkinson to Winfield Scott, 17 July 1832, ibid., 814–815.

123. Smith, "Indian Campaign of 1832," 161.

124. Henry Gratiot Journal, 15, 17 July 1832, Whitney, *Black Hawk War,* vol. 37, 1304, 1306n23; Albert S. Johnston, Journal, 19–20 July 1832, ibid., 1318; Smith, "Indian Campaign of 1832," 161; Atkinson to Winfield Scott, 21 July 1832, *Black Hawk War,* vol. 37, 840; Atkinson to Justin M. Harlan, 20 July 1832, ibid., 833; Atkinson: Order No. 61, 20 July 1832, ibid., 833; Roll of Potawatomi Indians in United States Service, *Black Hawk War,* vol. 35, 560; Whitney, *Black Hawk War,* vol. 37, 958n2.

125. In one of the more notorious episodes of the war, Dr. Addison Philleo, the Galena newspaper editor and physician, killed one Indian and collected two scalps during these initial encounters. Although one account maintained that Philleo shot an invalid while he begged for mercy, *The Galenian* celebrated the exploits of its "scalping editor" in his absence. Wakefield, *Wakefield's History of the Black Hawk War,* 109–110; Bracken, "Further Strictures on Gov. Ford's History of the Black Hawk War," 408; Whitney, *Black Hawk War,* vol. 37, 844n3.

126. Bracken, "Further Strictures on Gov. Ford's History of the Black Hawk War," 410; Reuben G. Thwaites, Winnebago Notes, US Mss 7E Folder 3, Wisconsin Historical Society, Madison, 13–14.

127. Dodge to Atkinson, 22 July 1832, Whitney, *Black Hawk War,* vol. 37, 843, 844n7.

128. Minutes of an Examination of Prisoners, 19 August 1832, ibid., 1028; Jackson, ed., *Black Hawk: An Autobiography,* 133.

129. John Shaw, "Sketches of Indian Chiefs and Pioneers of the North-West," in WHC 10, 218.

130. Dodge to Atkinson, 22 July 1832, *Black Hawk War,* vol. 37, 843. Satterlee Clark accompanied the Portage Ho Chunks and reported the collection of only three scalps. Clark, "Pierre Paquette: The Early History of Fort Winnebago," 5.

131. Decorah, "Narrative of Spoon Decorah," 453.
132. Whitney, *Black Hawk War*, vol. 37, 878n4.

### 7. FINAL BLOWS

1. George Boyd to George B. Porter, 13 June 1832, *The Black Hawk War, 1831–1832*, ed. Ellen M. Whitney, vol. 36, Collections of the Illinois State Historical Library (Springfield: Illinois State Historical Library, 1973), 581–582.

2. Boyd to Porter, 23 July 1832, George Boyd, "Papers of Indian Agent Boyd," in *Collections of the State Historical Society of Wisconsin*, ed. Reuben G. Thwaites, vol. 12 (Madison: Democrat Printing Co., 1892) (hereafter WHC 12), 275–276.

3. Elbert Herring to the Acting Secretary of War, 11 June 1832, *The Territorial Papers of the United States: Michigan Territory, 1829–1837*, ed. Clarence Edwin Carter, vol. 12 (Washington, D.C.: U.S. Government Printing Office, 1945), 487–488. Stambaugh desired to remain in the service of the Indian Office but would only do so as a treaty commissioner. He was appointed Indian agent during a congressional recess and fell victim to partisan politics when the Senate failed to ratify his appointment upon reconvening. Francis Paul Prucha, "Army Sutlers and the American Fur Company," *Minnesota History* 40, no. 1 (Spring 1966): 26.

4. Stambaugh to Porter, 7 June 1832, *Black Hawk War*, vol. 36, 545.

5. George Porter to Lewis Cass, 3 February 1832, National Archives, Letters Received by the Office of Indian Affairs, 1824–81: Green Bay Agency, 1824–1880, Microcopy No. 234, Roll 315: 1824–1832 (Washington, D.C.: National Archives and Records Service, General Services Administration, 1959), F710-743; Samuel C. Stambaugh, "Report on the Quality and Condition of Wisconsin Territory, 1831," in *Collections of the State Historical Society of Wisconsin*, ed. Reuben Gold Thwaites, vol. 15 (Madison: Democrat Printing Co., 1900) (hereafter WHC 15), 405; Albert G. Ellis, "Some Account of the Ad-

vent of the New York Indians into Wisconsin," in *Second Annual Report and Collections of the State Historical Society of Wisconsin for the Year 1855,* ed. Lyman C. Draper, vol. 2, Collections of the State Historical Society of Wisconsin (Madison: Calkins & Proudfit, Printers, 1856) (hereafter WHC 2), 415–449; David R. M. Beck, *Siege and Survival: History of the Menominee Indians, 1634–1856* (Lincoln: University of Nebraska Press, 2002), 90-108; Albert G. Ellis, "Fifty-Four Years' Recollections of Men and Events in Wisconsin," in *Report and Collections of the State Historical Society of Wisconsin, for the Years 1873, 1874, 1875 and 1876,* ed. Lyman C. Draper, vol. 7, Collections of the State Historical Society of Wisconsin (Madison: E. B. Bolens, State Printer, 1876), 210–215, 223–225.

6. Stambaugh to Lewis Cass, 10 June 1832, National Archives, Letters Received by the Office of Indian Affairs, 1824-81: Green Bay Agency, 1824-1880, F792-797.

7. Grizzly Bear's Talk, 22 June 1832, *Black Hawk War,* vol. 36, 650.

8. Ibid.

9. Ibid.

10. Boyd to Atkinson, 23 June 1832, ibid., 657.

11. Atkinson to Boyd, 12 July 1832, *The Black Hawk War, 1831–1832,* ed. Ellen M. Whitney, vol. 37, Collections of the Illinois State Historical Library (Springfield: Illinois State Historical Library, 1975), 770.

12. Boyd to Porter, 23 July 1832, Boyd, "Papers of Indian Agent Boyd," 277.

13. Childs's testimony is suspect, however, for a number of reasons. First, he makes conspicuous but uncorroborated claims (such as personally accepting the surrender of Red Bird following the 1827 Winnebago War and holding "frequent" conversations with Black Hawk). Second, Childs's account belies any skill at dealing with Indians; he brags about calling Menominees dogs, throwing lit pipes at their faces, and chasing Indians with hot pokers—hardly the stuff of diplomacy. According to one Green Bay educator, Childs was a drunkard who "pushed himself into undeserved po-

sitions of trust, honor and profit." Ebenezer Childs, "Recollections of Wisconsin since 1820," in *Report and Collections of the State Historical Society of Wisconsin for the Years 1857 and 1858*, ed. Lyman C. Draper, vol. 4, Collections of the State Historical Society of Wisconsin (Madison: James Ross, State Printer, 1859), 175, 185-186; Ellis, "Fifty-Four Years' Recollections," 257.

14. Alanson Skinner, *Social Life and Ceremonial Bundles of the Menomini Indians*, vol. 13, part 1, *Anthropological Papers of the American Museum of Natural History* (New York: American Museum of Natural History, 1913), 108, 110.

15. Ibid., 20.

16. Boyd to Atkinson, 20 July 1832, Boyd, "Papers of Indian Agent Boyd," 270-271. William Powell, a métis lieutenant of the Green Bay contingent, placed the total force at 480 Menominees. William Powell, "William Powell's Recollections, in an Interview with Lyman C. Draper," in *Proceedings of the Annual Meeting of the State Historical Society of Wisconsin* (Madison: The Society, 1912), 164.

17. Although sixty-two Oneidas and Stockbridge Indians had furnished a company of auxiliaries during the 1827 Winnebago War, the New York Indians uniformly refused to proffer aid in 1832. Childs, "Recollections," 172-173; Boyd to George Porter, 23 July 1832, "Papers of Indian Agent Boyd," 277-278; Boyd to the Chiefs & Young Men of the sevl. Bands of New York Indians in Michigan Territory, 25 July 1832, ibid., 282.

18. Cutting Marsh, "Extracts from Marsh's Journal, during the Black Hawk War," in WHC 15, 64.

19. John Dean, "Wisconsin—Early History," George A. Hyer Newsclippings, 1820-1824, 1830-1860, Wis Mss AX, Wisconsin Historical Society, Madison, no. 5, 10-11.

20. Boyd to Porter, 20 July 1832, "Papers of Indian Agent Boyd," 273.

21. Boyd to Atkinson, 20 July 1832, ibid., 271-272.

22. Ellis, "Fifty-Four Years' Recollections," 245.

23. Augustin Grignon, "Seventy-Two Years' Recollections of Wiscon-

sin," in *Third Annual Report and Collections of the State Historical Society of Wisconsin for the Year 1856*, ed. Lyman C. Draper, Collections of the State Historical Society of Wisconsin (Madison: Calkins & Webb, Printers, 1857), 196.

24. Ibid., 199–200.

25. Ibid., 212; Louise Phelps Kellogg, *The French Régime in Wisconsin and the Northwest* (1925; reprint, New York: Cooper Square Publishers, 1968), 425–428.

26. Boyd to George Porter, 23 July 1832, Boyd, "Papers of Indian Agent Boyd," 279.

27. Whitney, *Black Hawk War*, vol. 37, 959n2; Powell, "William Powell's Recollections," 147.

28. Boyd to Porter, 23 July 1832, Boyd, "Papers of Indian Agent Boyd," 277; Grignon, "Seventy-Two Years' Recollections of Wisconsin," 294.

29. Boyd to Porter, 20 July 1832, Boyd, "Papers of Indian Agent Boyd," 273.

30. Boyd to Daniel Whitney, 21 July 1832, ibid., 274–275.

31. Boyd to Porter, 23 July 1832, ibid., 277.

32. Alanson Skinner, *Material Culture of the Menomini*, ed. Frederick Webb Hodge, Indian Notes and Monographs (New York: Museum of the American Indian Heye Foundation, 1921), 322–323.

33. Skinner, *Social Life and Ceremonial Bundles of the Menomini Indians*, 125.

34. Ibid., 48.

35. Ibid., 125.

36. Ibid., 125–126.

37. Skinner, *Material Culture of the Menomini*, 62.

38. Skinner, *Social Life and Ceremonial Bundles of the Menomini Indians*, 92.

39. Ibid., 78.

40. Ibid., 100.

41. Menominee warriors who fought for the Union during the Ameri-

can Civil War carried their bundles into combat with faces painted red or black. Ibid., 127.

42. Skinner, *Material Culture of the Menomini*, 227; Skinner, *Social Life and Ceremonial Bundles of the Menomini Indians*, 110.

43. Marsh, "Extracts from Marsh's Journal, during the Black Hawk War," 64-65. Cutting Marsh was one of two pioneer Presbyterian missionaries in Wisconsin. He worked extensively with the Stockbridge Indians.

44. Boyd to Stambaugh, 25 July 1832, "Papers of Indian Agent Boyd," 282; Boyd to Atkinson, 25 July 1832, *Black Hawk War*, vol. 37, 875.

45. Skinner, *Social Life and Ceremonial Bundles of the Menomini Indians*, 110.

46. Powell, "William Powell's Recollections," 166.

47. Stambaugh to George Boyd, 2 August 1832, *Black Hawk War*, vol. 37, 915-916.

48. Skinner, *Social Life and Ceremonial Bundles of the Menomini Indians*, 110-112.

49. Stambaugh to George Boyd, 28 August 1832, *Black Hawk War*, vol. 37, 1077.

50. Stambaugh to George Boyd, 2 August 1832, ibid., 915-916.

51. Stambaugh to Winfield Scott, 11 August 1832, ibid., 988.

52. Atkinson to Gustavus Loomis, 27 July 1832, ibid., 890.

53. Loomis to Henry Dodge, 25 July 1832, ibid., 880; Street to Thomas Burnett, 25 July 1832, ibid., 882; Burnett to Street, 26 July 1832, ibid., 883; Street to Atkinson, 28 July 1832, ibid., 902; Street to Atkinson, 3 August 1832, ibid., 925.

54. Mauchhewemahnigo, "Narrative of Walking Cloud," in *Collections of the State Historical Society of Wisconsin*, ed. Reuben G. Thwaites, vol. 13 (Madison: Democrat Printing Co., State Printers, 1895) (hereafter WHC 13), 464-465.

55. Joseph Ritner to Gustavus Loomis, 29 July 1832, *Black Hawk War*, vol. 37, 903; Henry Atkinson to Winfield Scott, 5 August 1832, ibid, 936; Reuben G. Thwaites, "The Black Hawk War," in *How George*

*Rogers Clark Won the Northwest and Other Essays in Western History* (1903; reprint, Williamstown, Mass.: Corner House Publishers, 1978), 180–181; Mauchhewemahnigo, "Narrative of Walking Cloud," 464.

56. Street to Atkinson, 31 July 1832, *Black Hawk War,* vol. 37, 908; Street to William Clark, 1 August 1832, ibid., 913.

57. Joseph M. Street, Report of Prisoners and Casualties, 2 August 1832, ibid., 918–919.

58. Joseph Street to William Clark, 3 August 1832, ibid., 926.

59. Loomis to Henry Atkinson, 31 July 1832, ibid., 907; Joseph Street to William Clark, 2 August 1832, ibid., 917; From Joseph Throckmorton, 3 August 1832, ibid., 927.

60. Perry A. Armstrong, *The Sauks and the Black Hawk War, with Biographical Sketches, etc.* (Springfield, Ill.: H. W. Rokker Printer, 1887), 467–468.

61. Atkinson to Roger Jones, 19 November 1832, *Black Hawk War,* vol. 37, 1210–1211.

62. Spoon Decorah, "Narrative of Spoon Decorah," in WHC 13, 453. John Wakefield appears to have been mistaken in his belief that the Ho Chunks provided no guides following the Battle of Wisconsin Heights. John A. Wakefield, *Wakefield's History of the Black Hawk War,* ed. Frank E. Stevens (1834; reprint, Chicago: Caxton Club, 1904), 134.

63. Dean, "Wisconsin—Early History," no. 5, 10–11.

64. From Joseph Throckmorton, 3 August 1832, *Black Hawk War,* vol. 37, 927–928; John H. Fonda, "Early Reminiscences of Wisconsin," in *Report and Collections of the State Historical Society of Wisconsin, for the Years 1867, 1868, and 1869,* ed. Lyman C. Draper, vol. 5, Collections of the State Historical Society of Wisconsin (Madison: Atwood & Rublee, State Printers, 1868), 261–263.

65. Philip St. George Cooke, *Scenes and Adventures in the Army: Or, Romance of Military Life* (Philadelphia: Lindsay & Blakiston, 1857), 187.

66. Council between Henry Atkinson and the Winnebago and Me-

NOTES TO PAGES 196-199

nominee Indians, 6 August 1832, *Black Hawk War,* vol. 37, 950; Roll of Menominee Indians brought to head Qrs. by Colo. W S. Hamilton, 4 June 1832, *The Black Hawk War, 1831–1832,* ed. Ellen M. Whitney, vol. 35, Collections of the Illinois State Historical Library (Springfield: Illinois State Historical Library, 1970), 563; Cooke, *Scenes and Adventures in the Army,* 187.

67. Henry Smith, "Indian Campaign of 1832," in *Report and Collections of the State Historical Society of Wisconsin for the Years of 1883, 1884, and 1885,* ed. Lyman C. Draper, vol. 10, Collections of the State Historical Society of Wisconsin (Madison: Democrat Printing Co., State Printer, 1888), 164.

68. Wakefield, *Wakefield's History of the Black Hawk War,* 140–141.

69. Ibid., 143.

70. Albert S. Johnston to Stambaugh, 7 August 1832, *Black Hawk War,* vol. 37, 958. Johnston repeated the order to return to Green Bay on 10 August. Johnston to Stambaugh, 10 August 1832, ibid., 979.

71. Stambaugh to Boyd, 28 August 1832, ibid., 1071, 1072; Powell, "William Powell's Recollections," 165. According to Stambaugh, he sent Alexander J. Irwin to Prairie du Chien; William Powell later recollected that he performed this duty. Offered to Lyman C. Draper in an interview forty-five years after the war, Powell's account is sometimes self-serving, and I have considered Stambaugh's correspondence more reliable.

72. Stambaugh to Boyd, 28 August 1832, *Black Hawk War,* vol. 37, 1072; Powell, "William Powell's Recollections," 165–166; Grignon, "Seventy-Two Years' Recollections of Wisconsin," 294–295.

73. Stambaugh to Boyd, 28 August 1832, *Black Hawk War,* vol. 37, 1073.

74. Ibid.; Powell, "William Powell's Recollections," 166–167.

75. Powell, "William Powell's Recollections," 167.

76. Stambaugh to George Boyd, 28 August 1832, *Black Hawk War,* vol. 37, 1073.

77. Skinner, *Social Life and Ceremonial Bundles of the Menomini Indians,* 114.

78. Stambaugh to George Boyd, 28 August 1832, *Black Hawk War,* vol. 37, 1073.
79. Powell, "William Powell's Recollections," 167.
80. Ibid., 161.
81. Grignon, "Seventy-Two Years' Recollections of Wisconsin," 295.
82. Leonard Bloomfield, *Menomini Texts,* ed. Franz Boas, vol. 12, Publications of the American Ethnological Society (New York: G. E. Stechert & Co., 1928), 55; Skinner, *Social Life and Ceremonial Bundles of the Menomini Indians,* 116.
83. Powell, "William Powell's Recollections," 167.
84. According to Powell, the women and children perceived that Robert Grignon was a white man and ran to him for protection, which he provided. He identified the prisoners as eighteen women, a boy of about eight years old, and three or four younger children. Ibid., 167–169.
85. Stambaugh to Boyd, 28 August 1832, *Black Hawk War,* vol. 37, 1073. Robert Grignon would survive and receive a disability pension. Thwaites, WHC 12, 279n2. Powell asserted that Robert Grignon was first shot by a Sauk, but he also mentions buckshot entering his left shoulder. Powell, "William Powell's Recollections," 168.
86. Powell, "William Powell's Recollections," 169.
87. Ibid., 170. The Menominee women exacted further vengeance from corpses that floated past Prairie du Chien following the Battle of Bad Axe. According to one of the army regulars, "The women of the friendly Indians manifested their hatred toward the prisoners by every indignity they were permitted to practice. . . . They were barbarous in their treatment of the bodies of the slain savages; for days after, as the dead bodies floated down by the Fort, they were dragged ashore by the squaws, beheaded, scalped, and danced around by the savages grown furiously brave over the dead bodies of their own people." Dean, "Wisconsin—Early History," no. 5, 12–13.

88. Minutes of an Examination of Prisoners, 20 August 1832, *Black Hawk War,* vol. 37, 1035; Whitney, ibid., 1037n6.

89. Dean, "Wisconsin—Early History," no. 5, 13; Smith, "Indian Campaign of 1832," 164; Charles Bracken, "Further Strictures on Gov. Ford's History of the Black Hawk War," in WHC 2, 414.

90. The Dakotas also claimed that only two men escaped, while Sauk prisoners indicated that forty-seven warriors and boys escaped the engagement. Minutes of an Examination of Prisoners, 20 August 1832, *Black Hawk War,* vol. 37, 1035; Minutes of an Examination of Prisoners, 27 August 1832, ibid., 1056; Joseph Street to Winfield Scott, 22 August 1832, ibid., 1041-1042; Donald Jackson, ed., *Black Hawk: An Autobiography* (Chicago: Illini Books, 1964; reprint, Chicago: University of Illinois Press, 1990), 140; John W. Spencer, "Reminiscences of Pioneer Life," in *The Early Day of Rock Island and Davenport,* ed. Milo Milton Quaife (Chicago: Lakeside Press, 1942), 74-75.

91. Joseph Street to Winfield Scott, 22 August 1832, *Black Hawk War,* vol. 37, 1042; Speech to Wabashaw's Band of Sioux, 21 August 1832, Joseph Montfort Street Papers, Iowa Department of Archives and History, Des Moines. The Dakotas were reluctant to surrender their prisoners to Street. After receiving two appeals from Street, Wabasha personally delivered most of the prisoners but successfully lobbied for permission to retain two, including an orphaned girl he had adopted. Street to William Clark, 12 June 1833, Transcripts from Indian Office Files, US Mss BN Box 65, Wisconsin Historical Society, Madison.

92. Speech to Wabashaw's Band of Sioux, 21 August 1832, Street Papers.

93. Jackson, ed., *Black Hawk: An Autobiography,* 140.

94. Samuel Stambaugh to George Boyd, 28 August 1832, *Black Hawk War,* vol. 37, 1075.

95. Ibid., 1075-1076.

96. William Whistler to Patrick H. Galt, 14 August 1832, ibid., 1006; Owen to Winfield Scott, 5 September 1832, ibid., 1110; Joseph M. Street, Report of the Delivery of Black Hawk and the Prophet, 27 August 1832, ibid., 1065; William Whistler to William Maynadier, 19 September 1832, ibid., 1165.

97. The particulars of Black Hawk's surrender or capture are the subject of contention, addressed fully by Nancy O. Lurie, "In Search of Chaetar: New Findings on Black Hawk's Surrender," *Wisconsin Magazine of History* 71, no. 3 (Spring 1988): 163–183. See also Joseph M. Street, Report of the Delivery of Black Hawk and the Prophet, 27 August 1832, ibid., 1065; Street to Secretary of War, 28 August 1832, Street Papers; Jackson, ed., *Black Hawk: An Autobiography*, 139; One-Eyed Decorah, Memoir by Wadze-hutta-kaw of Black Hawk's Surrender, Wis Mss GJ, box 1, folder 2, Wisconsin Historical Society, Madison, 1–2.

98. Joseph M. Street, Report of the Delivery of Black Hawk and the Prophet, 27 August 1832, *Black Hawk War*, vol. 37, 1067, 1067n3.

99. Decorah, Memoir by Wadze-hutta-kaw of Black Hawk's Surrender, 2.

## 8. LOSING THE PEACE

1. Henry Smith, "Indian Campaign of 1832," in *Report and Collections of the State Historical Society of Wisconsin for the Years of 1883, 1884, and 1885,* ed. Lyman C. Draper, vol. 10, Collections of the State Historical Society of Wisconsin (Madison: Democrat Printing Co., State Printer, 1888), 160.

2. Stambaugh to Boyd, 28 August 1832, *The Black Hawk War, 1831–1832,* ed. Ellen M. Whitney, vol. 37, Collections of the Illinois State Historical Library (Springfield: Illinois State Historical Library, 1975), 1077.

3. Scott to Samuel Stambaugh, 17 August 1832, ibid., 1018–1019.

4. Minutes of a Meeting, Petition to Congress by Citizens of Green Bay, 3 December 1832, *The Territorial Papers of the United States: Michi-*

*gan Territory, 1829–1837,* ed. Clarence Edwin Carter, vol. 12 (Washington, D.C.: U.S. Government Printing Office, 1945), 544; Henry S. Baird, "Recollections of the Early History of Northern Wisconsin," in *Report and Collections of the State Historical Society of Wisconsin for the Years 1857 and 1858,* ed. Lyman C. Draper, vol. 4, Collections of the State Historical Society of Wisconsin (Madison: James Ross, State Printer, 1859), 218.

5. Speech to Wabashaw's Band of Sioux, 21 August 1832, Joseph Montfort Street Papers, Iowa Department of Archives and History, Des Moines.

6. Minutes of Examination of Prisoners, 19 August 1832, *Black Hawk War,* vol. 37, 1029, 1032.

7. Patrick Galt to Owen, 21 August 1832, quoted in Owen to George Porter, 27 August 1832, Porter and Mason Letters Received, 1831–35, US Mss BN Box 59, Wisconsin State Historical Society, Madison, vol. 2, 22.

8. Henry Atkinson to Henry Jones, 19 November 1832, *Black Hawk War,* vol. 37, 1212.

9. Samuel Stambaugh to Winfield Scott, 13 August 1832, ibid., 996.

10. Stambaugh to George Boyd, 28 August 1832, ibid., 1075.

11. Scott to Winnebago Indians, 18 August 1832, ibid., 1022.

12. Minutes of an Examination of Prisoners, 20 August and 27 August 1832, ibid., 1036, 1055–1056.

13. Minutes of an Examination of Prisoners, 20 August 1832, ibid., 1035.

14. Scott to Lewis Cass, 19 August 1832, ibid., 1024.

15. Scott to Cass, 19 August 1832, ibid., 1026.

16. Street to Winfield Scott, 22 August 1832, ibid., 1042.

17. Zachary Taylor to Patrick H. Galt, 22 August 1832, ibid.

18. Gideon Low to Henry Atkinson, 10 August 1832, ibid., 979; Joseph Street to Atkinson, 13 August 1832, ibid., 998; Zalmon C. Palmer to Winfield Scott, 28 August 1832, ibid., 1070; Scott to Lewis Cass, 1 September 1832, ibid., 1092–1093; ibid., 955n2.

19. Street to Scott, 22 August 1832, ibid., 1042.
20. Second Council with the Rock River Winnebago, 12 September 1832, ibid., 1135.
21. Winfield Scott and John Reynolds to William Clark, 22 September 1832, ibid., 1186.
22. "The Winnebagoes and Black Hawk War," in *Report and Collections of the State Historical Society of Wisconsin, for the Years 1867, 1868, and 1869,* ed. Lyman C. Draper, vol. 5, Collections of the State Historical Society of Wisconsin (Madison: Atwood & Rublee, State Printers, 1868), 308.
23. Council with the Winnebago from the Fort Winnebago, Rock River, and Prairie du Chien Agencies, 12 September, 1832, *Black Hawk War,* vol. 37, 1138, 1137.
24. Second Council with Representatives of the Winnebago Nation, 13 September, ibid., 1140. Dodge, who had demonstrated himself to be a capable war leader and provided the Ho Chunks an opportunity for military service, momentarily enjoyed the respect and confidence of the Ho Chunks, but it would not last.
25. Treaty with the Winnebago, 1832, *Indian Affairs: Laws and Treaties,* ed. Charles J. Kappler, vol. 2 (Treaties) (Washington, D.C.: U.S. Government Printing Office, 1904), 346.
26. Ibid., 346–347.
27. Third Council with Representatives of the Winnebago Nation, 14 September 1832, *Black Hawk War,* vol. 37, 1147.
28. Ibid., 1150.
29. Winfield Scott and John Reynolds to Lewis Cass, 22 September 1832, ibid., 1187.
30. Citizens of Illinois to Lewis Cass, 10 July 1832, National Archives, Letters Received by the Office of Indian Affairs, 1824–81: Chicago Agency, 1824–1847, Microcopy No. 234, Roll 132: 1824–1834 (Washington, D.C.: National Archives and Records Service, General Services Administration, 1959), F248–249.
31. While Jackson was not the first to formulate the policy of removal, he earnestly endorsed and enforced it as president. Francis

Paul Prucha explains Jackson's rationale in his sympathetic essay, "Andrew Jackson's Indian Policy: A Reassessment," *Journal of American History* 56, no. 3 (1969): 527-539. For a more thorough and balanced treatment, see Ronald N. Satz, *American Indian Policy in the Jacksonian Era* (1975; reprint, with a new preface by the author, Lincoln: University of Nebraska Press, 2002).

32. Reynolds to Andrew Jackson, 15 August 1831, *The Black Hawk War, 1831–1832,* ed. Ellen M. Whitney, vol. 36, Collections of the Illinois State Historical Library (Springfield: Illinois State Historical Library, 1973), 140.

33. Cass to Scott, 15 June 1832, ibid., 592.

34. Reynolds to Cass, 26 October 1832, *The Governors' Letter Books 1818–1834,* ed. Evarts Boutell Greene and Clarence Walworth Alvord, vol. 4, Collections of the Illinois State Historical Library (Springfield: Illinois State Historical Library, 1909), 214.

35. Owen to George Porter, 3 September 1832, Porter and Mason Letters Received, 1831-35, vol. 2, 24.

36. Treaties with the Potawatomi, 20, 26, 27 October 1832, *Indian Affairs,* vol. 2, 353-354, 368, 374; R. David Edmunds, "The Prairie Potawatomi Removal of 1833," *Indiana Magazine of History* 68, no. 3 (September 1972): 243-244.

37. Robert A. Trennert, "A Trader's Role in the Potawatomi Removal from Indiana: The Case of George W. Ewing," *The Old Northwest* 4, no. 1 (March 1978): 7-11.

38. Porter to Elbert Herring, 16 March 1833, National Archives, Letters Received by the Office of Indian Affairs, 1824-81: Chicago Agency, 1824-1847, F324-326.

39. Porter to Lewis Cass, 19 January 1833, ibid., F308.

40. Porter to Herring, 16 March, ibid., F324-326.

41. R. David Edmunds, *The Potawatomis: Keepers of the Fire* (Norman: University of Oklahoma Press, 1978), 243.

42. Charles Bracken to Micajah T. Williams, 24 November 1832, *Territorial Papers,* vol. 12, 535.

43. Roger L. Nichols, *General Henry Atkinson: A Western Military Career*

(Norman: University of Oklahoma Press, 1965), 178; Atkinson to
Hiram M. Curry, 6 November 1832, National Archives, Letters Received by the Office of Indian Affairs, 1824-81: Chicago Agency,
1824-1847, F240; Atkinson to Owen, 16 November 1832, ibid., F241;
Owen to George Porter, 17 December 1832, Porter and Mason Letters Received, 1831-35, vol. 2, 37.

44. Owen to Atkinson, 11 December 1832, National Archives, Letters
Received by the Office of Indian Affairs, 1824-81: Chicago Agency,
1824-1847, F242-43; Reynolds to Lewis Cass, 13 December 1832, *The
Governors' Letter Books 1818-1834*, 220.

45. Owen to Porter, 9 January 1833, National Archives, Letters Received by the Office of Indian Affairs, 1824-81: Chicago Agency,
1824-1847, F309.

46. Report of Billy Caldwell and Alexander Robinson, 18 January 1833
(forwarded to Cass with endorsement by Owen 21 January 1833),
ibid., F292-293.

47. Observing Potawatomis concentrating on the Rock River in
March, John Dixon was sufficiently alarmed to request that Henry
Gratiot repair immediately to discern their purpose. John Dixon
to Gratiot, 27 March 1833, Transcripts from Indian Office Files, US
Mss BN Box 65, Wisconsin Historical Society, Madison, 1.

48. Nicholas Boilvin to Lewis Cass, 10 January 1833, National Archives,
Letters Received by the Office of Indian Affairs, 1824-81: Chicago
Agency, 1824-1847, F268-269; Henry Gratiot to Lewis Cass, 2 March
1833, Transcripts from Indian Office Files, Box 65.

49. Augustus Langworthy to John Reynolds, 6 April 1833, National Archives, Letters Received by the Office of Indian Affairs, 1824-81:
Chicago Agency, 1824-1847, F346-347. Among the sources of this
rumor was John Dixon, whose name appears in much of the rele-
vant correspondence.

50. Gratiot to Porter, 12 April 1833, Transcripts from Indian Office
Files, Box 65, 1.

51. One editorial asserted that four to five thousand *warriors* (exclusive of women, children, and the aged) of various tribes were as-

sembling forty-five miles north of Dixon's Ferry. *Galenian,* 2 April 1833, ibid.

52. Street to Clark, 24 July 1832, *Black Hawk War,* vol. 37, 872.

53. A fur trader opposed to removal and any economic disruption to the region, Kinzie steadfastly promoted Indian neutrality in the war. Stambaugh alleged that Kinzie (who was also the postmaster at Fort Winnebago) had deliberately failed to forward to Henry Atkinson several letters in which Stambaugh recommended the military employment of the Green Bay Menominees. Kinzie—who sarcastically referred to Stambaugh as the *"Menomonie Warrior"*— resigned his post rather than endure the investigation. Samuel Stambaugh to Henry Atkinson, 13 August 1832, ibid., 995; Henry Dodge to Kinzie, 5 January 1833, Transcripts from Indian Office File, Box 65; Kinzie to George Porter, 15 March 1833, ibid.

54. Henry Gratiot to William Clark, 12 June 1832, *Black Hawk War,* vol. 36, 78.

55. Gratiot to George Porter, 12 April 1833, Transcripts from Indian Office Files, Box 65, 1.

56. War wampum would have been painted red, black, or a combination of these colors. Gratiot himself had forwarded this rumor to Secretary Cass earlier in the month. Gratiot to Cass, 2 March 1833, ibid.

57. Gratiot to George Porter, 12 April 1833, ibid.

58. Juliette Kinzie, *Wau-bun: The Early Day in the North West* (1873; reprint, Philadelphia: Bibliobazaar, 2006), 210.

59. Kinzie to Elbert Herring, 22 March 1833, Transcripts from Indian Office Files, Box 65. The *Galenian* also printed Kinzie's complaint to the editor.

60. Kinzie to Herring, 22 March 1833, ibid.

61. Kinzie to Porter, 31 January 1833, ibid.

62. Owen to Herring, 22 June 1833, National Archives, Letters Received by the Office of Indian Affairs, 1824-81: Chicago Agency, 1824-1847, F300.

63. Porter to Herring, 16 March 1833, ibid.

64. Gratiot to Cass, 8 February 1833, Transcripts from Indian Office Files, Box 65.
65. Ibid.
66. Street to Secretary of War, 28 January 1833, ibid. Street most likely implied that the Ho Chunks would initiate "mischief" in the absence of a strong military presence to serve as a deterrent, but he shared the common perception that the U.S. Army was a peacekeeping force. In spite of his condescension and advocacy for removal, Street genuinely viewed himself as a friend (albeit an overbearing and paternalistic one) to the Indians.
67. William Campbell to Andrew Jackson, 13 July 1832, *Black Hawk War,* vol. 37, 788.
68. Kerry A. Trask, *Black Hawk: The Battle for the Heart of America* (New York: Henry Holt, 2006), 224-227.
69. Dodge to War Department (extract), 14 April 1833, in D. Kurtz to George Porter, 9 May 1833, Porter and Mason Letters Received, 1831-35, vol. 1, 53.
70. Ibid.
71. Mary Lee Stubbs and Stanley Russell Connor, *Armor-Cavalry, Part I: Regular Army and Army Reserve, Army Lineage Series* (Washington, D.C.: Office of the Chief of Military History, 1969), 7-9.
72. Kinzie to Herring, 22 March 1833, Transcripts from Indian Office Files, Box 65.
73. Interestingly, the modern armor branch of the U.S. Army can trace its contiguous lineage to the Black Hawk War. Although Congress raised federal cavalry forces during the American Revolution and the War of 1812 and made abortive provisions for a permanent cavalry force at various times, the War Department relied almost entirely on state volunteers to provide mounted soldiers through the end of the Black Hawk War, with disastrous consequences at Stillman's Run. Congress authorized Dodge's Battalion of Mounted Rangers as an expedient to help prosecute the war in June 1832. The Rangers proved helpful but undisciplined,

and Atkinson labored to command and control his force as mounted volunteers outpaced his infantry and artillery. Consequently, Congress completely federalized the force with the formation of the First Dragoons on 2 March 1833. The U.S. Army has retained regular cavalry (or armor) regiments ever since. Stubbs and Connor, *Armor-Cavalry, Part I*, 7-9.

74. Dodge to War Department (extract), 14 April 1833, in D. Kurtz to Porter, 9 May 1833, Porter and Mason Letters Received, 1831-35, vol. 1, 53.

75. Thomas J. V. Owen to George Porter, 3 August 1832, ibid., vol. 2, 15; Owen to Porter, 31 July 1832 and 9 August 1832, National Archives, Letters Received by the Office of Indian Affairs, 1824-81: Chicago Agency, 1824-1847, F218, F221; John Kinzie to Porter, 15 August 1832, Porter and Mason Letters Received, 1831-35, vol. 2, 19.

76. Kinzie informed Porter, "Many have lost their corn fields, (for want of attention) by this Indian war." Kinzie to Porter, 15 August 1832, ibid. As early as 13 August James C. Steele recorded in his journal that the residents of a Potawatomi village were "almost starved to death." (Steele mistakenly identified the village as belonging to the Winnebagos). Journal of James C. Steel, *Black Hawk War*, vol. 37, 1342.

77. Owen to Porter, 3 August 1832, Porter and Mason Letters Received, 1831-35, vol. 2, 15.

78. Kinzie pleaded for relief for the Ho Chunks of the Fort Winnebago Agency on 25 August, but the War Department did not approve his request until 7 November, and several additional weeks would pass before Kinzie could actually issue the authorized pork and flour to his charges. D. Kurtz to George Porter, 7 November 1832, ibid., vol. 2, 35.

79. Deep snow cover causes whitetail deer to "yard," or cluster, in predictable forage grounds, making them relatively easy prey in the harsh months of January and February. Native communities relied on such opportunities to sustain themselves through the win-

ter. Harold Hickerson, "The Virginia Deer and Intertribal Buffer Zones in the Upper Mississippi Valley," in *Man, Culture, and Animals: The Role of Animals in Human Ecological Adjustments*, ed. Anthony Leeds and Andrew P. Vayda (Washington, D.C.: American Association for the Advancement of Science, 1965), 58-59.

80. Kinzie to George Porter, 15 March 1833, Transcripts from Indian Office Files, Box 65.

81. Little Priest's band of the Rock River admitted that some of their young men stole ore and twenty-eight hogs, but Little Priest was penitent and promised indemnity. Gratiot to Cass, 2 March 1833, ibid.

82. Stillman to Reynolds, 4 January 1832, *The Governors' Letter Books 1818-1834*, 199-200.

83. S. C. Christy to Reynolds, 28 April 1833, National Archives, Letters Received by the Office of Indian Affairs, 1824-81: Chicago Agency, 1824-1847, F352-353; Nichols, *General Henry Atkinson*, 182.

84. Kinzie to Porter, 27 March 1833, Transcripts from Indian Office Files, Box 65; Memo. of a Talk held at Four Lakes, 28 April 1833, ibid.

85. Herring to Porter, 30 March 1833, ibid.

86. Herring to Porter, 13 March 1833, Porter and Mason Letters Received, 1831-35, vol. 1, 49.

87. Porter to Herring, 12 April 1833, Transcripts from Indian Office Files, Box 65.

88. Herring to Porter, 25 April 1833, ibid.

89. Treaty with the Winnebago, 1832, *Indian Affairs*, vol. 2, 345-348.

90. George Porter to Herring, 12 April 1833, Transcripts from Indian Office Files, Box 65.

91. Herring to Porter, 30 March 1833, ibid.; Herring to Porter, 3 April 1833, Porter and Mason Letters Received, 1831-35, vol. 1, 52.

92. Herring to Porter, 13 March 1833, ibid., vol. 1, 49.

93. Porter to Herring, 12 April 1833, Transcripts from Indian Office Files, Box 65.

94. Ibid.

95. Dodge to War Department (extract), 14 April 1833, in D. Kurtz to Porter, 9 May 1833, Porter and Mason Letters Received, 1831-35, vol. 1, 53.

96. Nichols, *General Henry Atkinson*, 183.

97. Joseph Street to Elbert Herring, 18 July 1833, Street Papers.

98. Kinzie to George Porter, 15 March 1833, Transcripts from Indian Office Files, Box 65.

99. Extracted from Charles Joseph Latrobe's "The Rambler in North America," in Henry H. Hurlbut, ed., *Chicago Antiquities: Comprising Original Items and Relations, Letters, Extracts, and Notes, Pertaining to Early Chicago; Embellished with Views, Portraits, Autographs, Etc.* (Chicago: Fergus Printing Co., 1881), 219.

100. Journal of the Proceedings of a Treaty between the United States and the United Tribes of Pottawottamies, Chippeways and Ottowas, 10 September 1833, Transcripts from Indian Office Files, Box 65, 16.

101. Ibid., 1-54; Treaty with the Chippewa, etc., 1833, *Indian Affairs*, vol. 2, 402-415; Anselm J. Gerwing, "The Chicago Indian Treaty of 1833," *Journal of the Illinois State Historical Society* 57 (Summer 1964): 117-142.

102. Hurlbut, ed., *Chicago Antiquities*, 228-229.

103. Correspondence, Articles, Miscellany on Wisconsin Indians, US Mss 7E Folder 3, Wisconsin Historical Society, Madison, 15.

104. Thomas P. Burnett to William Clark, 11 December 1833; M. S. Davenport to Clark, 18 December 1833; Burnett to Clark, 23 December 1833; Joseph Street to Clark, 12 April 1834, Transcripts from Indian Office Files, Box 65.

105. Joseph Street to William Clark, 12 April 1834, ibid.

106. On 18 December, the Sauks and Mesquakies requested "the approbation of our great Father and his people to make war on the Sioux when we find them on our own lands." Wa-Ke-Shaw-Shee's Speech, Rock Island, 18 December 1833, Transcripts from Indian

Office Files, Box 65. Shortly thereafter, the Mdewakanton Dakotas formed an alliance with the Menominees, Yanktons, and Sissetons. Thomas P. Burnett to William Clark, 12 February 1834; Burnett to Clark, 20 February 1834, ibid. On 27 February, Major John Bliss, commanding Fort Snelling, reported that the Mesquakies "have invited the Sauks and the Kickapoos to 'a general rendezvous' for their own foray against the Dakotas." Bliss to Alexander Macomb, 27 February 1834, ibid.

107. Henry Gratiot to Lewis Cass, 2 February 1834; John Bliss to Alexander Macomb, 27 February 1834; Marmaduke S. Davenport to William Clark, 21 February 1834; Bliss to Macomb, 19 February 1834, ibid.

108. Thomas Burnett to William Clark, 19 January 1833, ibid.

109. Gratiot to Cass, 2 February 1834; Bliss to Macomb, 27 February 1834, ibid.

110. Henry Gratiot to Cass, 2 February 1834, ibid.

111. Thomas Burnett to William Clark, 20 February 1834; Robert McCabe to Porter, 25 March 1834, ibid.

112. Talk of the Bald Eagle, 21 February 1834, ibid.

113. James P. Ronda, "Red-Head's Domain: William Clark's Indian Brokerage," in *Between Indian and White Worlds: The Cultural Broker,* ed. Margaret Connell Szasz (Norman: University of Oklahoma Press, 1994), 81–97; Landon Y. Jones, *William Clark and the Shaping of the West,* (New York: Hill and Wang, 2004), 285.

114. Herring to William Clark, 29 May 1834, Transcripts from Indian Office Files, Box 65.

115. Minutes of a Talk held at Jefferson Barracks Missouri on the 27th of March 1834, by General H. Atkinson with Keokuck and other principal Chiefs of the Sac and Fox Nation, ibid.

116. Nichols, *General Henry Atkinson,* 186.

117. Talk of L'Arc, Sioux Chief, 4 June 1834, Transcripts from Indian Office Files, Box 65.

118. Joseph Street to William Clark, 25 October 1834; Ethan Allan

Hitchcock to William Clark, 5 November 1834; Street to Clark, 18 November 1834, ibid.; "The Winnebagoes and Black Hawk War," 308.

119. Spoon Decorah, "Narrative of Spoon Decorah," in *Collections of the State Historical Society of Wisconsin*, ed. Reuben G. Thwaites, vol. 13 (Madison: Democrat Printing Co., State Printers, 1895), 462.

### 9. AN INDIAN WAR

1. Speech to Wabashaw's Band of Sioux, 21 August 1832, Joseph Montfort Street Papers, Iowa Department of Archives and History, Des Moines.

2. Atkinson to Winfield Scott, 9 July 1832, *The Black Hawk War, 1831–1832*, ed. Ellen M. Whitney, vol. 37, Collections of the Illinois State Historical Library (Springfield: Illinois State Historical Library, 1975), 753.

3. Council between Henry Atkinson and the Winnebago and Menominee Indians, ibid., 949.

4. Cass to S. T. Mason, 18 June 1832, Porter and Mason Letters Received, 1831–35, US Mss BN Box 59, Wisconsin State Historical Society, Madison, vol. 1, 8.

5. Stambaugh to George Porter, 7 June 1832, *The Black Hawk War, 1831–1832*, ed. Ellen M. Whitney, vol. 36, Collections of the Illinois State Historical Library (Springfield: Illinois State Historical Library, 1973), 545.

6. Porter to George Boyd, Detroit, 31 August 1832, Indian Office Files, US Mss BN Box 5, Wisconsin State Historical Society, Madison.

7. Thomas Forsyth, "Original causes of the troubles with a party of Sauk and Fox Indians under the direction or Command of the Black Hawk who is no Chief," 1 October 1832, Draper Mss T, vol. 9, Wisconsin Historical Society, Madison, 58–59.

8. Orlando Brown, "Causes of the Black Hawk War," in *Report and Collections of the State Historical Society of Wisconsin for the Years 1883, 1884, and 1885*, ed. Lyman C. Draper, vol. 10, Collections of the State

Historical Society of Wisconsin (Madison: Democrat Printing Co., State Printer, 1888), 225-226. According to Frank E. Stevens, Forsyth's opinion was not exceptional, and Atkinson drew considerable scorn for permitting the Dakotas to harrow the pitiful survivors of the Battle of Bad Axe. Frank E. Stevens, ed., *Wakefield's History of the Black Hawk War* (Chicago: Caxton Club, 1903), 210.

9. Burnett to Henry Dodge, 2 July 1832, *Black Hawk War,* vol. 37, 730.

10. Kinzie to Porter, 11 June 1832, National Archives, Letters Received by the Office of Indian Affairs, 1824-81: Michigan Superintendency, 1824-1851, Microcopy No. 234, Roll 421: 1832-1835 (Washington, D.C.: National Archives and Records Service, General Services Administration, 1959), F55-F56.

11. At the Rock Island treaty proceedings of September 1832, the Rock River chief Little Priest lamented that they had listened to Henry Gratiot, who encouraged the Ho Chunks to fight for the Americans, rather than Kinzie. "If all had done as the Portage Agent advised us, we should have avoided this scrape; but we listened to Mr Gratiot. In the future we will listen to the advice of Mr Kinzie." The Rock River band vindicated Kinzie's fear that, unless removed from the scene of the war altogether, young Ho Chunk warriors would ignore the objections of their elders and attack Americans to realize their martial ambitions. Second Council with Representatives of the Winnebago Nation, *Black Hawk War,* vol. 37, 1142.

12. Dodge to Atkinson, 30 June 1832, ibid., 716.

13. Building upon Gregory Evans Dowd's impressive scholarship on earlier nativist movements, Patrick Jung has argued that the Black Hawk War provides evidence of the persistence of an "ideology of resistance" and of a sense of Indian solidarity. Further, Jung suggests that American officials succeeded in defeating Black Hawk's resistance movement at least in part by exploiting intertribal divisions in the region. While Black Hawk no doubt entertained ambitions of replicating the earlier success of Pontiac and Tecumseh, this study suggests that Jung underestimates the depths of inter-

tribal animosity and, by extension, the plausibility of a broad Indian confederacy in 1832. More remote tribes, such as the Dakotas and Menominees, had yet to endure the sustained offenses of Anglo-American society that would have compelled them to surrender their traditional antagonisms in favor of intertribal unity. While Dowd's work provides a useful light by which to examine Black Hawk's resistance, James Drake's study of King Philip's War provides a better model for considering the actions of these tribes, which had not previously presumed that considerations of race trumped those of alliance. Patrick J. Jung, *The Black Hawk War of 1832* (Norman: University of Oklahoma Press, 2007), 4; Gregory Evans Dowd, *A Spirited Resistance: The North American Indian Struggle for Unity, 1745–1815* (Baltimore: Johns Hopkins University Press, 1992); James D. Drake, *King Philip's War: Civil War in New England, 1675–1676* (Amherst: University of Massachusetts Press, 1999), 14.

14. William Campbell to Andrew Jackson, 13 July 1832, *Black Hawk War,* vol. 37, 788.

15. Gary Clayton Anderson, *Kinsmen of Another Kind: Dakota-White Relations in the Upper Mississippi Valley, 1650–1862* (St. Paul: Minnesota Historical Society Press, 1997; reprint, with a new introduction), 254.

16. William Campbell to Andrew Jackson, 17 June 1832, *Black Hawk War,* vol. 36, 612.

17. Kerry A. Trask, *Black Hawk: The Battle for the Heart of America* (New York: Henry Holt, 2006), 280; Cecil Eby, *"That Disgraceful Affair," the Black Hawk War* (New York: W. W. Norton & Co., 1973), 201; Felix Keesing, *The Menomini Indians of Wisconsin: A Study of Three Centuries of Cultural Contact and Change* (Philadelphia: American Philosophical Society, 1939), ix.

18. Richard Bache to Gideon Low, 7 September, 1832, *Black Hawk War,* vol. 37, 1115; Treaty with the Potawatomi, 20 October 1832, *Indian Affairs: Laws and Treaties,* ed. Charles J. Kappler, vol. 2 (Treaties) (Washington, D.C.: U.S. Government Printing Office, 1904), 354;

Thomas J. V. Owen to George Porter, 3 September 1832, *Black Hawk War*, vol. 37, 1102; Atkinson to Samuel T. Matthews, 22 June 1832, *Black Hawk War*, vol. 36, 645.

19. Atkinson's orders were unspecific regarding the arming of the Indians and whether they would be permitted to keep their arms after the war. Joseph Street and George Boyd concluded that it was impracticable to reclaim the weapons from the Prairie du Chien and Green Bay contingents, respectively, and both forces retained their arms after the war. Street to William Clark, 7 June 1832, *Black Hawk War*, vol. 36, 547; Boyd to George Porter, 13 August 1832, George Boyd, "Papers of Indian Agent Boyd," in *Collections of the State Historical Society of Wisconsin*, ed. Reuben G. Thwaites, vol. 12 (Madison: Democrat Printing Co., 1892), 288.

20. Boyd to Stambaugh, 23 July 1832, *Black Hawk War*, vol. 37, 857.

21. Stambaugh to Boyd, 28 August 1832, ibid., 1076. George Boyd cited the precedent of the Winnebago War, during which the government paid its Indian allies, and further argued for compensation on the grounds that the Menominees were due no other treaty compensation during the year 1832, "which has been a sore disappointment to them." Boyd to George Porter, 13 August 1832, ibid., 993; Boyd to Porter, 2 September 1832, Boyd, "Papers of Indian Agent Boyd," 291.

22. Porter to Lewis Cass, 17 September 1832, *Black Hawk War*, vol. 37, 1160; Augustin Grignon, "Seventy-Two Years' Recollections of Wisconsin," in *Third Annual Report and Collections of the State Historical Society of Wisconsin for the Year 1856*, ed. Lyman C. Draper, Collections of the State Historical Society of Wisconsin (Madison: Calkins & Webb, Printers, 1857), 295.

23. Stambaugh to George Boyd, 28 August 1832, *Black Hawk War*, vol. 37, 1075.

24. Third Council with Representatives of the Winnebago Nation, 14 September 1832, ibid., 1151.

25. Second Council with Representatives of the Winnebago Nation,

13 September, ibid., 1144. Atkinson had, in fact, directed that the Ho Chunks receive "Twenty of the pack horses of the middle class." Atkinson to Zalmon C. Palmer, 2 September 1832, ibid., 1094.

26. "The Winnebagoes and Black Hawk War," in *Report and Collections of the State Historical Society of Wisconsin, for the Years 1867, 1868, and 1869,* ed. Lyman C. Draper, vol. 5, Collections of the State Historical Society of Wisconsin (Madison: Atwood & Rublee, State Printers, 1868), 306-309.

27. For contrasting interpretations of the evolution of Potawatomi political organization and chieftainship, see David Baerreis, "Chieftainship among the Potawatomi," *The Wisconsin Archeologist* 54 (1973): 114-134; James A. Clifton, "Potawatomi Leadership Roles: On Okama and Other Influential Personages," in *Papers of the Sixth Algonquin Conference,* ed. William Cowan (Ottawa: National Museum of Canada, 1975).

28. James A. Clifton, *The Prairie People: Continuity and Change in Potawatomi Indian Culture, 1665–1965* (Iowa City: University of Iowa Press, 1998), 273.

29. James A. Clifton, "Billy Caldwell's Exile in Early Chicago," *Chicago History* 4 (Winter 1977–1978): 224; R. David Edmunds, *The Potawatomis: Keepers of the Fire* (Norman: University of Oklahoma Press, 1978), 206.

30. James A. Clifton, "Merchant, Soldier, Broker, Chief: A Corrected Obituary of Captain Billy Caldwell," *Journal of the Illinois State Historical Society* 71 (August 1978): 210.

31. Ibid., 190, 206.

32. Citing the memoir of Hoo-wan-nee-kaw (Little Elk), Lucy Eldersveld Murphy has suggested that "military excursions on behalf of Euro-Americans were considered different and perhaps less important in an Indian man's life than Indian-initiated, inter-tribal battles." The cases of the Rock River Ho Chunks and Potawatomis support this assertion, while those of the Menom-

inees and, perhaps, Dakotas do not. Lucy Eldersveld Murphy, *A Gathering of Rivers: Indians, Métis, and Mining in the Western Great Lakes, 1737–1832* (Lincoln: University of Nebraska Press, 2000), 148.

33. Joshua Boyer, Journal of Joshua Boyer, Oct. 10–Dec. 10, 1832 with accompanying letter, Jan. 24, 1833, US Mss BM Folder 5, Wisconsin Historical Society, Madison, 23, 25.

34. Ibid., 32–33.

35. David R. M. Beck, *Siege and Survival: History of the Menominee Indians, 1634–1856* (Lincoln: University of Nebraska Press, 2002), 112–114.

36. Keesing, *The Menomini Indians of Wisconsin,* 41–42.

37. Beck, *Siege and Survival,* 109.

38. Alanson Skinner, *Social Life and Ceremonial Bundles of the Menomini Indians,* vol. 13, part 1, *Anthropological Papers of the American Museum of Natural History* (New York: American Museum of Natural History, 1913), 97.

39. Alanson Skinner, *Folklore of the Menomini Indians,* vol. 13, part 3, *Anthropological Papers of the American Museum of Natural History* (New York: American Museum of Natural History, 1915), 436.

40. Ibid.

41. Stambaugh to George Boyd, 28 August 1832, *Black Hawk War,* vol. 37, 1076.

42. William Powell, "William Powell's Recollections, In an Interview with Lyman C. Draper," in *Proceedings of the Annual Meeting of the State Historical Society of Wisconsin* (Madison: The Society, 1912), 161.

43. Skinner, *Social Life and Ceremonial Bundles of the Menomini Indians,* 127; Russell Horton, "Unwanted in a White Man's War: The Civil War Service of the Green Bay Tribes," *Wisconsin Magazine of History* (Winter 2004–2005): 18–27; Nancy O. Lurie, "Winnebago," in *Northeast,* ed. Bruce G. Trigger, vol. 15, Handbook of North American Indians (Washington, D.C.: Smithsonian Institution, 1978), 700.

44. John A. Wakefield, *Wakefield's History of the Black Hawk War,* ed. Frank E. Stevens (1834; reprint, Chicago: Caxton Club, 1904), 158.

45. Adèle Maria Antoinette de Perdreauville Gratiot, "An Interesting

Narrative: The Reminiscences of Mrs. Adele B. Gratiot," *Galena Weekly Gazette*, 2 May 1879, 5.

46. U.S. Bureau of the Census, *Population and Housing Unit Counts: Illinois*, 1990 Census of Population and Housing (Washington, D.C.: Bureau of the Census, 1990), 1; National Historical Geographic Information System: Pre-release Version 0.1, Minnesota Population Center, University of Minnesota, Minneapolis.

47. Jacqueline Peterson, "Prelude to Red River: A Social Portrait of the Great Lakes Métis," *Ethnohistory* 25, no. 1 (Winter 1978): 59.

48. Alice E. Smith, *From Exploration to Statehood*, ed. William Fletcher Thompson, vol. 1, *The History of Wisconsin* (Madison: State Historical Society of Wisconsin, 1973), 144.

### EPILOGUE

1. Thomas Forsyth, "Manners and Customs of the Sauk and Fox Nations of Indians etc. with Anecdotes, etc.," Draper Mss T, vol. 9, Wisconsin Historical Society, Madison, 31.

2. Charles Whittlesey, "Recollections of a Tour through Wisconsin in 1832," in *Collections of the State Historical Society of Wisconsin*, ed. Lyman C. Draper, vol. 1 (Madison: Wisconsin State Historical Society, 1855; reprint, with the addition of a memoir of Dr. Draper and the early records of the Society, Madison: Wisconsin State Historical Society, 1903), 81.

3. Roger L. Nichols, *General Henry Atkinson: A Western Military Career* (Norman: University of Oklahoma Press, 1965), 187; R. David Edmunds, *The Potawatomis: Keepers of the Fire* (Norman: University of Oklahoma Press, 1978), 250-251.

4. Henry H. Hurlbut, ed., *Chicago Antiquities: Comprising Original Items and Relations, Letters, Extracts, and Notes, Pertaining to Early Chicago; Embellished with Views, Portraits, Autographs, Etc.* (Chicago: Fergus Printing Co., 1881), 249.

5. Edmunds, *The Potawatomis: Keepers of the Fire*, 250-252; Nichols, *General Henry Atkinson*, 193-194.

6. Nichols, *General Henry Atkinson*, 201-205.

7. James W. Silver, *Edmund Pendleton Gaines: Frontier General* (Baton Rouge: Louisiana State University Press, 1949), 150–151.

8. Moses Paquette, "The Wisconsin Winnebagoes," in *Collections of the State Historical Society of Wisconsin*, ed. Reuben G. Thwaites, vol. 12 (Madison: Democrat Printing Co., 1892), 401–402.

9. Gary Clayton Anderson, *Kinsmen of Another Kind: Dakota-White Relations in the Upper Mississippi Valley, 1650–1862* (Lincoln: University of Nebraska Press, 1984; reprint, with a new introduction, St. Paul: Minnesota Historical Society Press, 1997), 151; Alice E. Smith, *From Exploration to Statehood*, ed. William Fletcher Thompson, vol. 1 of *The History of Wisconsin* (Madison: State Historical Society of Wisconsin, 1973), 145–146.

10. Nancy O. Lurie, "Winnebago," in *Northeast*, ed. Bruce G. Trigger, vol. 15, *Handbook of North American Indians* (Washington, D.C.: Smithsonian Institution, 1978), 699; John T. De la Ronde, "Personal Narrative," in *Report and Collections of the State Historical Society of Wisconsin for the Years 1873, 1874, 1875 and 1876*, ed. Lyman C. Draper, vol. 7, Collections of the State Historical Society of Wisconsin (Madison: E. B. Bolens, State Printer, 1876) (hereafter WHC 7), 359; Correspondence . . . on Wisconsin Indians, Folder 3, 15; Treaty with the Winnebago, 1837, *Indian Affairs: Laws and Treaties*, ed. Charles J. Kappler, vol. 2 (Treaties) (Washington, D.C.: U.S. Government Printing Office, 1904), 498–500.

11. Henry Merrell, "Pioneer Life in Wisconsin," in WHC 7, 393.

12. Nichols, *General Henry Atkinson*, 212.

13. William J. Peterson, "Moving the Winnebago into Iowa," *Iowa Journal of History* 58, no. 4 (October 1960): 362–375.

14. Nichols, *General Henry Atkinson*, 214.

15. Ibid.

16. De la Ronde, "Personal Narrative," 363.

17. Ibid.

18. Ibid.

19. Correspondence . . . on Wisconsin Indians, Folder 3, 15; Nancy

Oestreich Lurie, *Wisconsin Indians,* Revised and expanded ed. (Madison: Wisconsin Historical Society Press, 2002), 12.

20. James A. Clifton, *A Place of Refuge for All Time: Migration of the American Potawatomi into Upper Canada, 1830–1850* (Ottawa: National Museum of Man, 1975), 31.

21. Susan Sleeper-Smith, *Indian Women and French Men: Rethinking Cultural Encounter in the Western Great Lakes* (Amherst: University of Massachusetts Press, 2001), 116–138; Clifton, *A Place of Refuge for All Time,* 34.

22. Lurie, *Wisconsin Indians,* 9; Patricia K. Ourada, *The Menominee Indians: A History* (Norman: University of Oklahoma Press, 1979), 119–124.

23. Anderson, *Kinsmen of Another Kind,* 274–278; Robert M. Utley and Wilcomb E. Washington, *Indian Wars* (Boston: Mariner Books, 2002), 203–204.

24. R. David Edmunds, ed., *Enduring Nations: Native Americans in the Midwest* (Urbana: University of Illinois Press, 2008), 1–2.

25. United States Department of Defense, "Executive Summary of the 2003 Population Representation in the Military Services," (Washington, D.C.: Department of Defense, 2003), 3.

26. For an interesting consideration of Indian motives for serving in the modern U.S. military, see Tom Holm, *Strong Hearts, Wounded Souls: Native American Veterans of the Vietnam War* (Austin: University of Texas Press, 1996), 100–101, 118, 121.

## Acknowledgments

Undoubtedly, the greatest reward in writing this book has been the opportunity to enjoy the counsel, mentorship, and encouragement of some truly wonderful people. I begin by thanking my parents for instilling in me a love of books and learning. Even in the lean times, I never wanted for something good to read or the sense that I was spending my time wisely. If my parents encouraged me to read, Matthew Moten taught me to be a discriminating, critical reader. As a captain and major, he dismantled a young cadet's unwarranted convictions and replaced them with the seeds of historical curiosity. Years later, he was able to reap what he had sown when I returned to West Point to work for him as a member of the faculty. Personifying the ideal of the "soldier-scholar," Colonel Moten inspired me to pursue a career in history and helped make that career possible.

While I'm indebted to many members of the faculty at the University of North Carolina–Chapel Hill, I owe special thanks to Dick Kohn, Michael Green, Theda Perdue, and Joe Glatthaar. Their collaborative influence is manifest in this book, which I could not have written without any one of them. I am humbled by their erudition and selflessness, and I am honored to call them mentors and friends. It is also a privilege to acknowledge the late Don Higgin-botham as my graduate advisor. A gentleman in the most noble sense, Don always gave freely of his time—even when he knew so lit-tle remained. I dearly miss his charm, wit, and wisdom, but I will be forever grateful for his guidance and the time we spent together.

Thanks also to my colleagues and classmates from West Point and Chapel Hill. Their enduring camaraderie, friendship, support, and advice have proven invaluable. Similarly, I thank the faculty and my fellow students at the Bay Mills Community College. It is no exaggeration to claim that I could not have written this book without their influence; *gchi-miigwech*. I am further indebted to Joyce Seltzer, my editor at Harvard University Press, for her patient tutelage. It has been a joy and a privilege working with her, and I'm grateful that we'll be able to continue our collaboration.

Finally, I must thank my wife (and impeccable proofreader), Heidi. Many are familiar with the burdens borne by an army wife, and some can imagine the solitude of a "writer's widow," but few can appreciate the compound sacrifices made by a woman suffering both fates. For over seven years, I have cloistered myself in my study, emerging periodically but always scampering away at the first sign of domestic responsibility, casting convenient (if valid) excuses in my wake. Heidi has patiently awaited the publication of this book and the promised, concomitant return of her husband—only to learn that I've undertaken a second book. Nevertheless, Heidi re-mains the rock of our household, a devoted mother to our son, Connor, and my best friend in the world. I cannot thank her enough for everything she has done, and I love her more than she knows.

# INDEX